STUDIES IN ECONOMIC HISTORY AND POLICY
THE UNITED STATES IN THE TWENTIETH CENTURY
EDITED BY LOUIS GALAMBOS AND ROBERT GALLMAN

EUROPE, AMERICA, AND THE WIDER WORLD:
ESSAYS ON THE ECONOMIC HISTORY OF WESTERN CAPITALISM

VOLUME I

EUROPE AND THE WORLD ECONOMY

Europe, America, and the Wider World

Essays on the Economic History of Western Capitalism

VOLUME 1

Europe and the World Economy

WILLIAM N. PARKER

PHILIP GOLDEN BARTLETT PROFESSOR OF
ECONOMICS AND ECONOMIC HISTORY
YALE UNIVERSITY

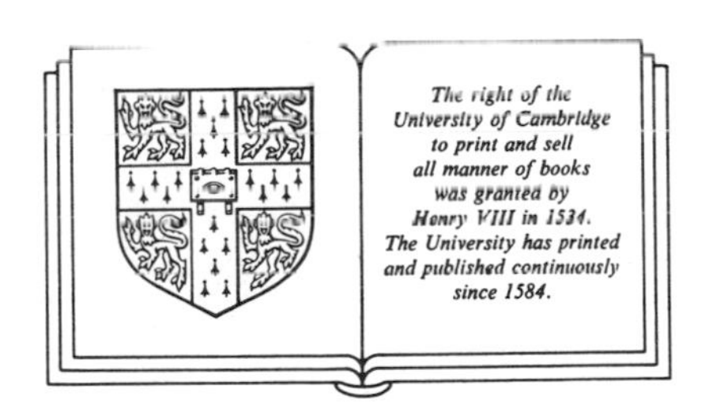

CAMBRIDGE UNIVERSITY PRESS

CAMBRIDGE
LONDON NEW YORK NEW ROCHELLE
MELBOURNE SYDNEY

Published by the Press Syndicate of the University of Cambridge
The Pitt Building, Trumpington Street, Cambridge CB2 1RP
32 East 57th Street, New York, NY 10022, USA
296 Beaconsfield Parade, Middle Park, Melbourne 3206, Australia

First published 1984

Printed in the United States of America

Library of Congress Cataloging in Publication Data
Parker, William Nelson.
Europe, America, and the wider world.
(Studies in economic history and policy)
Includes index.
Contents: v. 1. Europe and the world economy.
1. Economic history–Collected works. 2. Capitalism–
Collected works. I. Title. II. Series.
HC51.P37 1984 330.9181'2 84-3161
ISBN 0 521 25467 1 hard covers
ISBN 0 521 27480 X paperback

To Abbott Payson Usher, my teacher and friend, and to all those students of mine to whom I have tried to pass along his ideas, friendship, and affection – mingled with my own.

Contents

Editors' preface

This volume differs in four respects from those that have preceded it in this series: It is a collection of essays, whereas the others have been monographs; it is concerned with Europe, whereas the others have treated the United States; it contains several essays that deal with history before the twentieth century, whereas the earlier volumes focus on the twentieth century; it is not exclusively concerned with policy issues (at least not explicitly), while the earlier volumes are.

The last three differences appear to remove the present volume from the purview of this series, which after all is entitled *Studies in Economic History and Policy: The United States in the Twentieth Century.* Even were appearance reality, the editors would not be unduly concerned over this incongruity, so pleased are we to have the collected essays of such a distinguished economic historian as William N. Parker. But appearance, in this case, is not reality. The present volume is the first of two, the second containing essays on the American scene. Both volumes, which are closely related, range widely over space and time, but the two together constitute a coherent and original interpretation of Western economic development, raising finally large questions about the nature of modern capitalism and about the future of American political economy. Thus they are concerned with the fundamental issues that animate this series.

William N. Parker is Phillip Golden Bartlett Professor of Economics and Economic History at Yale University. He has served as editor of the *Journal of Economic History,* as president of the Economic History Association, and as president of the Agricultural History Society. Sixteen of the essays published here have appeared before in print; three are published now for the first time.

LOUIS GALAMBOS
Professor of History
The Johns Hopkins University

ROBERT E. GALLMAN
Kenan Professor of Economics and History
The University of North Carolina

Preface

Essays such as these are supposed to be the chips for a workshop, after the masterpiece has been carted away. But as Cornelia said of her children to the ladies who came showing off their jewels (in our Columbus, Ohio, high school Latin book and in a phrase repeated on a statue in the State House yard, showing her as Ohio, spreading her arms over lesser statues of Grant, Sherman, and Sheridan, Ohio's great Civil War heroes): *Haec sunt aurae meae* – These are my jewels. (The trouble with that statue was that there was a circular bench around its base, where the bums who lived in the State House yard, their toes sticking out through the newspapers in their shoes, used to sun themselves, sharing with the generals Cornelia's indiscriminate bounty.)

Perhaps these essays are more like those lesser jewels. I love and relish them but they are not going to win the civil war that now rages on the battlefields of historical scholarship. For that task, I would rather trust to my generals – an album full of Ph.D. students. The work of nearly all of them is in many respects proving better than mine; perhaps they had better teaching or an earlier start and have been pounded out on a forge of scholarly controversy that has made their sparks fly. The tiny share I have had in their extraordinary work constitutes my five-foot shelf of great books.

In any case, these "pieces" are chips indeed from that workshop – the classroom and the conference room. They were written for occasions or on request; only that fear of disgrace against a deadline, that prospect of hanging, could concentrate my mind. Except for the next to last one (Chapter 12) they were written rapidly and without much agony, and as I proceeded on in each of them I was perpetually surprised that I had so much to say. I discovered what I seemed to think as I went along. Each left me feeling I had said my say, and indolence or discursiveness kept me from returning to improve them, to make them into a book. You often find if you try to do this, to routinize, model, categorize the pictures and the ideas, that – as I say of others here –

> You pick the flow'r,
> The bloom is shed –

which means of course that it was a delicate bloom – not quite a "joy forever" – but still worth something.

Perhaps these are worth a reprint. I am heartened by a realization that underneath the incidents, jokes, passions, puzzles, and methodological riddles of scholarly life, something in my mind has, I fancy, always sought structure, and this despite a deep and abiding affinity with anarchy and diversity. My senior essay in college – in English literature – on "Burke's Style in the Light of Ancient Rhetoric" – started off with the sentence, "In discussing an author's style, one must begin by erecting a structure of explanation to show its categories, their interrelation with each other and with their own origins. . . ." (That wasn't the sentence. The essay was in a box of papers in my cellar. I glanced over it once many years ago and was shocked to read its first sentence; that was its general gist, and it fit exactly what I felt I have tried to do, decades later, in economic history. I cannot quote it verbatim now because carpenter ants, or their entomological equivalent, got in the box and ate ribbons through the contents – having presumably their own ideas about structure.) In any case, that senior essay attempt naturally failed – and my disgust with what seemed to me then the intellectual vacuity and wordy insubstantiality of literary criticism sent me into economics. *Naturam expellas furca, tamen usque recurret.*

On re-reading and selecting this set of papers, I am conscious of a structure, or an effort to produce one, although it gets lost when it strays too far from concrete and partial trends, "threads" – as my teacher, Abbott Payson Usher, called them – in the historical record. Can I state it here? No. I must try to let it emerge, if the reader is patient enough to persevere through the obscurity, occasional detail, and not infrequent repetition of ideas and even of images and phrases where these essays overlap on one another's terrain. I have not tried very hard to prune them to follow one another in chapter-like fashion. Readers' eyes are the best pruning shears, and modern readers know – almost too well – how to skip. I have retitled most of them and rearranged their order to mark what – as I read them over – seems to me to show the evolution of an underlying structure. I have ventured to show this in schematic form in some "plumber's nightmare" diagrams in the last paper. I have gotten much comfort and guidance from these diagrams, though I have never had a student who let me feel he or she bought the whole package. The independence and variety of students' thought is to me a great source of both annoyance and satisfaction, humiliation and pride. In any case, the humility that I think I feel at so pretentious an effort as this volume and its companion is a quality of which it is self-contradictory to boast. Readers must (and will, I well know) judge it – what it has outlined and what it may have obscured – for themselves.

Acknowledgments

Quentin Skinner, a Cambridge philosopher, historian, and wit, once wrote in a review of a professor's collected papers, "As professors grow older they write less and less and publish more and more." This collection is an example of that; nevertheless three of the pieces appear here for the first time, and all have been arranged with altered titles in an effort to give some degree of coherence to the whole. In particular, Chapters 3 and 4 have been abbreviated. These constitute two chapters from a four-chapter portion of a book, and maps and tabular material, essential to the book but unessential to my present purpose, have been omitted.

The list of acknowledgments is too long to cite, but two immediate debts cannot be overlooked. I am most grateful to the Australian National University, in particular to Professor Noel G. Butlin and his group, for support and encouragement during two months spent there, during which this volume was assembled and completed, and to my wife for handling a confusion of affairs during that time at home. I wish to thank, too, the editors of the several scholarly journals and publishing houses who gave me their prompt and gracious permission to reprint as well as the editorial staff of the Cambridge University Press in New York, who helped to beat the manuscript into shape. Carolyn Jull, Yale '85, compiled the index and helped with sources and references. Ann Collins typed and retyped, without word processor, much of the manuscript.

PART I

The Renaissance and the twentieth century

I

What historians must explain

On the historian's map, a civilization that Marxists call "capitalist" and others call "Western" lies in the space between the fifteenth and the early twentieth centuries. For perhaps five centuries before the fifteenth century, Christian thought and belief – pessimistic and otherworldly – dominated philosophy and infused art and popular attitudes in Roman and Germanic Europe. A fragmented political structure was supported by force on a local scale and stabilized by habits of deference and acceptance of status within agrarian communities. A stagnant technology and high risks and costs of overland transport kept economic movements in check or focused them on a few notable commodities and lines of trade. Only a very thin ecclesiastical, military, or commercial elite operated the loose hierarchies of church, kingdom, or empire, or dealt in markets more than a few miles from town or manor. From these Europeans the globe's Western Hemisphere with civilizations similar to those of the Near East or Europe three thousand years earlier lay hidden, separated by an ocean, by timid navigation, and erroneous concepts of geography.

In the medieval world, there were economic elements we recognize as "capitalist," and elements in thought and even art that one recognizes as "modern." The "capitalist spirit," as Weber and Sombart described it, is an endemic phenomenon in human history, as are the other elements that went into the synthesis of the fifteenth- and sixteenth-century Renaissance humanism: individualism, in the sense of the exercise of a powerful individual will; and science, in the sense both of experiment and useful improvement and of rational speculation based on sense data about the physical world. Society, one may fancy, in some Hegelian fashion, contains all its elements, at all points and times simultaneously, *in posse* if not *in ease*. But in any society over centuries of stability, the social (and some claim, the physical) climate slowly changes, and new strains of thought and behavior are born, as if by genetic transmutation, and survive. In a mechanical rather than a biological analogy, a certain slippage occurs between the civilization's interlocking parts. And the internal structure of these changes (which are simply manifestations of the immanent but suppressed tendencies of the human animal living with his fellows) is such as to allow not simply a few new forms and personalities, but a whole generation and after it, another generation (in which old patterns of behavior and values no longer predominate, and sets of forms to contain social life and of attitudes to motivate it, previously deviant, eccentric, and rare, appear and appear together, cohesive and mutually supportive), furnishing the behavioral substratum, the functional interrelationships, and the very dynamic of a new civilization.

At such a point in the historical record, one becomes aware of transformation. Within half a century, business, government, religion, many social relationships, art, literature, even music – are rapidly altered in form, style, and content. No exact science of society tells us the reason, the prime cause, or the transmission mechanism for the widespread emergence of novelties, with marked structural and psychological similarities, in so many different spheres of life. But the extent of the changes and the many analogies between their different manifestations suggest powerful connecting undercurrents, deriving, it may be, from some single spiritual source. Some historians, indeed, have been quick to evoke such a single and transforming spirit, an altered *Geist,* a new *Mentalité.* The words *medieval, Renaissance, modern,* and *bourgeois* seem unavoidable when one takes one's eye even a short way above the surface of history. They serve to reveal an underlying unity of form among phenomena widely scattered in social space but concentrated in historical time. They emphasize, too, that change is not simply evolutionary but also cataclysmic, that there are periods in which it accelerates up to the point that some new balance is attained, or some momentum is acquired.

I would go too far afield to write here of the new sixteenth-century "humanist" sensitivity among scholars. Then, as now, universities were conservative, monkish institutions that sheltered a few radicals who had rediscovered the art, literature, philosophy, and science of antiquity and were in their hearts no longer medieval Christians. A counterpart to humanism (or that to which it was a counterpart) appeared in the church, where Luther returned to the spirit of the Christianity of the early church, where Calvin reverted to St. Augustine, and where numerous sectarians staged fundamentalist revivals until, with John Wesley in the eighteenth century, the last of the major evangelical Protestant denominations was born. The Renaissance in religion, and the born-again Christians, depended, like the new scholars and scientists, heavily on ancient authority, claiming to displace the visible, tangible, political authority of Catholicism with a higher source and a truer interpretation – of Aristotle, Plato, Vergil, Jesus, or the early Fathers. The expression in both spheres had in common the rejection of an external, contemporary structure of authority. Gradually but irresistibly in all spheres of belief, authority came to mean a reliance on the piety, the learning, the reasoning of individual contemporaries whose particular expression of piety, or of knowledge or of humanity, appealed to the individual man, in his soul, his reason, or his humane and esthetic sensitivity.

The Renaissance is so called because it saw the rebirth of the ancient world's learning, its texts, its knowledge. But the spirit in those texts was not that which allowed submission to external authority, even the authority of the texts themselves, even, that is, Aristotle or the Bible. The spirit, which, molded to the circumstances, social forms, and human material of the fifteenth, sixteenth, and seventeenth centuries, was called classical or Greek was a radical individualism resting all salvation, all expression, all attainment on the God or gods men found in themselves, or in their perceptions of and reasoning on nature, or ultimately on no God at all, except man, and among men, upon one's self.

In political life, wherein ultimately all was controlled, where men could be killed though they could not be made alive, individualistic self-confidence, this delight in reason, and this appreciation of the variety of human life and aspiration was to develop first in petty despotisms by princes ambitious to throw off church and empire. Dukedoms and principalities grew active in Germany and Italy and imposing kingdoms established themselves in Spain, England, and France. In those areas where the religious and intellectual development failed to consolidate its gains politically – either in the Reformation cities of Geneva, Edinburgh, Boston, or the Dutch Republic, or in the national churches of England and France – in, that is, the Empires of Spain and Austria and in the church-dominated lands of Italy, humanistic scholarship, the intellectual enterprise of modern science, the blooming capitalism in business life, and the classicism in art were crushed, or slid into decline after 1600; cultural, economic, and political vitality in Europe moved north of that line which Braudel has demarcated as the "zone of the grape and the olive." But the state that ruled through the local monopoly of force and divine right in a national or regional monarch proved a transitional form. In breaking with the authority of medieval church and empire, in effectively nationalizing the feudal structures, the masters of mercenary armies and household guards had destroyed the supernatural basis of their own legitimacy in the eyes of a citizenry of growing wealth, to whom individual freedom was the new superstition. In the series of revolutions – Dutch, Puritan, French, Central European of 1848, and finally in the revolutions of Russia and of Germany in 1917–18, state power slipped from Europe's hereditary rulers, the agrarian nobilities and royal houses, into the forms of a propertied liberalism, with constitutions, laws, and parliaments. Then in Russia immediately and in Germany with a decade's delay, the spirit of rebellion, transmuted through notions of popular democracy, was used by a fanatical oligarchy in lawless politics to destroy the forms of personal liberty that in the West had protected the individualistic spirit and property holdings of the Renaissance.

In the essays that follow, I wish to detail more clearly the evolution of the industrial capitalism that developed with this evolution of Western materialistic and rationalistic civilization and thought. Economic forms have, it will appear, also a course of progress within the appointed five-century span of capitalist growth. But within that span, development of those forms, as with development of Western scientific method, Western art and literature, and Western political forms, was in a sense, all of a piece, the working out of principles and interactions implicit in the original Renaissance conceptions. So it may be said that people of affairs of the nineteenth or early twentieth century could have understood their fifteenth- or sixteenth-century counterparts. Clemenceau or Bismarck could have understood Machiavelli; Rutherford or even Einstein lay in the scientific tradition of Galileo; the listener who can enjoy even Wagner or Ravel is not likely to shut his ears totally to the court and church music of the Renaissance, different though they are in style and emotional content. The portraits of Titian, Reynolds, and Sargent form a single though degenerating line. So too, as Alfred Chandler perceptively noted, "The American businessman of 1840 would find the environment of 15th Century Italy more familiar than that of his own nation seventy years later."[1]

A consistent though evolving style, and pervasive underlying values, through the working out of whose logic the evolution proceeded, establish Western civilization then as a single history in its development and reproduction from the great divide of the Renaissance. The striking, indeed, the unique and ultimately deceptive, feature of that civilization and its associated characteriological, ideological, and social phenomena – science, capitalism, national and martial spirit, its optimistic assertions of human power – was its apparently endless dynamism. The empires of the ancient world – Egypt, Babylon, China, Greece, Rome, Moghul India, and the Ottoman Middle East – all spread over a few centuries in a period of fluorescence by reproducing over a wide geographical area a body of fixed, centrally controlled, military and bu-

[1] A. D. Chandler, *The Visible Hand* (Cambridge, Mass., 1977), 455.

reaucratic institutions. Their expansions were geographic, but within their boundaries the forms and patterns of control and deference were fixed and stable. Their art rapidly lost spontaneity and creativity and became a craftsman's stale repetition of a fixed style. Even where this was not true – in China of A.D. 900–1200, as Needham has described it, or in the spiritual life of the Near East and the Indian subcontinent – the economy and technology, reproducing itself over a wide but ultimately limited area, showed few dynamic features. Production techniques remained unchanged, and wealth accumulated more through taxation and conquest than through expansion in productive capacity or variety.

But for five hundred years the West appeared to expand in a kind of dynamic equilibrium – externally overseas, internally through cycles of population growth, while experiencing continuing accretions of wealth and productive power and enjoying (if that is the word) continuing transformation of techniques. The earlier empires had expanded geographically up to certain notable limits while remaining internally stagnant in spirit, political structure, and economic life. The system of beliefs and behavior that burst forth in the Renaissance in Western Europe had an empire not of this world. Its ambitions, its materialism, its science, its view of man and of nature, its optimism and violence, its individualistic ethic expanded over half the globe and thoroughly infiltrated the rest while remaining, within itself, fragmented and in turmoil. The secret of this external chaos and this internal strength and penetrative power lay in the strength and fecundity of the Renaissance ideals and in the simplicity and flexibility of the economic forms that translated them into material life.

In this way, the evolution of Western civilization threw in the path of its capitalism an unending succession of opportunities for creating capital, wealth, and social output. These opportunities are examined in later essays in this volume. What is of interest here is not their detail but their recurrence. The overseas expansions; the discoveries of gold, spices, and furs, then of forests, slaves, and fresh soils, of vast native populations, strange flora, and at length, of the world's subsoil resources of minerals and fuels; and the mercantile trades that responded to these attractions are for Europe itself perhaps the smaller part of the story, though the one more convulsive in its effects on the planet as a whole. In Western Europe, as populations grew, as new ideas spread, as wars altered the map and revolutions rearranged internal social structures, richer markets and a more abundant labor supply began to draw out of the ancient arts of agriculture and industrial crafts a more productive body of practices, techniques, and equipment. And by the mid-eighteenth century, the modern Industrial Revolution – the continuous transformation of productive technology, supported by engineering and scientific traditions both deep and rich – created modern industry, modern transportation, modern urban structures and ultimately, after long delays, modern agriculture. And since the productivity of capitalist economies was in good part a matter not of productive ideas pure and simple but of the scale on which they were carried out, the worldwide expansion of this civilization, the doubling and trebling of its effective market size and resource base, continued to feed the furnace of its expanding economic opportunity.

Was this huge parade of opportunity created by capitalism itself – taking capitalism as the organization and body of motivation by which economic life was carried on? Or is the history better conceived as the introduction of opportunities from other human activities – war, speculation, family life – to which economic men could make a response? The answer may not seem very important except to historians, who are concerned with framing a philosophy of history and a model of social change that permits them to write a narrative that does no violence to the facts and the relationships that their intuitions suggest. In such an effort, one reaches the chicken-and-egg problem. One searches for the first cause of social change, the "primitive accumulation" of commodities, the primitive transformation of ideas and behavior traits from which the rest of the change takes its impetus. Yet it is no mere historian's issue, and it is one which historical evidence can hardly settle. The compartments of Western development were closely, if bafflingly, linked. Not one could have gone far along the path it took without a characteristic body of action, of response, within itself and in interaction with the civilization's other components. If, for example, the early trading ventures had not been actively pursued, if the Incas' gold had not been put into circulation, the expansion of Northern Europe might have been slower; and the mass of commerce and finance that had accumulated by 1750 could not have thrust itself so powerfully into the new lands and new techniques of the nineteenth century.

We come then to the question that has powerfully agitated social thought and historical research since the beginning of the twentieth century. Since scholars share the troubled environment they examine, it is the fundamental question for our view of the contemporary world. The question is simply this: Are we observing and experiencing in the twentieth century a closing in of Western civilization's horizons of opportunity, a breaking up of its forms of organization and expression, a transmutation of its individualism, its optimism, its faith in reason and in self – are we in effect living through the Renaissance in reverse? No doubt some actual reversions to the medieval are observable in the world today. In music, dance, painting, even literature – those most sensitive of indicators – bourgeois humanism has splintered between abstract styles, elitist and aristocratic in appeal, and works of frenzied or vulgar popularity. The forms of religious expression, too, appear as the saintly mysticism of the few and the mass emotion of a mob. Hierarchy, authority, and status have returned with a vengeance to the political and economic structure. One may trace back in the historical development of the West since 1870 the rewinding of many of the threads of the medieval synthesis that had been loosened and unraveled in the Renaissance and its succeeding centuries. But since history never repeats itself, though it gives the observer of its dreamlike stream of events the frequent experience of déjà vu, there are many new strands as well. Perhaps the phenomenon is not really a reversion to medieval forms but the crossing of another great cultural divide into the next age.

Society in the last hundred years, as in the late Middle Ages, has been living on a geologic fault, experiencing earthquakes as the strata settle into a new position. The tremors were felt first a hundred years ago, in the midst of the great half-century of capitalist expansion in European philosophy, art, and science, then in the political structures, in the social class structure within which capitalist economy worked, within which families are formed and tastes, motivation, and personalities generated. The world had been explored, its empty spaces settled; European population growth leveled off; only technological change continued moving relentlessly with the growth of science down its twentieth-century path, creating shortages and relieving them, scattering destruction and marvelous creations alike across the path of social development.

A historian can only look cross-eyed at the history of the last hundred years. It is too close for comfort. If Communist revolutions had been successful outside of Russia in 1917, or if the German and Japanese empires had been the winners in 1945, the job would be much simpler. Then a historian, writing like a monkish chronicler in the Dark Ages, would trace a clear dénouement to the drama of the West. The *Abendland* would have experienced *Untergang* and the organizational problem would be settled once and for all. The "role of the state" would not be a matter of discussion, and all the false starts, the brave ventures, the experiments of "mixed systems," the schemes of worker participation, all the patter and vaporings about capitalism and freedom and creeping socialism would be buried in an oriental despotism in the name of the proletariat or the Aryan (and Japanese) manifest destiny. Or, suppose the American army had done in 1945 what a few of its officers urged it to do – simply kept going, and ridden and flown on to Moscow – thus fulfilling the fantasies of Stalinist paranoia. What an ending then for Western history! For a military coup of such magnitude – had it succeeded – would have overturned American institutions as well as European, and an American fascism would very likely have substituted for the German and Japanese.[2]

In short, we see the world today terribly divided: in international politics, between East and West; in domestic economy, between bureaucratic socialism and market freedom, between huge organizations and little men; in spirit, between liberty and order, between rash venture and savings bank timidity, between family and self, between materialism and mysticism, between science and superstition. All these divisions are taken by many as cracks in the temple, indications of an imminent collapse. But it may be that the struggle, even the external enemies, are the conditions of the West's own transformation, the internal chaos a mask not of decay but of vitality. It has all come about in any case because in its two twentieth-century cataclysms, "the West" did not go under. Had it done so, the historian could have built a brilliant explanation, if "the historian" had been around to tell the tale.

But what, one may ask, has happened within Western capitalism, while this struggle against its enemies has been going on – against the childish militarism of the Central Powers, against the antiquated arrogant ideology of Stalinism, and internally against those symptoms of change, taken to be symptoms of decline but now perhaps to be seen as the experiences of a transformation? Between 1945 and 1970 the capitalisms of Continental Europe; North America; the western rim of the Pacific in Asia, the Mediterranean, and the Middle East; Australia; South Africa; and even to a degree the massive and creaky economy of India[3] all expanded faster, transformed more ardently, traded more vigorously, and invested more radically and more variously than ever before. Compared to the twenty-five years after World War I, the contrast

[2]No doubt this scenario portrays the Soviet state and German fascism in excessively monolithic terms. Each country, had it dominated the West, would have had its own history. The strictly economic problem of centralization and decentralization is not radically different in a planned communism than it is in the West under a mixed system. The element of private property is of course absent, but it is absent, too, in a world of corporate capitalism. The history of a Nazi world would probably have resembled that of an oriental empire, a chronicle of rapine and oppression, punctuated by fierce and petty struggles for succession.

[3]Because capitalism, as structured in these countries, flourished does not mean that socialism failed. Growth in the Soviet Union and some parts of Eastern Europe was also high. Moreover the word "capitalism" in every decade has meant something slightly different in a world economy of large organizations and government programs, incentives, and controls. To explain a growth record, one must penetrate below surface correlations and superficial nomenclature to see whether economies grew because of their institutions or in spite of them, and the institutional mix itself must be pulled apart into its dynamic and retardative elements.

could hardly be sharper. Yet those difficulties of the 1920s and 1930s, the ways they were overcome, the new forms of organization and state policy, the new science and art, the shattering changes in social characteristics, especially those specific to sex and to social class, the inflations of the early twenties and the long bellyache of unemployment of the thirties – all the excitements and miseries, the gaudiness and bleakness of these two decades, made a difference. Capitalist growth after 1945 is not simply the continuation of the British world economy of 1914. One cannot remove the interwar decades, like a piece of leaky pipe from the plumbing of history, and splice together the ends in a single conduit. Looking before 1914, one can even now see some of the shifts under the nineteenth-century surface, like shifting tectonic plates under the earth, which produced the volcanoes and the earthquakes of the twentieth century. And the history since 1970 shows, too, that we no longer live in the simple, free, expanding capitalism and the stable, structured culture of the "British century" between Napoleon and the Kaiser. Historians and sociologists have perceived this since the 1890s, but economists, businessmen, and political leaders are lighter-hearted creatures, readily misled by a decade or two of optimism and success.

The study of history is reputed to assist in the understanding of contemporary events. That no doubt is true in the same way that any deep and thorough study gives one a more sensitive, a more profound, more subtle appreciation of one's own environment. But history seems to assume a pattern and a form in our minds partly because, since it happened long ago, much of its detail is lost, and because we are not immediately involved in its past outcomes. No one – a historian least of all – can trace definitively the chaotic historical transition in which we are caught. This is true because we are all caught in it, and what we write as well as what we do reflects the underlying disorder. Historians, or socio-scientific pundits, Marxist or bourgeois, who think otherwise, compose vain rhetoric and empty, pompous, imprecise theory. It is commonplace to regret the narrow specialization, the loss of scope in scholarship; our inability to see what is happening and to assert with conviction that we do itself is a symptom of what we feel – the breakup of Renaissance ideals of learning and scholarship, and the groping in the dark toward a new synthesis and understanding in scholarship and a new stability and spirit in social life.

PART II

Europe's industrialization: the pre-history

2

The pre-history of the nineteenth century

THE FORMS OF LATE MEDIEVAL INDUSTRY[1]

Industrial activity in Europe in the late fifteenth century fell typically into five forms. Two of these were destined to decline over the following several centuries; one was to continue a vigorous life over the whole period covered in this essay, then virtually to disappear; and two, under

Originally published in Peter Burke (ed.), *The New Cambridge Modern History*, XIII, Compan. Vol. (Cambridge: Cambridge University Press, 1979), 43–79.

[1]Recent surveys have made this body of experience somewhat more accessible to English-language readers. On the subjects treated in this and the following section, see: Fernand Braudel, *Capitalism and Material Life* 1400–1800 (New York, Harper & Row, 1973); *The Cambridge Economic History of Europe* (London, Cambridge University Press, 1952–67); Jan De Vries, *The Economy of Europe in an Age of Crisis 1600–1750* (London, Cambridge University Press, 1976); Hermann Kellenbenz, *The Rise of the European Economy* (London, Weidenfeld & Nicolson, 1976); Gino Luzzatto, *An Economic History of Italy from the Fall of the Roman Empire to the Beginning of the Sixteenth Century* (London, Routledge & Kegan Paul, 1961); H. A. Miskimin, Jr., *The Economy of Early Renaissance Europe 1300–1460* (Englewood Cliffs, New Jersey, Prentice-Hall, Inc., 1969); Domenico Sella, 'European Industries 1500–1700' in C. M. Cipolla (ed.), *The Fontana Economic History of Europe*, vol. 2 (London, Collins/Fontana Books, 1974) and Sylvia Thrupp, 'Medieval Industry 1000–1500' in volume one of the same series (1972).

Among the many articles, see: Max Barkhausen, 'Government Control and Free Enterprise in Western Germany and the Low Countries in the Eighteenth Century' in Peter Earle (ed.), *Essays in European Economic History 1500–1800* (London, Oxford University Press, 1974); Eleanora Carus-Wilson, 'The Woollen Industry' in M. M. Postan and E. E. Rich (eds.), *The Cambridge Economic History of Europe*, vol. II (London, Cambridge University Press, 1952); Hermann Kellenbenz, 'Rural Industries in the West from the End of the Middle Ages to the Eighteenth Century' in Peter Earle (ed.), *Essays in European Economic History 1500–1800;* Herbert Kisch, 'The Impact of the French Revolution on the Lower Rhine Textile Districts – Some Comments on Economic Development and Social Change', *Economic History Review*, 2nd ser., 15 (1962), 304–27, and 'Textile Industries in The Rhineland and Silesia, A Comparative Study', *Journal of Economic History*, 19 (1959), 541–69; Marian Malowist, 'The Economic and Social Development of the Baltic Countries from the Fifteenth to the Seventeenth Century', *Economic History Review*, 2nd ser., 12 (1959), 177–89; Joan Thirsk, 'Industries in the Countryside' in F. J. Fisher pressures from changes in technology, were to blend together to create the industrial technique and organisation, larger-scale and continuously dynamic, that we recognise as characteristically modern.

The *village industry,* descended from the specialised crafts on manorial estates, was perhaps the most widespread of these forms. The serf status of the artisan, continued or restored in eastern Europe, had been permanently transmuted in the West to that of free worker owning his tools and materials. But markets were local, pay was often made in kind, and the artisan, particularly if he held a bit of land from a lord or one of his subtenants, was effectively immobilized. The shoemaker, the smith, the carpenter, the thatcher, the mason, the miller, the butcher, the baker, the weaver – all were distributed in local markets over the countryside, drawing upon the locality for most materials and serving the households of village and rural families. Their work was supplemented by the industry of itinerant craftsmen who transported their capital – i.e. their skills and a few tools – from place to place, eating their way through the countryside, sometimes in the training years of an urban apprenticeship, sometimes in a permanently gypsy-like existence. Below the level of village industry, the primitive *industry of peasant households* for their own or local consumption continued in many more remote areas. Except for the basic tasks of food preparation, it is difficult to find in fifteenth-century Europe, or thereafter, examples of the degree of self-sufficiency in a rural household that characterised the extreme conditions of the American frontier. The village form of social organisations was designed, one might almost suppose, to avoid it, and to afford to an agriculture of low productivity the means to release a few specialised workers for industrial tasks.[2]

(ed.), *Essays in the Economic and Social History of Tudor and Stuart England* (London, Cambridge University Press, 1961); Herman Van Der Wee, 'The Structural Changes and Specialization in the Industry of the Southern Netherlands, 1100–1600', *Economic History Review,* 2nd ser., 28 (1975), 203–21; H. Van Werveke, 'Industrial Growth in the Middle Ages: The Cloth Industry of Flanders', *Economic History Review,* 2nd ser., 6 (1953–4), 237–54.

For older literature, see: Karl Bücher, 'Gewerbe' in the *Handwörterbuch der Stattswissenschuften,* vol. 4 (Jena, G. Fischer, 1892) and *Industrial Evolution* (1901; reprinted 1967; New York, Burt Franklin); J. U. Nef, 'Industrial Enterprise at the Time of the Reformation, c. 1515–c. 1540' and 'Mining and Metallurgy in Medieval Society' in *The Conquest of the Material World* (Chicago, University of Chicago Press, 1964); George Unwin, *Industrial Organization in the Sixteenth and Seventeenth Centuries* (1904; reprinted 1965; New York, Augustus M. Kelley); Max Weber, *General Economic History* translated by Frank Knight (New York, Greenberg, 1927).

[2]The standard references on the history of Renaissance technology are the rather widely known and compendious volumes: Maurice Daumas (ed.), *A History of Technology and Invention,* vol. 2 (New York, New Crown Pub-

An immense gap in skill and organisational complexity existed between village and peasant industry and that of the *workshops of urban artisans*. In north Italian cities and the Flemish towns they are as well known to us through the history of the decorative arts, including at their highest the masterpieces of painting and sculpture of the Italian and north European Renaissance, as through the history of useful industry. The form of organisation was much the same in the fine and the practical arts and had not much changed since the flourishing of the craft guilds in the twelfth to fourteenth centuries. A master workman trained journeymen and apprentices, the latter bound to him, almost as family members, for a period of years. The master in turn was controlled to a degree through the guild, which set prices, terms of apprenticeship and standards of quality. The master workman had his own customers, or dealt with a merchant who also brought in supplies. The system, like the village agriculture of the period, remained a mixture of group control, individual initiative, and private property. The resurgence of princely authority since the late Middle Ages had destroyed some of the political power of the guilds but in many cities in 1500 they still formed an important component in town government.

A fourth industrial form present at the outset of the expansive period of European capitalism was *Montanindustrie*, mining, smelting, charcoal burning and quarrying, located with reference to the sources of supplies of the natural raw material. Since these were deep in the mountains and forests, the industries exploiting them tended to be part of landed estates, with labourers closer still to a serf-like status and controls altogether less capitalistic than in the village or urban workshops.

lishers, 1969); T. K. Derry and T.I. Williams, *A Short History of Technology* (London, Oxford University Press, 1961); Melvin Kranzberg and C. W. Pursell, Jr (eds.), *Technology in Western Civilization*,vol. I (New York, Oxford University Press, 1967); Charles Singer *et al.* (eds.), *A History of Technology*, vol. 3 (London, Oxford University Press, 1957).

My own knowledge owes most to A. P. Usher's classic treatment, *A History of Mechanical Invention* (revised edn, New York, McGraw-Hill Book Company, Inc., 1954) and to the books and articles of J. U. Nef, especially *The Rise of the British Coal Industry* (London, G. Routledge & Sons, Ltd., 1932) and his essays reprinted as *The Conquest of the Material World* (Chicago, University of Chicago Press, 1964); also to C. M. Cipolla's interesting little books, *Clocks and Culture 1300–1700* (New York, Walker and Company, 1967) and *Guns and Sails in the Early Phase of European Expansion 1400–1700* (London, Collins, 1965) and Samuel Lilley, *Men, Machines and History* (London, Lawrence & Wishart, 1965) as well as his chapter 'Technological Progress and the Industrial Revolution 1700–1914' in C. M. Cipolla (ed.), *The Fontana Economic History of Europe*, vol. 3 (London, Collins/Fontana, 1973) and Hermann Kellenbenz's chapter 'Technology in the Age of the Scientific Revolution 1500–1700' in volume two of the same series.

The iron industry, often considered in this category, was in fact only partly so. Small iron deposits in shallow diggings were exploited at many scattered locations. Iron production was located with reference to ore and charcoal supplies and, with the fifteenth- and sixteenth-century development of the blast furnaces and rolling mill, to waterpower sources as well. But the further working of bar iron occurred at forges near market locations.

Finally, *merchant-organised networks combining rural and urban labour* were widely employed. In the medieval wool trade a famous division of labour had existed between England, which grew the wool, Flanders, which spun and wove it, and Italy, which dyed and finished it. The growth of the Italian woollen industry in the fourteenth century had displaced this trade by putting out materials within the Italian countryside. But in East Anglia and the west country in England, and in patches on the Continent – in Flanders, Switzerland, parts of northern France – forms of a putting out system had begun to flourish wherever rural labour could be put to use or where waterpower in the fulling operation had drawn that part of the finishing trades to the countryside.

In 1500 the forms of industrial organisation in western Europe then were the following: (a) village and local specialised industry; (b) peasant industry for the household; (c) urban artisan industry; (d) materials-oriented industries in the countryside; (e) merchant-organised systems, combining rural and urban labour. All these forms had been present in the thirteenth century, and all persisted in one corner of Europe or another up through the nineteenth century. The changes of the early and middle modern period, i.e. from 1500 to 1800, which are the subject of this essay, occurred steadily throughout these 350 years, in response to a number of economic and technical factors, in particular as a result of the interaction between market growth and technical change. Before the mid-eighteenth century much the major causative factor, insofar as it is possible to weigh such things, was, as Adam Smith discerned, the steady growth of markets – the increase in the volumes of industrial goods which could be sold.

THE GROWTH OF THE MARKET

To analyse the reasons for the market growth would lead the discussion far into the total economic, social and political history of the early modern period. Evidently a mass of self-reinforcing expansionary processes lay implicit in the European environment and social system of the fifteenth century. They have been only very incompletely laid bare. Population growth, resuming its upward course after the catastrophes of the fourteenth century, must have expanded the margin of cultivation, and in so doing have increased the absolute surplus available to support a non-agricultural workforce. If then economies of scale were present in industry taken as a whole, a rise in industrial productivity would ensue and with it a rise in the market for both manufactures and agricultural products. Or again the growth of the state – the notable feature of Western political history in the sixteenth and seventeenth centuries – centralised and magnified demand for certain specific industrial products – for military equipment, for ships, for coinage, for the constructions and luxury consumption of princely courts. The stream of landed revenues must have been in part diverted to the hands of those who demanded goods with a higher skill and materials component and a lower component of sheer labour services. The growth of taxes, with royal imposts piled on top of feudal dues, must have increased the slice taken from the peasantry whose localised demand patterns were less favourable to concentrated industrial activities. In this same category of explanation must be placed the famous sixteenth-century inflation – perhaps four-fold over the century and affecting agricultural goods more strongly than manufactures. Whatever the distortions produced in the distribution of income, it would not be surprising if a price rise in the presence of some reserves of rural underemployment should have stimulated total demand. It would be interesting, too, to speculate on whether larger supplies of the precious metals and the growth in credit instruments and forms of debt did not themselves extend the market simply by facilitating trade, encouraging the conversion of barter transactions to monetary ones and permitting the accomplishment of trading transactions which under a scarcity of money would not have been consummated at all.

The growth of trade itself may be looked on as an exogenous prime mover insofar as improvements in navigation, ship construction, and the increase of geographical knowledge were involved. Here within the growth of trade itself occurred a reciprocal process, moving from its expansion to the knowledge, growth, and technical changes which made further trade possible. Beyond that, the distributional shifts and social and organisational changes accompanying the trade expansion both affected the growth of the market for industrial goods and the changes in the organisation forms within industry itself; this will be shown in more detail below. Directly, one can attribute major economic effects before the eighteenth century not to the overseas expansion, but to the growth of trade within Europe, the Dutch–Baltic trade, and the trade between the North Sea and the Mediterranean. Yet the overseas trade – round Africa and to the Americas – must have acted as an important exogenous stimulus, whose effects were multiplied within Europe itself. Closely related were the social and intellectual changes which, intertwined with the contemporary religious and political change, made western Europe in the sixteenth century a seedbed of individualistic mercantile and capitalistic industrial enterprise.

The market growth then was accompanied by changes in the shape of demand, by the development of forms of business and market organisation, and by a spirit of enterprise which, taken within its institutional forms, we call capitalistic. It should be emphasised that the effects of market expansion were felt in the sixteenth to eighteenth centuries not only in the mercantile sector, but in industry as well. Village and peasant industry for immediate consumption probably did not flourish, although it maintained its share of local markets until the displacements produced by the technical changes of the eighteenth and nineteenth centuries. But urban workshops, mines, and smelting works prospered, the latter benefiting from some notable technical improvements. To them were added, particularly in the France of Colbert, the royal manufactories, the mints, arsenals, potteries, and textile factories under royal sponsorship and finance. Growth of a state sector was accompanied by the sponsorship of a technical discovery and of science, described in the following section.

Among the industrial forms, it was the merchant-organised and merchant-dominated rural industry which enjoyed the greatest expansion. Where trade and mercantile influence was strongest – in the Midlands and the north of England and along the great river of industry that ran from the Low Countries up the Rhine, across south Germany and over the north Italian plain – the activity was most striking. The actual penetration of the countryside, the use of surplus rural labour, the complex movements of materials and foods had gone far beyond the mere absorption of seasonally idle agricultural workers, or of women of farm households. A rural industrial labour force was present in these locations engaged in full-time industrial activity for the market. Tasks were divided, small pieces of capital intruded themselves at each point. The demand patterns, wealth patterns, and especially the demographic behaviour of this labour force were radically different from those of a peasantry or of industrial workers in cities. At the same time, an alternative system of industrial organisation had not died out. Urban workshops, mills and mines, royal manufactories had increased in number and benefited from the technical changes of the sixteenth century more perhaps than the cottage industry could.

THE PATH OF TECHNICAL CHANGE

Modern industrial society takes its origin in the eighteenth century at the intersection of two historical processes which, though never completely separate from one another, had developed during the Middle Ages and Renaissance in relative independence. One of these was the organisational development identifiable as early capitalistic enterprise. The other was the complex and uncertain process of technical changes.

That these two features of industrial history had existed in isolation in earlier periods is undeniable. Trade and production for private profit occurred in ancient Greece, in South Asia, and in medieval Europe, together with the introduction and diffusion of money as a means of payment. Technical changes were not notable in mercantile capitalism of this sort; indeed it is not clear that the mercantile mentality with its quick calculations and short time horizons is best suited to understanding and fostering the uncertain, obscure, and capital- and skill-intensive activities by which production processes are improved. On the other hand, technical changes had appeared in societies – for example in China – where the drive for maximum profit or the pressure of market failure was relatively remote. The very slowness of technical change over mankind's history, its spottiness, the lack of ready diffusion of its results, may be attributable to the relative isolation of peasant producers, royal households and craft workshops from the force of competition on capitalistically organised markets. So long as merchants dealt in the natural surplus of a region's agriculture, or in goods produced in the local monopolies of the countryside or the guild-dominated city, capitalist competition did not systematically penetrate the structure of production. Technology remained largely a matter of the transmission of the considerable body of hand skills, the arts of industry and agriculture, acquired painfully over thousands of years of industrial history and held tenuously in the brains and trained muscles of the living generation of craftsmen or in the pages of a very few hand-copied texts and treatises. In technology's long and uncertain development before 1800, new ideas appear rarely and when they do, it is as if in the thought processes of an absent-minded man. They do not diffuse readily over space, nor are they followed up in all their refinements and implications even at their points of origin. There is a lack of concentration in the history, a lack of cumulative effect in the development.

Nevertheless the industry of the sixteenth century benefited from an accretion of inventions that had occurred in Europe during the preceding 500 years. Among power sources, to be sure, no striking innovation occurred. Only in the development of firearms was the expansive power of gases harnessed to any use. Wind and water remained, and were to remain till the late eighteenth century, the only inanimate prime movers with appreciable industrial use. Except for water in mill ponds and dams, they could not be stored; hence industrial operations beyond the strength of men or beasts were as dependent on the variability of natural forces as was agriculture. In the face of this restriction, the main development in the sixteenth and seventeenth centuries was the diffusion, development and generalisation in a variety of uses, of the water wheel. In mining, in iron working, in fulling and other operations requiring a stamping and hammering motion, the water wheel hitched to many ingenious gearing devices came into much wider use.

Connected to this development were several improvements in the other components of an integrated technology: the provision of raw materials and the transmission of power. Materials supplies were increased in the sixteenth century by improvements in mining, in paper-making, and through the development of the blast furnace, which spread probably from the neighborhood of Liège up the Rhine to the south-east, and also north across the channel. The largest branch of industry – textiles – remained dependent, however, on traditional raw materials: wool from England and Spain, flax from the North Sea coast, and a little cotton from Egypt and the Middle East. It was the extension of trade within Europe and the geographical exploration overseas rather than technical change that widened European industry's resource base. Precious metals from the New World, and increased supplies of Baltic timber and Swedish bar iron were important accessions.

On the whole industry improved most through the further development of mechanisms for the transmission of power. Here the structure of the technology was, in a sense, best able to yield to the pressures and incentives of a growing demand. The lathe, that marvellous late medieval tool, was developed, improved and adapted to many uses. The products of the smithy, forge and machine shop were not the complex forms of machinery for further production known to the late eighteenth century, but direct consumer goods: firearms, clocks and watches, scientific instruments, furniture, hardware of all sorts, crude agricultural implements. No invention in the operations of the textile industry in its many branches approached that late medieval invention, the spinning-wheel, in productivity-raising effect. Where inventions occurred, for example, the stocking frame and the ribbon loom, they had a striking, but rather localised impact. Diffusion was slow, and the basic operations of cloth-making remained unaffected. Most characteristic of the sixteenth and seventeenth centuries was the strenuous activity of the industries involving the largely unmechanised assembly of parts and materials – construction and ship-building. Here organisation was important; although designs, styles and materials altered, the crafts and their tools remained much as the Middle Ages had left them.

In the three centuries prior to 1750, then, some changes occurred in the three branches of technology: power generation, power transmission and materials production. Particularly between about 1450 and

1600, a mini-revolution may be identified in the application of water-power in mining and iron-making, the developments in smelting, and in the invention of ingenious mechanisms, especially in branches of production specifically stimulated by a spreading luxury demand – firearms, printing, clocks. Many of the improvements originated in south Germany, and the diffusion of inventions was fairly rapid after the invention of printing and where the items themselves moved in trade. In the imaginative notebooks of Leonardo da Vinci sketches of these Renaissance inventions went far beyond actual practice, but retained that scattered quality characteristic of all pre-modern technical change. They depended in no respect upon the introduction of any drastically new scientific or engineering principle, such as was to characterise invention in the late eighteenth and early nineteenth centuries, and they had little interaction with one another. No chains of rapid inventive progress were forged to pull productivity along in one industry after another, with the steady upward movement that became the mark of the Industrial Revolution and the industrial history that followed it. The productivity growth may have contributed to the relatively less rapidly rising prices of industrial goods in the sixteenth-century inflation but the growth of demand appeared still largely dependent on the factors mentioned above – population movements, political change, geographical discovery, the increase in trade. Technology was learning, in a sense, to respond to market incentives, but it could not yet lead the way to continuous market growth.

THE GENERATING INSTITUTIONS OF SCIENTIFIC AND TECHNICAL KNOWLEDGE[3]

The historian, at least when he works on a period where data are scarce, is always part-novelist, employing a narrative rhetoric in which the tone

[3]Some useful references from the large literature in this field include the following: J. D. Bernal, *Science in History*, vol. 2 (London, Penguin Books, 1969); A. F. Burstall, *A History of Mechanical Engineering* (Cambridge, Massachusetts, M.I.T. Press, 1965); E. A. Burtt, *The Metaphysical Foundations of Modern Physical Science* (New York, Doubleday, 1955); Herbert Butterfield, *The Origins of Modern Science 1300–1800* (London, G. Bell and Sons Ltd., 1950); G. N. Clark, *Science and Social Welfare in the Age of Newton* (second edn, London, Oxford University Press, 1949) and *The Seventeenth Century* (New York, Oxford University Press, 1961); A. C. Crombie, *Mechanical and Early Modern Science*, 2 vols. (New York, Doubleday, 1959); A. R. Hall, *The Scientific Revolution, 1500–1800* (Boston, Beacon Press, 1956) and 'Scientific Method and the Progress of Techniques' in E. E. Rich and C. H. Wilson (eds.), *The Cambridge Economic History of Europe*, vol. IV (London, Cambridge University Press, 1967); Peter Mathias, "Who Unbound Prometheus? Science

and emphases of the discussion and the arrangement of its parts contribute to its interest and its verisimilitude. At this point in this essay, it would be appropriate and straightforward to move directly into the English Industrial Revolution. When we do that, in the following section, it will become apparent how readily that central development follows upon the general market growth, the articulated economic institutions and the rather diffused technological change of the sixteenth and seventeenth centuries. For a treatment, which encompasses the nineteenth century, even in part, on the Continent, however, it is necessary to consider another early modern development, whose connection with the inventions of the fifty years following 1750 is thought by most scholars to have been tenuous, but whose underlying importance for the path of modern industrial development as a whole can hardly be denied. This development is, of course, the growth of fundamental science, with a particular body of social institutions to carry it on, and a particular mentality, a way of looking at the world that we now recognise as 'modern'.

Scientific thought is akin to the rising capitalism of the Renaissance in several respects. Both are materialistic philosophies *of this world,* and both – at least in their European form – were conceived as activities of individuals rather than of social or corporate entities. Both began to grow in European society before the Protestant Reformation and were indeed part of the social and intellectual ferment out of which the Renaissance, the Reformation, and the modern national state arose. Both involved a trust in tangible sense data and both were rebellious against authority, especially when it interfered with the individual pursuit of gain, or of scientific truth. The medieval Catholic world had furnished not only a relation of man to God and His Church, but also a sense of the social whole. It was a world in which ideally every part and

and Technical Change, 1600–1800' in Peter Mathias (ed.), *Science and Society 1600–1900* (London, Cambridge University Press, 1972); R. K. Merton, *Science, Technology and Society in Seventeenth Century England* (New York, Harper Torchbooks, 1970); René Talon, *Reason and Chance in Scientific Discovery* (New York, Philosophical Library Inc., 1957); A. N. Whitehead, *Science and the Modern World* (New York, Pelican Mentor Books, 1948); Edgar Zilsel, 'The Sociological Roots of Science', *American Journal of Sociology,* 47 (1942), 544–62.

On the ancient argument over Protestantism and Capitalism, an article by Herbert Lüthy, 'Once Again: Calvinism and Capitalism', *Encounter,* 22 (1964), 26–38, contains a new point of view which I have adopted here. A recent thoughtful statement of a different, but by no means contradictory view, is made by Albert O. Hirschman, *The Passion and the Interests* (Princeton, New Jersey, Princeton University Press, 1977).

person depended upon every other, the whole bound together by a common belief in another world, and by a common magic – the magic of the church and its sacraments, as much as in any primitive society studied by anthropologists in recent times. Against this social sense, with its supernatural sanctions, capitalism put the pursuit of individual gain, without regard to just prices, usury restrictions, or any ultra-mundane devotion. Science, though long retaining a magical and religious aura, depended in Galileo or Bacon on an individual mind's search for truth by observation and experiment. The Protestant Reformation, expressing a similar individualism in the search for the soul's salvation, achieved a rapid, religious symbiosis with both capitalism and science which Catholicism never could attain.

Yet neither capitalism nor science could avoid or dispense with the institutionalisation of their thought and behaviour patterns, the regularisation of the norms by which both money-making and truth-finding might be legitimately achieved and success tested and identified, and the development of devices for communicating their culture to others and to successive generations. These tasks were vested only partially in the state; private business activities, private agreements and codes of behaviour, private meetings and correspondence formed the basic stratum of a developing modern culture in the economic and intellectual life of northern Europe in the seventeenth and eighteenth centuries. The small peer groups – companies of merchants, societies of amateur scientists, corresponding members of university faculties – began to form a significant social class, an aristocracy of money, enterprise or intellect within which the rewards and sanctions exceeded anything that a king or his courts could have imposed.

The free European market both in goods and ideas developed, however, in the presence of – one might almost say under the very nose of – a state apparatus which in the sixteenth and seventeenth centuries did not remotely resemble that of the nineteenth century when capitalism and science had become dominant. The relation to this state – the royal and centralist state of sixteenth-century England and seventeenth-century France – was ambivalent and, like most ambivalent relationships, stormy. Merchants and manufacturers depended on the growing power of the central government for many things: first, for special privileges, grants of monopoly, contracts and trading rights; second, for the establishment of a currency system and the chartering and protection of financial institutions; third, for the legitimising of commercial contracts, the protection of property, and to a considerable degree the control of the labour force. On the other hand, their interests were not synonymous with those of the state, and the presence both of the landed interest and the monarch himself ensured a conflict. Clearly for commercial expansion, the optimal arrangement was that experienced in the Dutch Republic after its successful revolt against the Spanish emperor and in England after the 'Glorious Revolution' of 1688: i.e. the substantial hegemony of the mercantile interest in the conduct of government. In France, the policies of Richelieu, Mazarin, and Colbert directed toward fostering trade and industry were a rather weak substitute for the stimulus given to trade by the provision of a greater degree of bourgeois freedom in the Protestant lands.[4]

However, for the development of science, as distinguished from practical improvements in technology, it is not clear that the dominance of society by the commercial classes was the most favourable arrangement. The role of scientist, even in the amateur or non-institutionalised science of the Renaissance, is closer to that of the theologian or scholar-priest than to that of the inventor of practical technology. He is the elaborator of the true view of the world, employing a method involving both reasoning and appeals to sense data, to give men an understanding of where they are in relation to the universe, and what is the ultimate constitution of matter and material forces. The sponsorship of such an institution devolved naturally upon those who in previous ages had sponsored the church and ecclesiastical foundations and activities. Included among these foundations were the universities, which in the sixteenth and seventeenth centuries were beginning to change from the monkish groups of the Middle Ages engaged in theological disputation into the general purpose institutions of knowledge we know today.

Science then, of the more or less 'pure' variety – the natural philosophy which investigated astronomy, mechanics, and even chemistry – found the growing interest in its methods and its findings institutionalised and sponsored in several directions: first, in small private groups and societies of interested men, rich enough to pursue such a hobby; second, under specific sponsorship and financial support by noblemen and monarchs and even by wealthy bankers or merchants, as part of a general sponsorship of the arts; third, in the universities, as separately endowed foundations under royal or ecclesiastical patronage. In the Protestant states, private groups with some royal sponsorship were largely responsible for the growing body of experimentation and research; in southern Europe, science had to live under the watchful eye of the church and the Inquisition; in France, a characteristic mixture of Catholic and Protestant forms, in this as in many other things, offered perhaps the most favour-

[4]Nothing has surpassed the treatment of French and other mercantilisms by C. H. Wilson in 'Trade, Society and the State' in E. E. Rich and C. H. Wilson (eds.), *The Cambridge Economic History of Europe*, vol. IV (London, Cambridge University Press, 1967).

able climate for the development. The Inquisition was absent; sponsorship by the crown, eager to exhibit itself as the source of all knowledge and all light, was generous, yet a spirit of free rationalism was not smothered. By the eighteenth century, these institutions had matured into a strong network of intercommunicating groups. Even in Prussia, Russia, and Austria, the monarchs of the Enlightenment, affected by a culture that had its home and origin in France, founded schools and academies. At length that Black Prince of the Enlightenment, the Emperor Napoleon I, in France itself, established a legal, educational, and professional structure for the country which crystallised and routinised the seventeenth- and eighteenth-century practice.

From Galileo to Darwin, then, European science participated in, and even led, the general development of a triumphant and glorious secular culture, its rationalism animated by a glowing faith in reason, its materialism made endurable by a strongly felt esthetic, its potentially corroding individualism checked and channelled by an emergent nationalism, by strong state power, and the sense of participation internationally in a developing bourgeois culture, replacing the universal aristocratic and ecclesiastical culture of Catholic Christianity. In this cultural climate the Protestant sects – Lutheran, Calvinist, Puritan, Baptist, and even the national churches that had broken with Rome – flourished. But the back of ecclesiastical domination of thought and science, and the fine arts had been broken by Luther's revolt and Henry VIII's bullying, and by the wars of religion in the Netherlands, France, and the German states. Theology was no longer the queen of the sciences. Catholicism was no longer Europe's state religion. Despite the emphatic personal ethics of its sixteenth- and seventeenth-century founders, and the persistence of such an ethic far into the nineteenth century, Protestantism was in fact a much weaker form of social control than Catholicism had been. By the nineteenth century, the scientist, the political economist, the politician, and the businessman had replaced the courtier and the priest.

From the viewpoint of industrial history, it is not clear that European science until the middle of the nineteenth century was of much practical value. Industrial technology, and agricultural technology too, developed by 'tinkering', i.e., by rather random experimentation aimed at some useful object. The details of the process are considered in the next section, where it becomes evident that the accumulation of various series of such efforts, produced at length the climax of interaction that we call the Industrial Revolution. The scientific investigation of nature proceeded along somewhat different lines. Yet parallelisms or interconnections between technological and scientific progress may be observed. For one thing, it seems quite apparent that much the same attitudes of mind motivated and guided both processes. A rational faith in the orderliness and predictability of physical processes and the stability of physical materials was combined with a refusal to accept any evidences of this faith except those offered by direct observation and material demonstration – a rejection of authority and of history, of all that could not be personally and individually seen, communicated, and made available to be confirmed by others. The difference between scientists and practical men before the nineteenth century lay in the scientists' effort to generalise their results with the instrument of mathematics, so as to produce 'laws' of nature. Where technological change stopped with the development of a useful device, process, or material, going on only to employ it in further uses or in other inventions, the effort of scientists was to produce a general statement which would state the enduring relationship, preferably with a formula showing the magnitudes of the quantities and effects involved.

Given the similarities in the basic animating attitudes, it is no accident that both 'pure' science and applied technology experienced a lift in the intellectual climate of the centuries in which protestantism and capitalism grew, and a culture of rational humanism spread out from Italy over western and northern Europe. Nor is it an accident that the branch of science and technology which was first to yield up its secrets to the curiosity and contrivances of men in these centuries was that in which natural forces and materials are most ostentatiously displayed to the naked eye: the science and art of mechanics. By the eighteenth century, both the science and the art were well advanced, and one can then see forming between the two, the profession so important for nineteenth-century development, the mechanical engineer, acquainted with scientific principles, possessed of an adequate knowledge of mathematics, concerned with the exact and quantitative statement of a phenomenon or relationship, and interested in relating this knowledge and technique to the improvement of the useful arts, of machinery construction, bridge-building, road-building, mining, navigation. The development of such a profession requires that both the science and the technology in a field be at a certain point of development, each having arrived there separately to a degree and by empirical methods, a point which makes it possible to relate theory and practice in a stream of systematic improvements. But to say that this relationship could occur, first in mechanics, then in hydraulics (a branch of mechanics), then – beginning in the mid-nineteenth century in chemistry, finally in electricity, and the life sciences – is not to argue of either scientific progress or of technological change that one was the cause of the other. Bits of interconnection can of course be found. The devices and materials developed in industry were available for scientific experimentation, and the demands of scientists had a stimulating effect on the development of measuring, timekeeping, and other instrumental equipment. But relative to industrial markets generally, the demands of scientists were but one of many luxury demands of individuals and the state – like the demand for fine tapestries, firearms, china – which a developing body of industrial crafts could serve. By and large, in the seventeenth and eighteenth centuries science and technology grew up together like twins in a family out of a common culture which had deep-hidden social and socio-psychological, and ideological, origins.

THE INDUSTRIAL REVOLUTION: TECHNOLOGICAL ASPECTS

The brilliant mercantile expansion of northern Europe in the seventeenth and eighteenth centuries was accompanied by a measure of technical change. Europe was here involved in a complex social process in which three aspects were of predominant importance: mentality, scale and feed-backs. Of the mentality we have already spoken: an inquisitiveness about nature and a greedy desire to improve on her workings for practical ends. The scale depended partly on the diffusion of these attitudes and the links of communication between inventors and producers at points as distant as Italy and England, Sweden and Spain. With the economic and industrial awakening of northern Europe after 1550, a sharp increase had occurred in the area and in the population over which trade and the exchange of ideas and devices of technology were diffused. The growth in intra-European trade, plus the small but marginally very significant links with the nascent overseas empires in the Indies, the African coast, and the Americas, meant a growth in market size which had many economic and productivity-raising effects. These depended largely on the spreading of fixed costs in tangible and intangible social capital of which the new nation states could avail themselves. Rivers, harbours, shipyards, dock facilities became more crowded and more fully used. Knowledge of ship construction, the shipping lanes, and navigation became more widely spread and shared. As shipping routes became more complex, with numerous burgeoning ports of call, waste space and empty return hauls diminished.[5] The states grew strong enough to war on each other, which was a waste, but also to suppress internal tolls, bandits and marauders on land and sea, and to establish that chief public good of the modern state, internal peace and order, so as to permit the easy development of commercial practices, and laws of property and contract, enforced by the king's courts.[6] The growth of navies made possible the convoying of

[5] D. C. North, 'Sources of Productivity Change in Ocean Shipping', *Journal of Political Economy*, 76 (1968), 45–69.

[6] D. C. North and R. P. Thomas, *The Rise of the Western World* (London,

unarmed merchant ships, and the use for cargo of the space previously taken up by guns and fighting men. As such extensions of scale lowered production and transport costs, incomes rose and the effective scale of the market was further increased. This purely economic feedback, dependent upon the phenomenon of decreasing social costs, was not, however, the most important effect of the expansion in the European economy and its interconnected commercial and industrial culture. To understand the crucial effect on the process of technological change, it is necessary to consider the process in a little more detail.[7]

Technological change, at least before the age of the research laboratory and a developed engineering and scientific base, depended upon the unorganised ideas and obsessions of individual inventors. These men came from various occupations, and often were themselves tool-users, conversant with some branch of production and observant of means of improving it. They became characteristically seized with a specific problem – the mechanising of stocking knitting, the casting of large pots, the working out of a control mechanism for a clock, the smelting of iron ore with coal – which they pursued with single-minded intent. Whether they solved it or not was partly a matter of luck, but it was also dependent on the ideas, materials, instruments and auxiliary devices with which their minds and their workshops were furnished. Given that an inventor was seized by a problem, his efforts to solve it were carried

Cambridge University Press, 1973); W. S. Holdsworth, *A History of English Law,* vol. 8, 10, 11 (7th edn revised, London, Methuen & Co. Ltd., 1973, 1966, 1973).

[7]See references cited in note 2, pp. 16–17. A good bibliography on all the subjects in this and the following section is given in David Landes' contribution to *The Cambridge Economic History of Europe,* 'Technological Change and Development in Western Europe, 1750–1914', in vol. VI, part 2, H. J. Habakkuk and M. M. Postan (eds.) (London, Cambridge University Press, 1965), extended and published separately, without bibliography, as *The Unbound Prometheus* (London, Cambridge University Press, 1969). The role of science and technology has been re-examined by A. E. Musson and Eric Robinson, *Science and Technology in the Industrial Revolution* (Manchester, Manchester University Press, 1969) and D. S. L. Cardwell, *Turning Points in Western Technology* (New York, Science History Publications, 1972) and *The Organisation of Science in England* (revised edn, London, Heinemann, 1972). The coal technology and its effects on industrial skills and locations have been the subject of researches by J. R. Harris and his students. See J. R. Harris, 'Skills, Coal and British Industry in the Eighteenth Century', *History,* 61 (1976), 167–82; Jennifer Tann, 'Fuel Saving in the Process Industries during the Industrial Revolution', *Business History,* 15 (1973), 149–59. Two other recent treatments with new materials are R. L. Hills, *Power in the Industrial Revolution* (Manchester, Manchester University Press, 1970) and C. K. Hyde, *Technological Change and the British Iron Industry, 1700–1870* (Princeton, New Jersey, Princeton University Press, 1977).

out on a stage which was set by all that he knew, and all the equipment and materials available at the time. At some point, in a successful invention, a moment arrived when, after weeks or years of conscious and unconscious concern with the solution, the combination of elements in the environment was hit upon, by accident, even in a dream, or sometimes with conscious design, which provided a feasible, economical solution. Following this, a period, called by Usher the period of 'critical revision', occurred in which the invention was refined, ancillary improvements were introduced, a model was made, a patent acquired and production begun. Even here, and in the early stages of the production process, many small inventions, small novelties were introduced. The whole was an act of creation perfectly analogous to the creation of a pure work of art or of the intellect.

Now the function of the environment in this process was to provide the inventor both with the problem and the means and stimulus for its solution. But the availability of such ideas and materials depended much upon how wide was the inventor's world and vision. The growth in the scale of the economy, and of western European industrial society, was a widening of this world. To provide in England, Swedish iron, or ideas published in German books, was to offer to English inventors materials and information which greatly facilitated their efforts. The function of scale expansion then, apart from spreading the fixed costs of equipment, transport, public goods, and knowledge, was to increase the communication of such ideas and the availability of such materials and equipment. Across western Europe, in all the industrial areas, a race of inventors appeared in the wake of the industrial and commercial expansion. But it required a particular intensity of economic life, a rather strong concentration of industrial opportunity, a rather close-knit nexus of communication to produce a flowering of inventive activity. The combination of attitudes, ideas, knowledge, ambitions, commercial opportunity and the protective institutions of property and patent rights – all this was required to coax out invention and then, once it was begun, to give it its head.

Hence it was that 'the' Industrial Revolution occurred not in the old industrial areas of the continent, in royal factories, or towns dominated by princes or the remains of guilds – but in England where trade expansion, capitalist institutions, a pragmatic view of the world, and a social structure that gave common tradesmen and mechanics appreciable freedom, were all simultaneously present and on an adequate scale. The Netherlands, a closely analogous case in many respects, could not furnish so large an internal market or so broad a base in industry and industrial resources. England, on the other hand, which had shared but not dominated the European expansion in scientific knowledge, main-

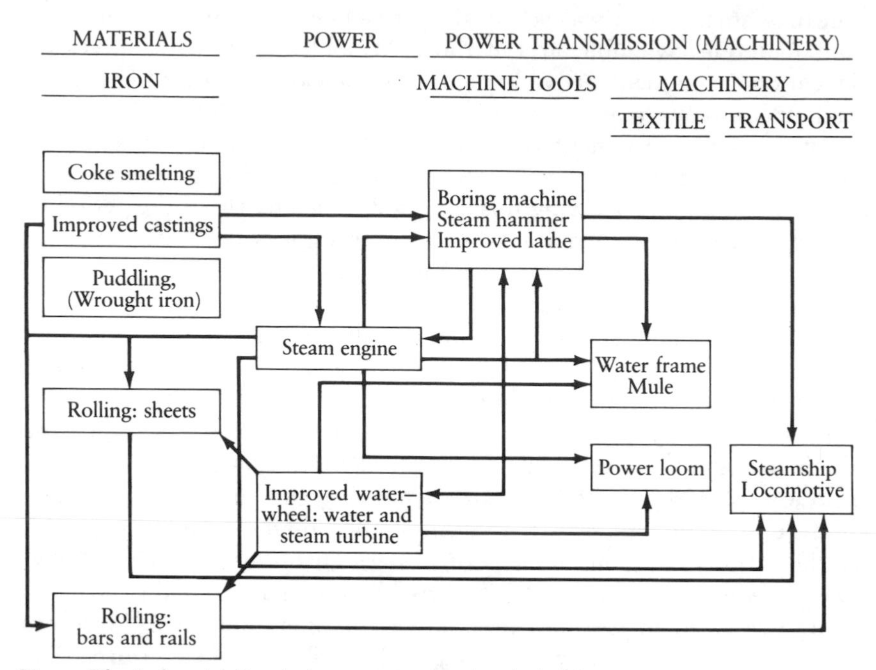

Fig. 1. The Industrial Revolution: sequence and technical interconnections, 1750–1850.

taining her connection with the intellectual sources of invention, offered a commercial climate in which the activity could flourish.

Given this locus for inventions, it is of interest to examine their specific interconnections. Figure 1 divides inventions into three groups: the production of materials, the generation of power from inanimate sources, and the transmission of power – its 'harnessing' to move the right part, at the right speed in the right direction. These branches of technology in the eighteenth century existed in what may seem by some retrospective standard to have been uneven states of development. The third, being mainly the province of mechanical technology, was the most advanced. Using parts made of wood or of iron, employing the power of animals (including men), of gravity, generally with the medium of falling or moving water, or of the wind, a body of equipment had developed since antiquity, which under the inducements of the sixteenth and seventeenth centuries had acquired considerable sophistication. Until the middle of the nineteenth century, it was these mechanisms which showed the greatest development. Most of the industrial revolution was the extension of machinery – now built of iron – into new types of operations and new branches of manufacture and agriculture. Underlying the whole development of the mechanical side was the elaboration of machine tools and the development of a profession of mechanical engineering whose calculations could improve design and efficiency. The mechanical inventions of the period 1760–1850 make a very long list indeed, and developed partly out of one another, employing parts, devices, or ideas to produce a widening array of products.

Alongside these inventions, the other two branches of technology have only two major changes to offer: in materials production, the improvement and cheapening of iron through smelting, refining, and further working; and in power generation, the development of the steam engine, itself largely a mechanical invention except for the novel power source employed. The important improvements in the water wheel came largely as the result of careful application of principles of mechanical and hydraulic engineering to an old device. It may be thought a convenient formulation to call these 'enabling inventions,' which occurred at just the time and to just the degree to permit the mechanical industrial revolution to flourish.

It would take a long book to begin to specify all the interconnections among the mechanical inventions. The story of Watt's dependence on Wilkinson's boring machine to give him cylinders machined to a fine enough tolerance is but one example. Through the mass of technical interrelations an evolving body of machine technology was initiated. Its creation required a number of economic, social and intellectual conditions, notably: (1) a moderately large and well-organised market sufficient to make invention profitable; (2) within that market, some bottlenecks focussing attention on specific points in the technical processes of manufacture, offering rewards for the solution to specific technical problems; (3) a body of skilled mechanics, tool-users, and ingenious practical men who kept in touch with one another and with manufacturers; (4) means of finance at least at the very modest levels required in this sort of research and development; (5) an absence of interference or excessive direction or planning from a central authority, whether the state or money market. In these circumstances, invention could become a kind of folk activity, done repeatedly, on a very small scale, by very many different operators. An attack of this kind on the secrets of nature is sometimes called a 'shotgun approach'–the firing of many small missiles at the target. Obviously such a process entails great individual loss, many bankruptcies and much suffering. In the absence of full knowledge of the underlying science, no other way of guiding invention was possible.

Given this social technique of invention, it was certainly no accident that mechanical invention flourished while subtler forms and problems of technology–in chemistry or physics, animal breeding or the plant sciences for example–lay untouched. Most of its basic knowledge goes back to Aristotle and Archimedes and the development of mechanisms for specific tasks was not a matter of research but of contrivance. Ingenuity and imagination were required, but the instrument of observation was the naked eye and, unlike the case in agricultural sciences, the success or failure of an experiment could be immediately known. No historian of technology has yet arrayed discoveries in various branches in order of their inherent difficulty, or in relation to the capital equipment in instruments, scientific knowledge, and experience required to bring them to light. Yet such an investigation must underlie the understanding of why modern technology developed in the forms and sequences that in fact it did.

The fact that mechanical inventions came first, employing iron and moved by waterpower or by the steam engine using wood or coal is, however, a fact of vast significance for modern industrial history. Its significance for the development of the organisational form of modern industry – the factory – built around a central power source is considered in the next section. Equally important was the way it reinforced, almost as if by design, the commercial supremacy of England for the hundred years after 1770. The technology of coal and iron was, by modern standards, a crude and simple technology which favoured, locationally speaking, areas well-endowed with those minerals. Such accidents happen in economic history where the effects of resources, techniques, and commercial culture are so closely intertwined. How different might the picture of industrial location in the nineteenth century have been had not coal, but oil, been the first prime industrial fuel, and water power or water vapour figured less prominently! The large coal and ore resources conveniently located near water transport in Great Britain set the seal, as it were, on the predominance that Britain's commercial expansion had already initiated. Other coal and iron areas at that period of history had generally one raw material or the other, but not both, or were themselves remote from intense commercial activity, and British capital was not yet moving out to such locations with the vigour and abundance that appeared in its worldwide expansion after 1850. Other strongly commercial areas, the Netherlands or later New England, did not overlay, in close contact, the extensive subsoil deposits that could create a local mining industry. In Britain, both parts of the puzzle fell into place and a complex industrial development suffered no check from any direction. But while all this is true, it was also the case that Britain really held no secrets in the minds and equipment of her inventors which others could not readily copy. If the Industrial Revolution was built on a combination of aggressiveness and physical advantage, there might come a time when others who had or could acquire similar endowment could adopt the attitudes that produced so exciting a result. The British development was like the growth of a tropical forest in a favourable climate and on the soil of a shallow technology which proved exceedingly fertile for a short space of historical time. As technology advanced in step with a developing body of science and scientific techniques of gaining more knowledge, its roots went deeper, its variety became richer, and its applications in the world's areas came to depend less on climate, harbours and mineral wealth at home, and more upon the adaptability to local conditions that a profound knowledge of the ways of nature would permit.

As the Pandora's box of modern technical knowledge was opened, the creatures which lay on top swarmed out first. And the situation was made the more complicated by the fact of not one, but two Pandora's boxes – one labeled Technology and one labeled Science. It is not fair to English science to suppose that because inventions poured out of the Technology box in such profusion, the Science box lay unopened. But in fact for British technology the commercial opportunities in the late eighteenth and early nineteenth centuries were so rich that the mass of inventions of immediate practicality darkened the sun. Like rich lumps of ore lying on the surface of a deep deposit, the mechanical inventions, involving simply the physical relations of one piece of visible matter to another, lay open, shiny and attractive, available at the cost of a little ingenuity and cleverness. What lay below the external appearance of matter, what forces bound it together, even giving it life, could not be known and worked for the practical power it gave over nature until the Science box had been opened for several generations. A science of mechanics could be developed in the eighteenth century, and a mechanical conception of nature, originating in the study of celestial mechanics, could take hold of men's imaginations at the same time that mechanical technology could proliferate in practical uses. As the profession of mechanical engineer developed, the science could even be of use in the art of invention, particularly in perfecting its details and increasing its efficiency. And purely empirical research could go a long way towards harnessing even forces as remote and dangerous as electricity or the chemical processes of metallurgy or the explosive power of gunpowder or combustible vapours. But as the mechanical technology presupposed a certain level of familiarity with mechanics, these later technological developments came about in the presence of an advancing science already looking into their essential nature and causes. The growth of that sort of knowledge in turn required experience with, and improvements on, the methods, instruments, and language of science itself.

THE INDUSTRIAL REVOLUTION: ORGANISATIONAL ASPECTS

The path of mechanisation and its attendant industrial change through the industries and regions of western Europe is sketched briefly in the final section of this essay. Before discussing the spread of technology, however, it is important to specify more exactly the old and the novel elements in the socio-economic organisation which surrounded, permitted, and even stimulated it, and ultimately were so strongly shaped by it. Changes in the status and condition of the working class were the most sensational social effects of the new industrial forms and techniques. A subtle analogy exists, however, between the balance of liberty and authority in labour organisation and similar balances in capital markets and in the social and intellectual history more generally.

In all respects English society appears to have been freer, more fluid, closer to an ideal market economy, even in the eighteenth century, than were the kingdoms of continental Europe. Much erosion of medieval and even of mercantilist restrictions and conceptions had occurred with the development of trade and the working class. The almost purely capitalistic form on which English trade was conducted and financed promoted the diffusion of a money economy and market relationships and motions from international commodity markets into the markets for capital, technology, and labour. The wide extension of the putting-out system – the creation of mercantile enterprise – gave entrée for capital into industrial processes, but it was not wholly responsible for the revolutionary result. Putting-out existed on the Continent, too, without leading readily into a dynamic process of technical change. But the fact that some mobility of capital, ideas and labour was good does not imply that more would have been better. English society of the late eighteenth century must have contained a balance of mobility and rigidity, of fluidity and 'lumpiness', of freedom and authority very nearly optimal for economic growth in that stage of technology and markets. To make this point more explicitly, we must consider the function played by monopoly and immobilities in productive factors in three areas: the generation of technology, the accumulation of capital, and the organisation of the labour force.

Technological change.[8] In a competitive economy organised by small-scale producers, the generation of new techniques is both stimulated and directed by economic circumstance. If a new product or new process can be devised and temporarily or permanently monopolised by a producer, monopoly profit can be derived from it. The incentive to innovate should be high, particularly if the market is wide, but not so wide as to make its monopolisation wholly beyond the reach of any

[8]Some of the extensive literature on induced innovation and related topics is examined, and many important insights given, in Nathan Rosenberg's collected essays, *Perspectives on Technology* (London, Cambridge University Press, 1976) especially chapters 4–6.

single producer who can obtain a modest cost or sales advantage by an invention. Or in a competitive industry producers may be threatened with the narrowing of profit margins, or even with bankruptcy by sudden external developments. Competing products suddenly coming in from abroad or from regions opened up by transport improvements, a tightening of the labour market, or rises in raw materials costs, may produce this threat. Producers then may feel pressure to seek for innovations, to shift out of production, to find other sources of labour or supplies and to apply any other available profit-maintaining or cost-reducing devices.

Innovation induced in these ways is part of competitive producers' efforts to escape from the pressure of competition on profits by whatever means are at hand. The effectiveness of the incentive was recognised in England and on the Continent in the eighteenth century by the development of patent laws, themselves a device drawn from the arsenal of state mercantilist policy. Patents, by giving a monopoly, or property right, in an invention, need not have a total social effect of stimulating the competitive search for innovation or efficiency. The effects of royal grants of monopoly in the seventeenth century differed little from the effects of the guild restrictions of medieval industry. But given for a limited period in an atmosphere of competition, patents may offer the promise or the illusion of encouraging invention without perpetuating monopoly. On the whole patents appear to have added a bit to the incentive to innovate without much encumbering the spread of knowledge. Furthermore, as an unintended side-effect, patenting created a new product: technology, which could be licensed or sold. It helped to professionalise the trades of inventor and engineer and to separate invention from production, creating a specialised activity with its own organisation and rewards. This aspect of the development did not become prominent until late in the nineteenth century.

Now the special historical conditions under which patents and property rights in knowledge could have an incentive effect on the creation of new technology appear to have obtained in the hundred years from 1750 to 1850 in Great Britain. Most important in the result was the relatively small scale of production. An industrial production derived not from the monopolies of craft shops but in large measure from the mercantile organisation of the putting-out system was animated less by the 'instinct of workmanship' than by the drive for profits. Even in a monopoly, if a profit-maximising spirit is preserved, the possibility of adding to profits acts as an inducement to invention. But the atmosphere was one of a world not of monopoly but of small competitive ventures, each seeking to capture a bit of profit, as in a trading venture, and needing some special place in the production structure to do so.

Capital was fairly mobile within the trades and competition was keen. How much more then must the drive for profits have been active where profits were continually threatened, where competition or external developments brought the face of bankruptcy and ruin up close, pressed stark against every producer's window! Not monopoly, not pure competition, but the uneasy monopoly in a competitive world offered the economic – as distinct from a sheer intellectual – stimulus to invention.[9]

A rush to invention as a means to gain or to maintain profits in a competitive economy suggests that invention is in some sense easier to come by than the rearrangement of capital and productive factors through markets along different lines. Indeed this is what is meant when it is said that invention is spurred on by the fear of loss along a given line of production. Such loss can be felt only if productive factors are immobile, if sunk capital or acquired skills cannot be converted or liquidated and shifted to other use, if the supply of a factor to an individual producer is not perfectly elastic. In order for bottlenecks in production to arise, creating quasi-rents for some and threatening ruin for others, a degree of factor immobility is necessary, and it must appear to producers more nearly possible to break such bottlenecks cheaply, not by shifting factor proportions, or moving out of the industry, but by focussing inventive talent on some portion of the production process. Inventors must be, in a sense, more mobile than capital or labour, if economic circumstances as such are to produce a spur to invention. But in fact it is just this generalisation of mechanical and inventive talent, this flexibility and mobility that appear to have existed in eighteenth-century England and nineteenth-century USA – perhaps even more strongly in the latter where a 'jack of all trades' tradition had been stimulated by the conditions of the frontier.

The scale on which inventive activity occurs and the openness of lines of communication among inventors and between them and producers is also an important feature. Large-scale organisation, with good communications, makes for specialised activity which narrows an inventor's focus, but a large economy also provides a mass of industry over which inventive talent can work. Were the market to reign supreme, without other means of communication or other incentive to inventors, specialisation might become too narrow and invention too closely directed to specific ends. The inventor must see beyond the end of his nose, or of a profit and loss account. Were the market not to exist at all, an inventive culture might intercommunicate, but the spurs and the signals to move

[9] F. D. Prager, 'A History of Intellectual Property from 1545 to 1787', *Journal of the Patent Office Society*, 26 (1944), 711–60. See also the remarks in D. C. North and R. P. Thomas, *The Rise of the Western World* (London, Cambridge University Press, 1973), pp. 152–6.

and direct useful activity would be absent. Here, as at so many other points, an appropriate mix of market and non-market organisation and motivation appears to have been required for economic and industrial growth.

The incentive effect, as just described, is supplemented in modern technical change by another effect of economic circumstances, called by Rosenberg, 'focussing' – the steering of an inventor, or a group of inventors in an industry, toward a specific problem. In what has been said above there is no clear reason why the economy should cause invention to focus on one problem rather than another. Invention may be induced in response to external circumstance but in general not located or focussed by changed economic conditions. If labour grows expensive, there is no particular reason for producers looking for labour-saving techniques, rather than some other sources of savings. The structure of production and technology should adjust where it is weakest, i.e. where factors are most mobile or where technical changes are closest to the horizon. However, the small-scale competitive firms of eighteenth-century England utilised rigid and rather narrow techniques. If costs in a process rose, the option was not open to reduce costs in other firms or branches of production; the process itself had to be adjusted or the trade abandoned by the producer. In coke smelting, for instance, a rise in the price of charcoal might in theory have caused capital to move elsewhere. But in the smelting firms, it may plausibly also have focussed inventive activity on efforts to find a substitute fuel. A rise in the price of yarn, derived from increased demands of weavers using the flying shuttle in the eighteenth century, or by suspension of English yarn imports on the Continent in the Napoleonic wars, might have been compensated by some shifts of workers into spinning. But it would also understandably focus inventive activity on improving the productivity of the spinners already at work. And if, as it happened, that was just a place where invention was practicable, where the structure of the existing technology was relatively easier to change, then spinning inventions would be the result.

The mechanical technology of the eighteenth century appears to have been particularly susceptible to such economic inducements and focussing. The situation in industry indeed was not as dissimilar to that in agriculture as has sometimes been supposed. In both sectors the skills of workers trained in the specific trade since youth had formed the basis of the technology. In both sectors, the excitement of market growth, stirring the imagination of materialistic and money-minded men, encouraged efforts to improve existing techniques. In both cases under such pressures the body of existing technology proved itself capable of extensive improvement without undergoing striking change in fundamental principles. In industry the improvement was accompanied by the perfecting of a science of mechanics (which could later be applied to agriculture as well); both art and science were capable of being improved by the unaided power of the mind and the eye, by observation, thought, and contrivance, and the technology could move on within half a century to more complex realms.

Organisation of capital and labour.[10] Strictly speaking, a 'market for technology' did not exist before very recent decades in industrial history. In the eighteenth century there was a market for products, and not a very perfect market at that. But where it was active, thanks to mercantile activities, it made its influence and excitement felt backwards into the structure of production and even of technology. In doing so, the mixture of market and non-market elements, of old and new motives, of pockets of security and profit in the blowing wind of competition created an excellent environment for rapid, simple technological change. As the techniques were derived from production experience, so did they remain closely entwined with industrial activity, providing a growing inventory of tools and ideas for further development.

The situation was not greatly different with respect to the accumulation of capital. Capital was thought of as either very short- or very long-lived. The national wealth, when it was thought of at all, was viewed either in the mercantilist notion of a stock of precious metal, or in Adam Smith's enlightened view, as land improvements and public buildings, and the energies and skills of the population. Private capital was a merchant's stock in trade or a manufacturer's inventory of materials and goods in process or a fund of money to be turned over in trade or through wage payments in the somewhat more lengthy processes of manufacture. As in the case of technology, there was not so much a market for capital as a responsiveness on the part of capital to market

[10]The *loci classici* for a discussion of these subjects are the famous chapters in Adam Smith, *The Wealth of Nations,* book 1, chapters 1–3, and Karl Marx, *Capital,* vol. I, chapters 13–15. An interesting, and provoking, recent addition to the discussion is by S. A. Marglin, 'What Do Bosses Do? The Origins and Functions of Hierarchy in Capitalist Production', *Review of Radical Political Economics,* 6 (1974), 60–112. On the supply of capital to industry in the Industrial Revolution, see the essays collected by Francois Crouzet, with a valuable editor's introduction: *Capital in the Industrial Revolution* (London, Methuen & Co. Ltd., 1972). Management methods are discussed in Sidney Pollard, *The Genesis of Modern Management* (Cambridge, Massachusetts, Harvard University Press, 1965) and sociological aspects of labour force organisation in Neil Smelser, *Social Change in the Industrial Revolution* (Chicago, University of Chicago Press, 1959) and the work of E. P. Thompson, *The Making of the English Working Class* (New York, Random House, 1963).

facts and opportunities. The liquidity which a primitive capital market afforded, and the communication of knowledge of investment opportunities encouraged saving and directed capital into profitable uses. But most of the industrial capital in England appears to have derived from industrial operations; indeed in early firms the distinction between capital and income, or capital expenditures and current expenses, was not made at all clearly. Such a situation was conducive to industrial saving, and to reinvestment at points where a hard-headed entrepreneur could see prospects of a sizeable gain. Money and credit, and even mercantile banks, were essential to keep the system running, but one may wonder whether a sensitive market for industrial capital would have improved the rate of accumulation or the direction of its investment. As it was, with each firm depending largely on its own resources the incentive to save was high, and the investment was made by those with best knowledge of the opportunity. It is doubtful whether the collection of brokers and stock-jobbers accompanying the capital markets of the 1870s and 1880s would have either induced more saving or known how to advise investors more wisely than the entrepreneur-savers of the Industrial Revolution were able to do for themselves.

If the organisation of capital and enterprise in the Industrial Revolution involved no separation of ownership and control, the reverse may be said for the organisation of labour. I do not refer here to the notorious separation of the worker from his 'means of production', the tiny physical capital of which he had availed himself under the putting-out or craft shop systems of organisation. Within both those organisational forms, a hierarchical organisation prevailed, based on the hierarchical organisation of the family. In a shop the master controlled the labour of his family and, for the length of their terms, that of journeymen and apprentices. Within such tiny political units, each man had his duties and station, and no doubt customary rights and obligations assumed the form of informal law, just as had occurred on manorial estates on a larger scale. Similarly also in rural domestic industry, a man commanded the labour of his wife and children, subject to all the sanctions which through proximity and affection they could inflict upon him. Nor is it clear that the position of women was distinctly inferior to that of men in the peasant or peasant-industrial household. What distinguished the fully developed putting-out system from these was the intimate and customary tie of the head of the family or para-familial labour unit to the furnisher of the materials and the market. To the degree that the merchant employer held a regional monopoly over 'his' cottage workers, the latter were subject to close bargaining whether they 'owned' their tools or not. Materials could be allotted and piece rates fixed to keep labour's share at a minimum, and the difficulty of organising a group of workers established that preponderance of bargaining power on the side of the merchant employer, which was to become so marked in the developed factory and wage labour system.

In these conditions, the establishment of a few factories, i.e. collections of workers or worker family-groups under one roof and subject to one direction, may have made capitalist control of a labour force easier in the short run. But ultimately, as Marx first pointed out, factory organisation, though facilitating longer hours, stricter discipline and more careful supervision of time and materials, in the end removed the capitalist's great advantage over his workers: the difficulty they had in communicating with one another when they worked at dispersed locations. Instead of coming together at church or tavern on social occasions only, under the eye of priest or constable, the workers in a factory were thrown together in daily, intimate, professional contact. It is little wonder that workingmen's associations, which had led to a marginal existence among apprentices or rural workers, pushed beyond the limits of endurance, began to grow into regular and continuing bodies as factory organisation extended its scope. The titular loss of independence through loss of ownership of a few tools was finally more than balanced by the gain in easy access to the means of group solidarity, though this did not necessarily help the workmen immediately affected.

In those trades where the advantage of a factory organisation was confirmed by the grouping of complex geared and belt-driven machinery around a single power source, it was almost inevitable that the organisation would be carried out by a capitalist grouping workers at just the right points in the machine process, supplementing the failings of the machine by manual skills and human muscle power. The system indeed was preserved anachronistically within some early spinning factories, and systems of piece rate and time rate competed with each other for dominance. 'The market' appeared in the buying and selling of labour power as of any other commodity, but it is equally important to note the points into which the market did not penetrate. Labour was sold, but not by the minute on a perfect market, subject to close calculation and instantaneous renegotiation. The workers could not hire capital in the same sense that capital could hire workers; rather the hierarchical form of family organisation was preserved and transferred here, and without many of the protections that customary law in a small political unit gave to family and workshop. Workers sold themselves for a space of time, in a form of daily slavery, agreeing to do each day what job the employer required in exchange for a wage. Such an organisation is not truly a market organisation in the same sense as foreign exchange markets, for example, where supplies are offered and withdrawn at a slight titillation of the price, and negotiators change sides from supplier to demander as quickly as thought passes through the mind. The capitalist firm was a political organisation in its internal structure, bound by markets at either end.

The question is: how well was this form, derived so naturally from the historical circumstances in which the new technology was created, adapted to those techniques? It is not possible to argue that the techniques themselves were created and adapted to the form without ignoring the immanent constraints of the technology. Are we not rather in the presence again of one of those historical coincidences without which the surprising growth of modern industry could never have occurred? Remarkable developments require remarkable explanations and England's sudden industrial development in textiles and iron was a wholly unexpected and, in the long run, unsustainable and extraordinary event. Why then should it appear or yield to some deterministic and holistic explanation?

Whatever the explanation, it is possible to argue in retrospect that the adaptation was a good one for establishing machine industry and for insuring its spread. The factory built around a central power source – a water wheel or large steam engine – possessed significant technical economies of scale, particularly since the steam engine was never as successful as was later the electric motor in adapting to a wide range of capacities. The scale economies made it profitable to keep machinery in continuous operation – particularly water wheels during seasons when water power was strong. (In many cases the steam engine was first used to supplement water power in dry seasons.) It meant also attaching as much machinery as possible to the wheel or engine once its fixed installation was accomplished, and so of producing a large volume of output. These economies of scale were closely allied with economy of continuous operation, particularly evident to private owners of capital who thought in terms of turning over their stock. Whether working with his own or borrowed money, it paid a manufacturer not to let his equipment stand idle. But continuous operation had another aspect. While the machinery was attached to the power source, it all moved together. Belts or specific machinery might be temporarily detached, but on the whole workers had to operate with the machine and to time their motions to its requirements. This was the principal advantage that a wage system, with an authoritarian organisation, held over a system in which labourers might sell not their labour but their product as it passed from one form to another, or might renegotiate their labour contract minute by minute, or hour by hour. The resemblance of factory organisation to that of an army, in which each member had to respond quickly and on command, without knowing all the reasons why, did not escape notice. And, as in an army, the operation of the market principle within the organisation was rendered impossible, or at least unnecessary, by the fact that a few men – the managers – planned the whole operation and had no need of any inputs from below.

It remains to ask why, if slavery on the job was the technically most efficient status for the labourer, the freedom of the labourer off the job appears to have been wedded so closely to nineteenth-century industrialism. In Russia and in the American South, serf- or slave-operated factories were not unknown. Their limited success makes them the exceptions that prove the rule. The answer – that it is cheaper for an individual capitalist to avoid responsibility for workers off the job – is not wholly satisfactory since it confounds the individual with the social perspective. Unemployed or ill workers had to be supported by someone, and ultimately the capitalists would have to pay a sizeable share of the cost. The advantage of freedom over slavery for the workers in nineteenth-century growth appears to have lain in the value of mobility in an economy where new industries, firms, locations, and tasks were appearing every week. Where entrepreneurs were locked in to their already adopted technique and where capital was not nearly as liquid as it was later to become, ownership of workers by masters, or even binding patriarchal relations deprived an economy of an important element of flexibility. And, too, wherever freedom won out over slavery the drive to individual self-advancement could remain for workers as for entrepreneurs a strong engine of economic growth.

In England, the peculiar mixture of markets and authority could prevail because state controls had been relaxed to a greater degree than on the Continent. Here again the vestiges of an earlier, more authoritarian organisation remained, enough to preserve the regularity of life and of expectations. It is not that the state was weak; there was no question of who retained the monopoly of force. The central authority of the Tudor state, indeed of the Norman kingship, was retained. The writ of the king and the king's courts ran into every county, and the lords lieutenant and the state church kept watch on the vagaries of local and town government. Below that and well integrated into it, a social structure of classes sustained by a class deference derived from feudalism persisted in England as elsewhere in western Europe. The beginnings of a democratisation, or even a thorough embourgeoisement of this society were still a hundred years in the future, and a full modernisation and proletarianisation still further off. The difference between England and the Continent lay not so much in the balance of central and local authority as in who controlled that authority. Here thanks to the intrusion of a strong mercantile interest in the struggle between king and landed aristocracy, the power of the Renaissance and seventeenth-century monarch, so strong in France and on a miniature scale in the German states, had been balanced by the wealth of London and the Puritan independence of large areas of the countryside. The Revolution of 1688 was to set the seal on a political compromise which lasted till the Reform Act of 1832–rather less a compromise than a combination of the heavy weight of a Protestant landed interest and a Protestant merchant and banking aristocracy to establish a limited monarchy. With things so arranged on top, and with enough flexibility to adjust squabbles within the ascendant Whig and Tory aristocracy, a government of incredible strength and toughness evolved, able to survive and surmount financial instability and crises, massive fraud and corruption, wars on the Continent and overseas, the loss of one empire and the development of another, and finally to organise the conservative forces of the Continent to the defeat of Napoleon. Little wonder that such a structure could also almost unconsciously control and channel the forces of a rising industrial development. No doubt its congeries of policies and laws, a fantastic scrap basket of bits left over from feudal and medieval restrictions, mercantilist encouragements, and responses to the pressures of particular situations and interests, produced a less than ideal or optimal effect on the development. One thing was clear; it was fully capable of providing stable support for the evolving body of commercial law, for the 'rights' of the individual property-holder, and for domination over the labouring poor. It was not a 'tool' of the propertied classes in any conscious, planned, or conspiratorial sense; had it been so, its evolution into full parliamentary democracy and twentieth-century socialist industrial organisation would have been far less steady and more bloody. But in the eighteenth century and the early nineteenth, it produced just the balance of authority and free markets that an early and unsteady capitalistic industrial organisation required to take its first steps toward maturity, strength, and dominance. On the Continent, developments were otherwise, as the following section will indicate.

THE SPREAD OF MODERN INDUSTRY[11]

The spread of mechanical techniques through industries and through geographical regions is a pair of processes with many common charac-

[11] W. O. Henderson, *Britain and Industrial Europe 1770–1870* (2nd edn, Leicester, Leicester University Press, 1965) traces some of the direct lines of connection from Britain to the Continent. Rondo Cameron's original and well-researched book, *France and the Economic Development of Europe 1800–1914* (Princeton, New Jersey, Princeton University Press, 1961) and the monumental work of Maurice Lévy-Leboyer, *Les Banques Européennes et l'Industrialisation Internationale* (Paris, Presses Universitaires de France, 1964) treat the Continental industrialisation, as does the earlier work of A. L. Dunham, *The Industrial Revolution in France 1815–1848* (New York, Exposition Press, 1955) and the

teristics. The mechanisation of a new industry required adaptation of the power and inventions to harness power to specific operations. The spread of a given machine technique, e.g. mechanical spinning, from one region required interested entrepreneurs, favourable factor cost conditions, suitable government policy, and supplies of capital and workers adaptable to the machine process. It too required minor inventions to adapt the equipment to specific raw materials, markets, climate, and labour force. The timing, speed, and form of the diffusion in both cases depended on special technical, economic or sociological conditions of the industry or region in question. In the competitive economy of northern Europe, the spread of mechanisation among industries was in one sense the more fundamental sort of diffusion since the minimum physical cost locations of new industries were determined by cost characteristics of the new technique. Given these characteristics, the ultimate dispersion of an industry was largely a matter of economic geography. Social and economic differences – the availability of capital, the training and immobility of the local labour force, the policy of the region's government – determined the lags, however, before the 'natural' economic factors and the force of competition took effect. This was especially true where the natural locational advantage of one region over another was rather small. In textiles, for example, differences in the location of enterprise, capital, cheap labour, and close relations with overseas outlets could set the advantage.

Diffusion among industries. In an earlier section, indication was given of the path of the Industrial Revolution among industrial processes.

essays by Jan Craeybeckx and Claude Fohlen in Rondo Cameron (ed.), *Essays in French Economic History* (Homewood, Illinois, Richard D. Irwin, Inc., 1970). To the classic textbook of J. H. Clapham, *The Economic Development of France and Germany 1815–1914* (4th edn, London, Cambridge University Press, 1963) and David Landes' treatment of the western European area as a whole (see *The Cambridge Economic History of Europe*, vol. VI, part 2, H. J. Habbakuk and M. M. Postan (eds.) (London, Cambridge University Press, 1965) and *The Unbound Prometheus* (London, Cambridge University Press, 1969) have now been added very good chapters in A. S. Milward and S. B. Saul, *The Economic Development of Conti-Europe 1780–1870* (London, George Allen & Unwin Ltd., 1973) and in C. M. Cipolla (ed.), *The Fontana Economic History of Europe*, vol. IV, especially chapter 1, 'France 1700–1914' by Claude Fohlen, and 2, 'Germany 1700–1914' by Knut Borchardt. The conference volume of the International Economic Association, edited by W. W. Rostow, *The Economics of Take-off into Sustained Growth* (New York, St Martin's Press, 1965) also contains a number of valuable articles on early development in various countries as well as an evaluation of the 'take-off' hypothesis of W. W. Rostow.

One may observe certain clusterings in the history of its progress. One was the spread of the power process from cotton-spinning through other branches of the textile industry – to wool and linen, and after a delay to mechanised weaving. Hand processes in the garment industry – e.g. shoemaking and sewing – presented specific technical problems which yielded, one after another between 1800 and 1850, to British and American ingenuity and enterprise. All this development was brought on partly by the force of economic pressures within the structure of textile and clothing production which focussed inventive activity, and partly by the rise in the level of technical opportunity for solving problems through improvements in materials, machine tools and control mechanisms. The history of the development of the sewing machine may be cited as a notable example of the eco-technic process at work.

Beyond the 'light' industries – textiles, boots and shoes, machine tools, and farm machinery – the latter developing more rapidly under favourable market and terrain conditions in North America after 1850 – there lay the engineering problems of heavier equipment in transport and power generation. Continuous improvements in the steam engine increased its efficiency and extended the range of capacities and pressures generated and contained. Such improvements occurred at all the locations where engines were used and produced, in England, Wales, Belgium, Germany – even on the banks of the Ohio in America. The adaptation of steam to water navigation is a classic story in the history of invention, and from Trevithick to Stephenson, the development of locomotives, braking mechanisms, and all the vast array of railroad inventions created the mid-century transformation of land transportation. In stationary engines, the first half of the nineteenth century saw the development of the water and steam turbine in France and England through the inventions of Fourneyron and the thorough investigation of the science of thermodynamics by Carnot.[12]

We have seen that mechanical inventions, as they spread to various industries and locations in northern Europe and North America, presupposed a large interconnected industrial region. This was required to ensure both adequate market size and the mass of intercommunicating inventive activity necessary to keep economic expansion and technical change in motion. In the eighteenth century, it appears that central England itself was a large enough area. A striking fact about the Industrial Revolution is the speed with which improvement extended from iron and machinery production to the manufacture of machine tools. Machine tools lie deep in the production processes of modern industry.

[12]D. S. L. Cardwell, *From Watt to Clausius* (Ithaca, New York, Cornell University Press, 1971).

To make it worthwhile to devote efforts to improve the machines which make machines, a large market for machinery is essential. The increase in the productivity of machinery and in its durability when iron was used worked in exactly the reverse direction. A market for machinery of unusual scale must have been present to give the impetus. This is true in early nineteenth-century north-eastern United States, where the level of income, its distribution, the protection afforded by distance from English competition and (some allege) the scarcity of labour relative to capital, and of both relative to the ambitions of the population, helped also to allow an industry of specialised machine tool manufacture to grow quickly out of the machine shops of the textile mills. Once developed, the machine tool industry, employing water or steam power, improved and cheapened iron, and better and more closely machined parts in its own equipment could lift machine production out of the workshop of the mechanic and make it too a factory industry. The cheapening of machinery, rather than a fall in the rate of interest, has been largely responsible for the greater physical capital intensity of modern processes.

In England and Belgium, the close link of machinery production to the local iron industry cannot fail to be observed. With the possibilities of steam-powered machinery, an engineering industry was growing up around iron works, and the massive fuel requirements of coke smelting and puddling brought iron works to locations at coal beds. In Britain by 1850 most major coal beds were thus the site of iron smelting and fabricating industries. There can be little doubt that even before the steel inventions of the 1850s, the coal-based industrial complex was an economic unit. Because of the saving in fuel transport costs and the further advantages of agglomeration and communication in a concentrated area, its products could undersell those of producers at scattered locations. By 1850 the Industrial Revolution, as a revolution in both technology and plant and enterprise organisation, had spread from cotton-spinning to other 'light' easily mechanised industries, then to the heavier industries of transport equipment and machine production itself, the latter based also on the improvements in the iron industry that were part of the eighteenth-century development. Lodged between light and heavy industries, the machine tool companies expanded and extended the varieties and uses of their products. As these industries, particularly those using coal and iron, clustered around coal or ore mining areas, the typical industrial complex of the later nineteenth century was formed. The railroad added to the advantage of these dark and smoky districts even as it increased the demand for their products, and the Bessemer and open-hearth processes coming in after the 1850s ensured their stability for the half-century following 1870, not only in

Britain and Belgium, but around the coal beds of the valleys tributary to the lower Rhine, and the upper Ohio.

One must remember that the Industrial Revolution was based on a certain group of inventions and an accompanying organisational form, which could not spread beyond the industries where coal, iron and machinery could be introduced. In Britain in 1850 many industries and operations were not power driven, or mechanised. The largest component of the non-agricultural labour force in 1850 was, after all, domestic service, and the mechanisation of the household lay beyond anyone's imagination. Construction, including ship-building and road-building, was relatively untouched, similarly most food-processing operations and, of course, agriculture. The very growth of the larger-scale industries, and the swarming of populations to new locations gave occupation to vast numbers of small-scale producers, and furnishers of service. Office work, too – except for the development of the typewriter and the telephone and telegraph after 1850 – experienced no productivity increases, and the way was laid in all these respects not only for the perpetuation of the class of small shopkeepers and professionals, but also for the growth of the 'white collar' staff of the larger establishments. The whole society then was not industrialised, much less proletarianised. Industry, industrial capital, industrialists, and industrial wage workers assumed a place on the front bench of society and politics, constituting a special 'interest' alongside the interests of the mercantile community, the bankers, the professional and white collar class and the landed interest of ancient origin. It assumed a place beside the others, but did not crowd them off the scene.

Diffusion among regions of north-western Europe. The advances in the cotton, iron and machinery industries between 1780 and 1840 were the whole bases on which the English Midlands, with extensions in South Wales and Scotland, in 1850 rested a remarkable industrial leadership over the long-established industrial regions of the Continent. In textiles, technical obstacles which lay in the way of mechanising operations in flax, silk, or even wool did not obstruct the application of machinery to cotton. England's lead in the cotton industry then must be attributed to her superior trading position and access to markets and to raw cotton supplies. Possibly also, the long experience in wool made an easier transition to cotton than could be achieved by silk or linen producers. The development of a cotton industry on the Continent had to depend initially on the importation of English machinery and a few English workmen and plant designers – an expensive and unsatisfactory way to overtake a foreign competitor. Still machinery was eventually applied to the branches of textiles in which continental producers specialised and the slower pace of development in machinery and the iron industry on the Continent cannot be attributed to technical reasons. Clearly before 1840 the continental industrial regions – the cities with their workshops and the rather widely separated and disconnected areas of rural industry – lacked the intensity in industrial activity closely linked to machine shops, which gave British industry the critical mass necessary to a continuous and self-reinforcing economic and industrial development. The imported English spinning machinery at Ratingen in the Rhineland, in Normandy along the Seine tributaries, and later in Ghent, were sparks of modernisation which did not light a fuse to set off the fireworks.

The Belgian case is the exception on the Continent which proves the point at issue here.[13] In Flanders the dense textile industrial district lay close to a large foreign market and to the iron- and coal-based industry of Liège and the Belgian coalfield. Even under Napoleon, industrial development began, when the area was joined with the Dutch provinces in 1815, overseas markets were opened and access given to Dutch capital. The Dutch areas themselves failed to industrialise – possibly because of a history and social structure based solely on commerce, possibly also because of lack of cheap coal. Instead, the Dutch king invested in the Belgian areas which lay under his government between 1815 and 1830, and a little borrowing of workmen and machinery from England developed mechanised spinning and a domestic machinery industry. By 1850 – twenty years after the separation from Dutch rule, the Belgian Netherlands had become the world's second coal-based industrial district in which the light and heavy industries of the Industrial Revolution were joined.

The persistence of traditional and typically 'early modern' barriers to industrialisation on the Continent is shown best in France. The Revolution had swept away the remains of feudal forms – feudal land tenures and the power of the guilds in cities. It had destroyed, indeed it had confirmed, governmental centralisation and mercantilist policies of the state. The revolutionary governments and Napoleon had strengthened the state much as Louis XIV had done, though more intelligently, and much was provided for the new (and not so new) commercial and industrial bourgeoisie. Commercial and property law was regularised through the *Code Napoléon,* scientific and technical education was extended and strengthened. An educated scientific and engineering élite

[13] To the references cited in note 11, p. 45 above including an excellent chapter in Rondo Cameron's *France and the Economic Development of Europe* 1800–1914 (Princeton, New Jersey, Princeton University Press, 1961) may be added a recent treatment of the Belgian 'case' by Joel Mokyr, *Industrialization in the Low Countries* 1795–1850 (New Haven, Connecticut, Yale University Press, 1976).

was enlarged. The Bank of France helped stabilise the currency and brought French public finance up to the degree of modernity that England had achieved a hundred years earlier. Modernisation and regularisation of the tax system added greatly to the regularity with which business expectations could be pursued. By reducing its personal and arbitrary character, the post-Revolutionary government helped to create a climate of reduced uncertainty for mercantile and business interests.

The regimes from Napoleon I to Napoleon III offered also many direct opportunities to business enterprise. Interruption of trade with England from 1790 to 1815 reserved the Continental market to Continental – and largely to French or Belgian – producers. The inflation and the wars themselves offered the usual opportunity for short-term and individual gains. Enough venality was present, enough luxury demand, enough waste to nourish the greediest entrepreneur. Yet for all that, one cannot speak of any French government until the parliamentary democracy of the Third Republic, as an oligarchy like that in seventeenth-century Netherlands or eighteenth-century England. The peasantry, the church, the remaining aristocracy, the army, the bureaucracy – all were too strong to furnish a clear climate for modern capitalism. If the balance in England by 1780 was about right to allow an eco-technic, industrial revolution to proceed, the balance lay in France a bit too strongly on the side of what Marxists call pre-industrial economic formations. Much is made in history books of England's political gradualism, in contrast to France's recurrent revolutions. But in economic modernisation, it was in France that gradualism prevailed. Napoleonic government and its successors under the Restoration and the July Monarchy maintained a stance which combined liberalisation, protection, and paternalism until more classic liberal policies were introduced. By that time, industrialisation had developed into something different from what it had been seventy years earlier, and what France had preserved of the older forms and values – the system of technical education, the aristocratic spirit of scientific research, the balance between population growth and her own food supplies – began to pay off.[14] The nation then could lay the base for continued economic progress as a national unit, even up to the present day, through all the devastations of war and political and moral catastrophe.

The situation in the scattered German textile and metal-working re-

[14]French technical education is interestingly treated in F. B. Artz, *The Development of Technical Education in France 1500–1850* (Cambridge, Massachusetts, The M.I.T. Press, 1966). A recent dissertation by Bernard Gustin, 'The German Chemical Profession: 1824–1867' (Department of Sociology, University of Chicago, 1975) throws needed light on German chemical training and research before Liebig, and the role of the apothecaries in the development.

gions of the eighteenth century was not greatly different from that in France.[15] But they lacked two developments that English and French regions had experienced: incorporation in a national state, and within it a political revolution. Even by 1700, the physical depredations of the Thirty Years War had been repaired, but within the notoriously numerous political districts, a mixed medieval and Renaissance political economy survived and flourished. The states were not inactive in efforts to advance industry; they encouraged it by all the best principles of mercantilist economic policy. Nor was there any lack of skill or enterprise in many areas; we have seen earlier how extensive was the diffusion of the Renaissance technology in the south, central and western German states. Rhine merchants and bankers were active throughout the whole period before 1850, and in south-west Germany, the activity and ambitions of apothecaries, along with the princely sponsorship of 'pure' science in the universities, laid the foundations for Germany's later successes in chemicals. The tariff history, of which so much has been written, indicates that barriers to internal trade were overcome, but the Zollverein, too, was a mercantilist measure pursued from political motives, not only on the part of Prussia but also of the petty princes who hoped, in typically seventeenth-century fashion, to increase net revenues from a source outside the control of assemblies and nobility. Even after the industrialisation got under way in the Prussian territories and in the Empire, no one would ever have mistaken the Imperial German government for a businessman's state.

By 1850 what was lacking in both Germany and France in 1800 had been partially supplied. The social and political basis for modern capitalistic industry had inched its way toward a condition which could tolerate capitalist expansion without the continual drag of medieval or mercantilist restrictions or the unexpected and disrupting assertions of authority of divine right monarchs and their bureaucracies. Then between 1850 and 1870 two decades of classical liberal policies in both France and Prussia expanded trade, strengthened financial institutions, encouraged capital accumulation. What had been lacking in the earlier textile industrialisation was the opportunity to make the link with the iron industries, and this the railroad had only partly supplied. But the social and physical elements in modern industry were present – the in-

[15] See the articles by Herbert Kisch in note 1, p. 15 above and also Gerhard Adelmann, 'Structural Change in the Rhenish Linen and Cotton Trades at the Outset of Industrialization' in Francois Crouzet, W. H. Chaloner and W. M. Stern (eds.), *Essays in European Economic History* 1789–1914 (London, Edward Arnold Ltd., 1966). On metallurgy, see N. J. G. Pounds and W. N. Parker, *Coal and Steel in Western Europe* (Bloomington, Indiana, Indiana University Press, 1957).

tangible social capital of laws, skilled mechanics and engineers, educational institutions, a still disciplined labour force, and the physical capital of transport improvements. As contact between regions improved, the disadvantages of the small- and scattered-scale of the earlier textile and light machinery industries began to be overcome.

Into this atmosphere in the 1860s came as a supplement and substitute for wide geographical scale, the opportunity for heavy industry localisation. Through the accidents of politics north-western Europe's coal was distributed in bits across all of the major north-western countries. It had long been known and mined in spots – in the Saar, in the Liège region, and at a few shallow diggings in France. With the opportunity opened by market growth and the steel inventions of the 1860s, the clustering around these deposits began to take shape, and the immense industrial strength of the Franco-German–Belgian area began to make itself felt.

The development of coal, steel, chemicals and electricity on the continent belongs to the history of the latter part of the nineteenth century. It would take another chapter, or another book, to fill it in. It exhibits similarities in form and timing to the American development south of the Great Lakes, between Chicago and Pittsburgh in these same decades. But European industrial history prior to 1850 shows that it grew up on an industrial base very different from that of both England and the USA. Unlike the eighteenth- and early nineteenth-century developments in England, continental industrialisation after 1850 was not based simply on the scale economics of wide textile markets, and the accompaniment of a mechanical engineering technology. That was a combination which the continental locations, for reasons of economic and social organisation in the late eighteenth century, had not been able to achieve. But at length after half a century of sporadic, artificial, and pale imitations of British technology, continental industry hit upon a rich vein which its own tools and traditions were able to mine. In the technology of coal-based chemistry, in metallurgy scientifically developed, and in inventions leading into the lighter but even more science-based industry of the twentieth century, the Continent's long industrial traditions and its institutions of pure scientific research and of applied training could at last come into their own. With the concentration of activity around coalfields, the industrial strength was developed which, by permitting further developments away from coalfields, could lead continental industry into its upsurge after the calamities of the 1940s.

This essay develops ideas offered in lectures to graduate economics students at Yale University over a number of years, and exposed also at seminars at European and American universities since 1972. I wish to express thanks to many participants in those seminars for useful comments, and in particular to Richard Levin, Jan De Vries, Harry Miskimin and Quentin Skinner for reading and commenting on the manuscript. I am especially indebted to Peter Mathias, Eric Jones and Peter Burke for initial encouragement, even though they may, like St Peter, wish now to deny it thrice before the cock crows. The work could in any case not have been brought into this form without a generous grant from the Concilium on International and Area Studies and the Department of Economics at Yale, and the diligent and informed research assistance of Laurie Nussdorfer.

My debts to the authors in the field are only imperfectly acknowledged in the footnotes, but will be evident to anyone acquainted with some of the literature, including, I trust, the authors themselves. The footnotes indeed are intended not as source references or elaborations of the text, but as suggestions for further reading, primarily in English-language sources. A full bibliography of the main writings published in English, French, German and Italian since the publication of the major bibliographies of David Landes, *Cambridge Economic History of Europe,* vol. VI, part 2 (1965) and Maurice Lévy-Leboyer, *Les Banques Européennes et l'Industrialisation Internationale* (1964) is in preparation. I regret that I have been excluded from writings in Dutch and Swedish by 'ignorance, pure ignorance'.

PART III

Heavy industrialization in the European regions

3

The interruption of expansion

GROWTH BEFORE THE FIRST WORLD WAR

Following upon the revolutionary inventions of the mid-nineteenth century, in a generally expanding market, with adequate growth in supplies of trained personnel and of capital, and an increasing knowledge of the successive minor improvements in equipment and techniques, the producers of coal and steel in Western Europe found themselves continuously encouraged to expand output, to sink new mines and to build new plants. The decade of the 1880's passed with no appreciable discouragement to this general upward movement, and it continued with only short setbacks until the eve of the First World War. Then, with the year 1913, a sort of divide was reached, like that between the watersheds of two rivers, and here, as in so many other features of European life, a period of astonishing progress came to a sudden close.

Between 1880 and 1913, the annual rate of growth in coal production ran continuously at about 3 per cent; coke and pig-iron output grew at rates over 5 per cent, and beginning in 1890 – at which time the basic open hearth process was beginning to establish itself in the Ruhr and the Thomas converter process in French Lorraine – the average annual rate of growth in steel production was about 8 per cent for the next twenty-four years.[1] These rates compare with high rates of growth

Originally published in N. J. G. Pounds and W. N. Parker, *Coal and Steel in Western Europe* (London: Faber & Faber Ltd., 1957). Reprinted by permission.

[1]These rates are based on output by region, collected from a variety of government and trade association sources. Other statistics of output in these chapters are similarly derived. Full data and references are given in the author's article, 'Coal and Steel Output Movements in Western Europe, 1880–1956', *Explorations in Entrepreneurial History*, April 1957. The area covered by the data here is less than the area of the present Coal and Steel Community by exclusion of Italy and of the small output of Western German regions outside

in periods of rapid industrial expansion in the economic history of other countries.[2]

INSTABILITY AND STAGNATION SINCE 1913

The movement of output of all these products after 1913 presents the most striking possible contrast to this picture of steady and rapid growth. Production, shown in Figure 1, no longer moved continuously in any one direction, either up, down, or 'sideways' (i.e. remaining constant). Instead it moved from catastrophe to climax in three successive waves during the two world wars and the intervening Great Depression. The cataclysms of 1915–1925 were the most terrible and complex of all – several partial recoveries being succeeded by even deeper falls in output. The events of 1944–6 reduced production briefly to the lowest levels of this century, but were not succeeded by the serious interruptions of recovery which characterized the early 1920's. The depression of the early 1930's did not reduce production to the depths reached in 1919, 1923, or 1946, but it provided an effective check to the sharp upward movement of the late 1920's.

The wide swings in output since 1913 present the most spectacular contrast to the even movement of the peaceful decades before that date. A more significant, and superficially more disturbing fact, however, reveals itself on closer examination. Beneath this uneven record, one comes to suspect that – at least between 1914 and 1950 – some mighty

Rhineland–Westphalia. Data for 1956 where given are based on latest available estimates.

These rates of growth are, of course, reduced if combined with the much slower growth of cast iron and the absolute decline in puddled iron. The growth of pig-iron production represents more closely the growth in total output of iron for final use.

[2]Burns's measurement of the average annual growth rate in the United States for the period 1885–1929 is as follows:

	Percentage per annum	
Coal	3.7	(A. R. Burns, *Production Trends in the United States*, New York, 1934, 57–9.)
Coke	4.6	
Pig-iron	4.4	
Steel	7.2	

However, for the period 1880–1913, these rates were higher. See also the table of average annual rates of growth of these products in W. Hoffmann's calculations for Great Britain. W. Hoffmann, *British Industries 1700–1950* (M. O. Henderson and W. H. Chaloner, tr.), Oxford, 1955, p. 320.

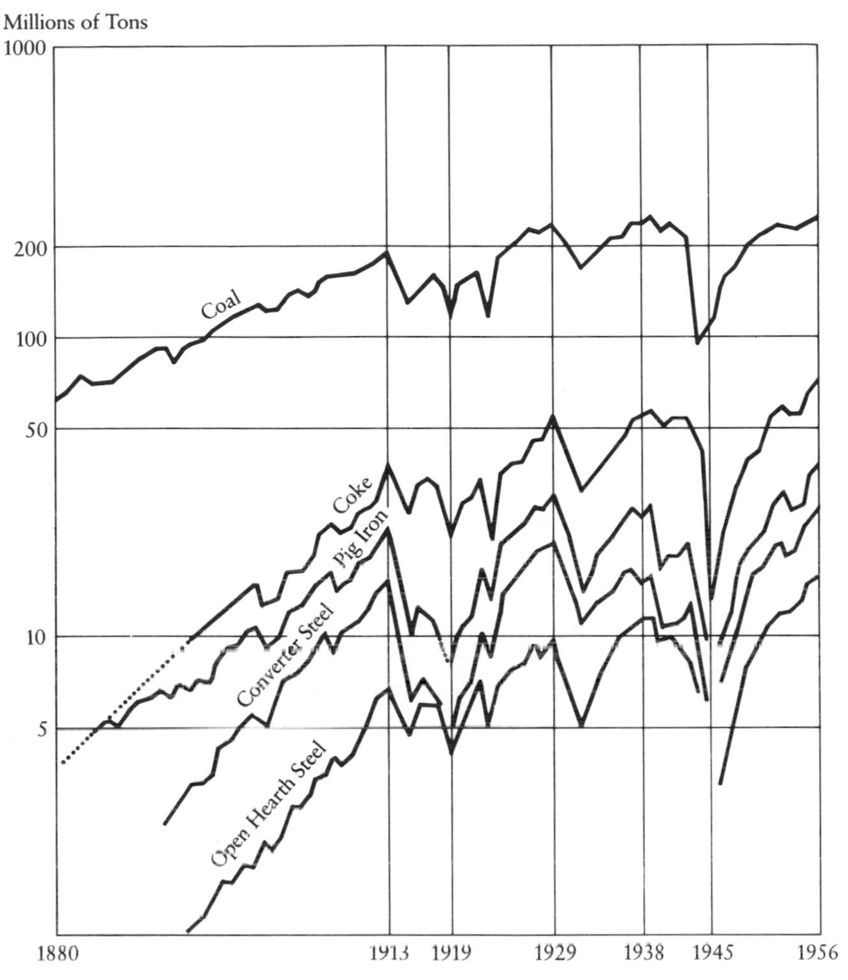

Fig. 1. Coal, coke, pig-iron and steel production of the West European countries (France, Belgium, Luxembourg, Netherlands, Germany).

force of propulsion, which produced not only steady, but strongly upward-moving trends of output for decades before 1913, had been seriously weakened. The continuation of pre-1913 trends of output would by 1929 have produced levels of output far beyond those actually achieved. The 1929 output levels, shown in Table 1, stood between 20 and 50 per cent above the level of 1913. The continuation of a steady average annual rate of only 3 per cent, however, would have yielded outputs over 60 per cent above 1913 in 1929. The conclusion is clear: the recovery of 1925–9 made up a portion of the increase in

Table 1 *Percentage growth in output between peak years, 1913–56, in Western Europe*

	Output in the peak year of the period:			
	1920–1934[a]	1935–1944	1945–1956[a]	1945–1956[a]
	as a percentage of output in the peak year of the period:			
	1909–1919[a]	1920–1934[a]	1935–1944	1909–1913[a]
Coal	119	103	102	125
Coke	148	101	129	193
Pig-iron	129	91	139	164
Steel				
Converter	141	85	158	189
Open hearth	142	119	138	235

[a] The peak years were 1913, 1929, and 1956 in all commodities for these periods.

production that had been lost, but did not continue long enough to represent a restoration of the pre-war long-run average rates of annual growth. Until the mid-1950's the year 1929 represents in general the best that the European economy could achieve. The recovery of the late 1930's, far from representing any growth above the maximum outputs of the late 1920's, barely met those levels in most products. Comparison of the first and last columns of Table 1 indicates however that since 1954 the 1929 ceiling has been decisively broken through.

Within the general pattern of output after 1913, certain differences occur among the records of the individual commodities – coal, coke, iron, and steel. Open-hearth steel production grew significantly from one peak year to the next; in converter steel and pig-iron, growth was stopped between 1930 and 1954. However, these movements of the products relative to one another represent in part the ascendancy in different periods of German as against French regions. The fluctuations in output since 1913 are also of considerable interest for the economic history of these troubled years. In each decade, the problems of these industries and the short-run aspects of the record present important subjects for research in the general study of industrial fluctuation. Attention in this and the following chapters, however, is directed largely to the long-run movement of output – the steady growth to 1913, and the movement from peak to peak in the succeeding years.[3] Here, par-

[3]The method and point of view here, though arrived at independently, resemble in some respects those of the much broader study by I. Svennilson, *Growth and Stagnation in the European Economy*, Geneva, 1954. Svennilson's analysis of the coal and steel industries (Chapters VI, VII) is based on national, rather than regional, statistics.

ticularly in the records of the producing regions relative to one another, the force of geographical and technological factors reveals itself. Treatment of some of the economic and social elements affecting the record is contained in the next essay.

INTERPRETATION OF THE OUTPUT RECORD

Growth to 1913, and a general stagnation since that time, are a reflection of the changing limits of economic opportunity for producers in these industries in Western Europe. The opportunity opened first by the great inventions of the mid-nineteenth century was sustained by the remarkable ore discoveries in Lorraine and by the increasing accessibility of Northern Sweden.[4] These developments reduced sharply the physical costs of production in mining and steel-making and opened the possibility for a growth in output even more rapid than the growth in the European economy as a whole. At the same time, the level of aggregate demand in Europe was rising over these decades. To be sure, the opportunity for a growth in output might have been destroyed by sharp rises in the prices of productive factors – labour, materials, equipment – or in the cost of borrowing money. For output to grow within the limits of the opportunity, an efficient industrial organization of individual skills and ambitions was also required. The record of output is sufficient indication that, taken all in all, these economic elements that limited opportunity, and these social elements, affecting the response of producers, were not unfavourable. The rising demand and the new inventions and ore discoveries may be considered *active elements* affecting the conditions of production; the failure of costs to rise and the presence of an industrial organization favourable to expansion were, in a sense, *permissive elements* enabling steady growth in output to occur in these years.

Europe after 1900 held few new surprises in techniques or sources of materials for producers in mining and metallurgy. Only the sharp upward movement in aggregate demand sustained the opportunity for expansion to the eve of the First World War. Until the reconstruction and new investment of the early 1950's, the capacity of mines and mills – expanded from a variety of motives in the 1920's – was to be fully utilized only in 1929, and in certain products and regions in 1938. Resources and techniques became largely passive elements in the long-run movement of output, while aggregate demand maintained a tyrannical sway, producing both the violent short-run oscillations and the general stagnation already observed. The movement of wage and other cost rates – not examined here – was almost certainly unfavourable in

[4]M. Flinn, 'Scandinavian Iron Ore Mining and the British Steel Industry, 1870–1914', *The Scandinavian Economic History Review*, II, 1954, 31–46.

the long run. In these circumstances of sharply narrowed economic opportunity, the industrial organization and individual effort by which the human response to opportunity is expressed became matters of secondary importance for interpreting narrowly the long-run output record in these industries. Minerals exploration, technological change, and movements of demand, however, must be closely examined. We focus attention here on the first two of these elements in the economic opportunity facing producers.

MINERALS EXPLORATION AFTER 1900

No decline in skill or ambition can account for Europe's failure to repeat after 1900 the sensational minerals discoveries of the nineteenth century. Differences continued to exist between the French and German methods of organizing minerals exploration. In France, much work was financed and organized by the State. In the mining districts, state engineers carried on exploratory work partly in connection with the preparation of the geological map of France.[5] Mining and steel companies, working in co-operation with state engineers or private drilling companies, obtained concessions; each concession, however, was in the form of a specific contract between the State and the concessionnaire. So long as the state supervision was efficient and honest, this system made for orderly and vigorous exploration. In Germany, the system based on the Prussian mining law of 1865 was considerably more free. Concessions were made automatically, as a matter of right, to the discoverer of minerals, under standard and rather liberal conditions.[6] By both systems, effective exploration was carried out in all regions.

[5]A similar official map was prepared for the Ruhr by the Preussische Geologische Landesanstalt, but much more work even of a purely scientific character appears to have been sponsored by the industry in Germany than in France. See *A. d. M.*, Ser. 7, IV, 375; Ser. 12, I, 257–65; Ser. 12, XVII, 119–66, and the long article by P. Lafay, Ser. 12, XVI, 179–235. Discussion and bibliography of German geological work is contained in P. Kukuk, *Geologie des niederrheinisch-westfälischen Steinkohlengebietes,* Berlin, 1938, 21–5, 631–93. An interesting comparison of French and German methods of exploration in the Lorraine ore field is given in J. Bichclonne and P. Angot, *Le bassin ferrifère de Lorraine,* Nancy-Strasbourg, 1939, 57–69.

[6]A comparison of the French, German and Belgian laws at the turn of the century is given in C. Dumanent, *Traité de l'Exploitation des Mines,* Brussels, 1898 (2nd ed. by A. Dufrane-Dumanet), III, 427–47. Some modifications of these laws were made after 1900, in the direction of closer control in Germany and greater flexibility in France; the essential differences, however, persisted. See *A. d. M.*, Ser, 10, XII, 217–31, where the 1907 modifications in the German law are discussed, and *Gluckauf,* 1937, 47–8, for later changes. A comprehensive study by H. Lanetois, *A. d. M.*, Ser. 13, XIII, discusses the changes in France, Germany, and the Netherlands (see esp. pp. 260–71, 321–5).

Closer survey of the extent of existing coal deposits produced in fact rather surprising results in all countries. Within a few years after 1893 in Dutch Limburg and 1901 in the Belgian Campine, the further extensions of the Aachen field were fully uncovered, amid considerable excitement. In Belgium, the discoveries were of special interest, since they contained a good proportion of coking coal, and were more easily mined than the Southern Belgian field.[7] In the Netherlands, the discoveries made mining on a significant scale possible for the first time.[8] German occupation of the major French mining regions during the First World War induced an extensive search for coal by the state engineers in the rest of France, with very meagre results.[9] In 1903–7, drillings in the region of Nancy showed the extent of the Saar–Lorraine field, and the intervening region was explored by Germans before 1914, and by French after 1919.[10] In Pas-de-Calais, although drillings continued, discoveries after 1905 were of little importance.[11] In the Ruhr, however, the continued mapping of the north-eastern extension of the deposit combined with drilling to greater depth there and west of the Rhine produced a sizeable growth in known reserves. Reserves to 1,000 metres depth were almost completely known by 1913.[12]

That these mineral discoveries were all extensions of existing basins reduced to some degree their effect on the conditions under which the coal industry operated. In Lorraine, conditions in the new deposits were as favourable as those in the Saar, although the quality of the coal was somewhat softer. The Northern Belgian–Dutch Limburg deposit could be much more cheaply mined than the Northern French–Southern Belgian field, which had been long in exploitation, and the quality of the coal was for some purposes superior. In the Ruhr, increased depths involved higher costs, but the proportion of coal of good coking quality in the reserves was not reduced. The balance maintained among the four major countries in the area in these discoveries is of special interest as evidence of the vigour and effectiveness of exploration in all of them. Since 1900, significant new coal reserves have been found in France (Lorraine), Belgium (Campine), the Netherlands (Limburg) and Germany (Ruhr). Within each country, the growth of mining at new loca-

[7]*A. d. M.* (Belg.) in 1903–4 (XI, XII), carries a full account of the early work and its results. See esp. IX, 208–23.

[8]Coal to shallow depths had been mined in Limburg much earlier, and drillings in 1858–63 and 1873–81 had produced several concessions. Extensive explorations began with the Orange-Nassau concession in 1893. *A. d. M.*, Ser. 7, X, 434–5; Ser. 10, VII, 123–32; Ser. 11, III, 357–9.

[9]*A. d. M.*, Ser. 11, XI, 379–80.

[10]Ibid., Ser. 12, XVI, 207–11.

[11]Ibid., Ser. 12, XVI, p. 191 and plate IV, following p. 238.

[12]P. Kukuk, op. cit., 631–2.

tions and the decline of the older parts of the producing regions was foreshadowed. Of the older regions – considering the Saar and Aachen as regions separate for their western extensions – only the Ruhr maintained and even increased its share of the reserves. These discoveries came as extensions of life to existing mining areas or to the coal industry of the various countries. Even if conditions of demand and money costs had been the same after 1900 as they had been earlier, these discoveries could not have offered opportunities as extensive as the minerals discoveries of the preceding century. They are evidence rather of continued intellectual and commercial enterprise under conditions of diminishing returns in a soil that had been well worked over.[13]

COMMUNICATING TECHNOLOGICAL CHANGE

In the modern process of technological change, each participant receives from the world at large far more than he gives. Communication, therefore, is the matter of first importance. Throughout the twentieth century – to a large extent even in war-time – the communication network linking Western Europe, Britain, and America has been maintained in a tolerable state of repair. It has consisted of three elements: text-books and technical schools, trade association journals and meetings, and the activities of equipment producers. These elements have all been closely related to the national societies of the Western countries. National schools, national trade associations, national equipment industries have been largely responsible for the state of technical knowledge within national boundaries. Despite this fact the degree of competition and communication between national units has generally been sufficient to join them all to a single international gridwork, with a remarkable resistance to the occasional indolence of industrialists and the recurrent oppressions of politicians.

At the beginning of the century, engineering education in Europe was of high quality.[14] In Germany, a great reform of technical education had been completed; the *Technische Hochschulen* with their specialized courses of study were empowered in 1899 by imperial decree to grant diplomas in engineering, and shortly thereafter the German *Dr. Ing.*

[13]Diminishing returns to minerals exploration are evident in the German search for iron-ore during the 1930's, and in French explorations for coal and ore throughout the period between the two wars.

[14]In 1905, A. Pelleton, deputy-director of the École des Mines (Paris), was sent on an official mission to Germany to compare instruction in the Technische Hochschulen and the Bergakademie with that in the École des Mines. His report, and the discussion provoked by it (*R. d. M.*, 1904, 1 ff.; 1906, 445 ff.; 1907, *passim*), are especially lively and revealing. One sees here at their source many of the finer points of French and German national differences.

began to be released upon the world.[15] Development in education had followed a different course in France, where the curriculum of the *École Polytechnique* clung to mathematical studies, and even the *Écoles supérieures des Mines* at Paris and Saint-Étienne stressed general, rather than specialized engineering education. These differences in method can be overemphasized; both trained excellent engineers, and perhaps each was best adapted to the peculiar features of its students' previous education and outlook, and to the industrial system in which they were later to work.[16]

An engineer, graduated and working in a plant, was kept abreast of developments by the periodicals of the trade and professional associations – *Stahl und Eisen* and *Glückauf* in Germany, the *Revue Universelle des Mines* in Belgium. In France, the obsessive secrecy of industrialists – a trait which persists to the point of childishness to this day – kept this form of public communication at a minimum. The *Annales des Mines* (Paris) and the *Revue de l'Industrie Minérale* (Saint-Étienne) furnished an official outlet for some publication, especially by members of the Corps des Mines; the *Revue de Métallurgie,* founded in 1904 by the

[15] *R. d. M.,* 1908, *Extraits,* 555. A useful survey is given in an American consular report: E. C. Meyer, *Industrial Education in Germany,* U.S. Department of Commerce and Labor, Special Consular Reports, XXXIII, Washington, 1905, with bibliography. On Belgium, see Société de l'Industrie Minerale, *Bulletin,* 1907, 223–92, extracted in *R. d. M.* 1907, 67.

[16] This fascinating subject cannot be pursued further here. Certainly in mining and metallurgy excellent texts were available in both French and German. Despite the enormous amount of German work on mining, probably no single text was as complete or successful as the French one of Haton de la Goupillière, *Cours d'Exploitation des Mines,* Paris, 1st ed. 1884–5, 2nd ed. 1896, 3rd ed. 1905–11, 4th ed. 1928–36. E. Treptow, *Grundzüge der Bergbaukunde,* Vienna and Leipzig, 1903, and G. Köhler, *Lehrbuch der Bergbaukunde,* Leipzig, 4th ed. 1897, are examples of one-volume German works. Two Belgian works, A. Habets, *Cours d'Exploitation des Mines,* Liége, 1902, and C. Demanet, *Traité d'Exploitation des Mines de Houille,* Brussels, 1899, are somewhat less impressive. Despite the great original French contribution to metallurgy, the *opus magnum* was certainly H. Wedding's *Handbuch der Eisenh üttenkunde,* Brunswick, 2nd ed. 1891–6. This was in origin an adaptation of Percy's *Metallurgy of Iron and Steel* and was a work of reference rather than a text. Despite translation into French of Bell's *Principles of the Manufacture of Iron and Steel* (tr. Paris, 1895) and Lebedur's *Handbuch der Eisenh üttenkunde,* Leipzig, 1st ed. 1894, 5th ed. 1905 (tr. Paris, 1898), a few French texts were in use (e.g. H. Noble, *Fabrication de l'Acier,* Paris, 1st ed. 1905, 2nd ed. 1918; L. Gage, *Traité de Métallurgie de Fer,* Paris, 1898; U. le Verrier *La Métallurgie en France,* Paris, 1894; A. d'Auriac, *Leçons de Sidèrurgie,* Paris, 1920). Deficiencies in textbooks alone, even if they existed, would not be conclusive evidence of inferior instruction. The moral of all such partial comparisons is that national educational, social and industrial systems must be viewed as single systems of many interdependent elements – a fact which makes international comparison of elements in isolation especially odious.

genius of Henri Le Chatelier, owed something to official as well as to industrial sponsorship.[17] Nevertheless, the regional trade associations in Lorraine and the Loire, and the *Comité des Forges* offered some means of communication,[18] and the foreign publications were of course open to all who read English and German. The British Iron and Steel Institute developed this international communication to a high point; it included a large number of foreign members, and held meetings on the continent periodically.[19] Frequent trips to the United States were reported in both French and German publications;[20] American methods of coal-washing and ore mining and dressing at the turn of the century were special subjects of study.[21] The unusual capacities of some new American equipment and innovations in blast-furnace and open-hearth practice did not go unnoticed. Textbooks and journals reported fully developments in mine and mill practices, and, supplemented by bulletins of the research institutes, they also made available the results of fundamental chemical and physical research.

Development and advertisement of new equipment was actively carried on by the equipment manufacturers. In coking, the equipment producer's handbook was an important guide to practice.[22] In France, Germany, and Belgium a national industry furnished most kinds of mining, coking, and steel-making equipment to the national producers,[23] but

[17]J. Tribot-Laspière, *L'industrie de l'Acier en France,* Paris, 1917, 290, claims the Comité des Forges as the patron. Le Chatelier, however, was a professor at the École des Mines. For some references to the journal's origins see *R. d. M.*, 1904, 1 ff.

[18]J. Tribot-Laspière, op. cit., pp. 47–9. The main purpose of these groups, however, was to disseminate industrial information concerning wages, markets, legislation, etc.

[19]In 1879 the Iron and Steel Institute included among its 1,026 members, 36 French, 29 German, and 18 Belgian members (*J.I.S.I.*, 1880, No. 1, 4–5). By 1913 the Institute's membership had doubled, and among the 632 foreign members were 71 German, 61 French, and 37 Belgian members (*J.I.S.I.*, 1914, No. 2, xxi). Meetings of the Institute took place at Düsseldorf (1880, 1902, 1936), Vienna (1882, 1907), Paris (1889, 1900, 1921), and Brussels (1894, 1913, 1934), *Handbook and List of Members of the Iron and Steel Institute,* London, 1955.

[20]See *R. d. M.*, 1905, 601, 816, for an example.

[21]For example, H. Lenicque, *État Actuel de la Préparation Méchanique des Minerais,* Paris, 1904. Lenicque points out that the secrecy of French firms often causes French students to visit plants in Germany, from which they return convinced of German superiority. Thus American techniques also become known in France, but he points out, 'les procédés américains de réussissent pas toujours en Europe, même quand ils sont recommandés par les Allemands' (p. 8).

[22]L. Cambon, *L'Allemagne du Travail,* Paris, 1909, 48.

[23]This subject deserves more study than has been given to it. Coke oven producers exploited domestic markets to a large extent in all countries (e.g. Otto, Coppée, Simon-Carvès Semet-Solvay), and all had a considerable export

this curious fact did not keep producers from exhibiting in fairs and exhibitions in one another's countries,[24] and important differences in equipment furnished could not exist where communication among customers was so close. In no region could suppliers of equipment fall very far behind the developments of the times.

This organization of knowledge has been maintained and extended in Europe down to the present, despite formidable obstacles and occasional set-backs. After 1913, the obstacles were undeniably more numerous; the First World War to some extent cut off German technicians, but it intensified their own work. Increased government finance in the Kaiser Wilhelm Institutes and the laboratories of the universities and *Technische Hochschulen* had the effect of directing research toward problems in the interests of the national industry as a whole.[25] The war

business. The German steel-making machinery firms (e.g. Gutehoffnungshütte, Duisburger Maschinenfabrik) were well known, but in France much equipment was made by Frnch producers like Delattre et Frouard. Further research could show the extent to which national markets were reserved to national machinery industries, the financial and sociological reasons for this phenomenon, and its effects on national production.

[24]The voluminous reports of several observers at these exhibitions are important sources of information. For the 1870's two reports by a Hungarian nobleman, Anton, Ritter von Kerpley, are of special value (*Eisen und Stahl auf der Wiener Weltaufstellung*, 1873, and *Eisen und Stahl auf der Weltaufstellung in Paris*, 1878). In the 1890's F. Laur reported on the exhibitions at Brussels in 1897 and in Paris in 1900 (*Les Mines et Usines à l'Exposition Internationale de Bruxelles en* 1897, Paris, 1897; *Les Mines et la Métallurgie à l'Exposition Universelle de* 1900, Paris, 6 vols., 1900). References to innumerable other expositions, in Brussels, Düsseldorf, Vienna, St. Louis, Liége, etc., are scattered through the trade and technical journals.

[25]'75 Jahre Verein deutscher Eisenhüttenleute', *S. u. E.*, 1936, 1296–1303, 1346–53, 1390–5, 1428–35. Before 1913, research in coal and mining in Germany was carried on especially at the Bergwirtschaftliches Laboratorium (Bochum), and in the Bergakademie at Clausthal; research in metallurgy was carried on in the Technische Hochschulen at Aachen and at Berlin. Many plants also had laboratories, and the Materialprüfungsamt—the Prussian Bureau of Standards—also performed experiments. (See *R. d. M.*, 1908, *Extraits*, p. 717). Only in 1914 was the Kaiser Wilhelm Institut für Kohlenforschung founded at Mülheim (Ruhr), and in 1918 its counterpart for ferrous metallurgy in Düsseldorf. The Gesellschaft für Kohlentechnik, created by the Ruhr mines in 1913, was a centre for work on coking in the 1920's, while the work at Mülheim under Fischer's direction centred on coke by-products, especially synthetic fuels.

Laboratory facilities in France before 1913 for metallurgical work were probably better, and, the work better directed than in Germany. The laboratories of firms (Schneider, Châtillon-Commentry, Terre Noire) were notable. (*R. d. M.*, 1904, pp. 1 ff.; Comité des Forges, *Bulletin*, No. 168 (1881), p. 311.) The state schools and the engineers of the *corps des mines* supported much research in had similar effects in other countries, and strengthened for a time communication among the Western Allies. These phenomena are difficult to assess. Most of the channels of communication were kept open until the outbreak of war in 1939, and research and teaching continued; the perfectness of communication and the standards of research, however, may not have been maintained.[26] In Germany, research was turned even further toward providing an increased self-sufficiency. In France, it was probably equipment producers rather than teachers, writers, or plant engineers, who failed to keep up with new developments elsewhere.[27] Lack of competition among national industries and lack of incentive in a stagnant market affected the quality of European equipment even where the institutions responsible for teaching, research, and communication of information remained intact. The 1939–45 war and Nazi domination brought development nearly to a standstill.[28] Since 1945, the restoration of technical communication, of the quality of new equipment, and of native research organizations has been slow and painful. Perhaps too much emphasis in this period has been put on the imitation of American techniques and too little on the restoration and improvement of native European institutions of research and training.

MAIN LINES OF TECHNOLOGICAL CHANGE[29]

From the minds of individuals in plants, schools, and research institutes in all Western countries, the network of communication took innumerable bits of knowledge about products and processes and suggestions about design and operation of equipment and plants, and spread them throughout Western Europe. This knowledge and these suggestions differed in kind from the technological changes of the nineteenth century. The steel-making inventions of Siemens and Bessemer, the by-product

their laboratories and test stations. There can be no doubt, however, that German plant engineers pursued special subjects avidly and delighted in communicating their results. In addition to *Stahl und Eisen,* the Verein deutscher Eisenhüttenleute published voluminous special reports, forming after 1927 a separate periodical, the *Archiv für das Eisenhüttenwesen.*

[26]A survey of the international exhibitions, fairs, etc., mentioned in the *Revue de Métallurgie* and in *Stahl und Eisen* shows a marked falling off in their frequency after 1930.

[27]See, for example, the criticisms of Charles Berthelot, *R. d. M.,* 1937, 170–6.

[28]This at least is the general impression. Certainly progress in Nazi-occupied Europe was almost nil. On the work in Germany, see the FIAT Review of German Science, W. Eilender, *Ferrous Metallurgy* (Hq. T-Force, Control Commission for Germany, British Element), Bielefeld, 1948.

[29]No comprehensive survey of technological developments in mining, coking and ferrous metallurgy, with special reference to the period since 1880 in conti-

coke oven and the modern design of the coke-oven battery, the development of the heated blast and the higher blast-furnace, directly and radically altered production techniques. Compared to them, even the Thomas process was a more limited sort of invention – an adaptation of the Bessemer principle to permit the use of phosphoric ores. Much of this earlier work was carried on by empirically-minded inventors and engineers without complete chemical and physical analyses; nevertheless, the 'revolutionary' discoveries were quickly found to be superior to previous equipment in most situations. A radical change in costs under a variety of different cost conditions was their characteristic effect on production opportunity.

Improvements after 1880 were somewhat different in their origins and noticeably different in their effect. They originated partly in the results of fundamental research into the chemistry and physics of products and processes. Partly too they constituted an application of materials and techniques developed in other, related industries. Of the ideas originating with mining and metallurgical engineers, many were adaptations of standard equipment and practice to particular situations, and so were lacking in general applicability. Whatever the origin, each individual change had a relatively minor effect on production costs. Even

nental Europe, is in existence. On ferrous metallurgy, O. Johannsen, *Geschichte des Eisen*, Düsseldorf, 1st ed. 1925, 3rd ed. 1953, contains some useful material. (See esp. 3rd ed., pp. 341–578.) However, it is largely devoted to earlier periods, being based in part on the famous work of L. Beck (*Die Geschichte des Eisens*, 5 vols., Brunswick, 1884–1903). Works with intriguing titles by noted technologists, e.g. Sir Robert Hadfield, *Metallurgy and Its Influence on Modern Progress*, London, 1925, and Léon Guillet, *L'Evolution de la Métallurgie*, are extremely disappointing to the historian. Brief notes on specific topics are contained at the outset of some of the technical articles and books (e.g. the chapter by O. Johannsen, 'Die geschichtliche Entwicklung der Walzwerkstechnik', in J. Puppe and G. Stauber, eds., *Walzwerkswesen*, 3 vols., Düsseldorf and Berlin, 1929–39, Vol. I, Ch. 2).

The source material for such a history lies in the technical journals and in standard texts (see p. 65, note 16, above) and monographs of the period. The bibliography in R. Durrer, *Die Metallurgie des Eisens*, 1st ed. 1931–4, 2nd ed. 1940, 3rd ed. 1943, in the series Gmelins 'Handbuch der Anorganischen Chemie', provides some guide through this material, for ferrous metallurgy, but no comparable guide exists for mining or coking. The text of this section is based on the French and German monographs on special topics and on numerous articles in *Stahl und Eisen*, *Glükauf*, and the *Revue de Métallurgie*. The attempt has been made to avoid dependence on works in English and on very recent works, so as to get at the development as it was seen by the mining and metallurgical engineer on the Continent. The collections of this material available at the libraries of the Verein deutscher Eisenhüttenleute (Düsseldorf), Glückauf (Essen), the École des Mines (Paris, the Iron and Steel Institute (London), and H.M. Patent Office (London) have been used for this purpose.

the accumulation of change did not produce an effect comparable to that of the group of nineteenth-century inventions.

Fundamental research was carried on by chemists and metallurgists in plant laboratories and research institutes. Here the use of the microscope, improved pyrometers, and other equipment yielded some important results to successive generations of trained workers. The most fruitful work was done in the study of the structure of metals – specifically, the effects of alloys and heat treatment of the structure of steel. For the first time, a general explanation of the properties of iron alloyed with increasing amounts of carbon could be given. Refinement in the adaptability of steels to different industrial uses could be made. At the same time, alloys of steel with the whole range of non-ferrous metals were studied and the variety of special-purpose steels greatly extended. Similar studies were made into the physical and chemical composition of coal. Here the problem of analysis was complicated by the organic nature of coal substance. No two bits of coal have the same chemical or physical composition, and even a comprehensive classification of coals was difficult to achieve. A more exact separation of coals according to heat content, gas content, friability, readiness to ignite, ability to yield good coke, and other qualities was made; coals could then be more finely graded and sorted for distribution to their most appropriate uses. The behaviour of coal during coking was a subject of special study; understanding of the 'coking principle', relating the qualities of coke produced to the nature of the coals charged, however, remained incomplete. The work yielded some improved tests and standards for metallurgical coke, and certain recipes for mixing coals to produce good coke. The study of coal chemistry produced spectacular results outside the ordinary uses to which coal is put, i.e. in the further treatment of chemical products extracted from coal during its distillation. This work, however, lay outside the limits of the coal and coke industries as such.

Studies of the chemical composition of coal were most easily carried on as the coal was being burned or coked. Study of the behaviour of coal during coking yielded the discovery of so-called 'low-temperature' coking. Closer examination of the processes of coking and combustion – especially measurement of heat transfer and heat loss – also yielded improvements in coke oven and furnace design. In metallurgy, however, reactions during smelting and steel-making were impossible either to observe closely in a plant, or to reproduce satisfactorily in the laboratory. In open-hearth steel-making, methods of observation and testing were developed, so that practice could be placed more nearly on a scientific basis. Yet here, and even more in the converter and blast-furnace plant, the art of the skilled operator – like that of a cook in a kitchen – was not replaced by instruments and automatic control.

Along with a knack and a 'feel' for the operation, acquired by an experienced instinct, went doubtless also a great deal of humbug and superstition. Operators tended to set a high value on uniformity of materials, and sometimes to underrate the adaptability of their plant to changes in the quality of inputs.

High-quality steel improved the equipment in mines and in the steel plants where it was manufactured. The steel winding-cable in the mine permitted an increase in the capacity of shafts, and so in the volume of underground operations connected to a single shaft. Steel rolls, although not wholly replacing iron, were an important innovation in the rolling mill. Improvement in refractories for the lining of coke ovens, blast furnaces, and steel-making equipment was rather slow, change was not always beneficial in all situations, and only in the open hearth was progress clearly evident. Of the changes originating outside the steel industry itself, the introduction of electricity had certainly the widest effects. Its use as a source of heat – permitted by the development of the electric steel furnace and even electric smelting – was sharply restricted by cost. Electric power, however, could be introduced on a large scale; it not only lowered power costs but also increased greatly the kinds of operations which could be efficiently mechanized, and the weight of single loads that could be handled. At the same time the power plant formed a convenient part of the economy of the mine and steel-mill. The gas-engine, running on producer or blast-furnace gas, as well as the steam-engine could be used to run the dynamo. Where connection was made with a regional power grid, excess power could be sold, and peak load requirements in the plant were more easily met. The development of the steam-turbine extended even further the economic possibilities of electric power.

Changes of wide applicability were thus suggested by the work in laboratories and by the improvements in materials and techniques of power generation. Their introduction into the coal and steel industries was the work of the mining and metallurgical engineer, working for an equipment producer or in a particular mine, cokery, or steel plant. Faced with a specific production problem, the engineer devised specific solutions; the problem faced by the industry at large was that of generalizing these solutions and testing their applicability in other locations and under other conditions of cost.

Where production conditions permitted erection of a new large integrated plant, the work of engineers was most effective. Reference has already been made to the increased size of mines permitted by improved winding-cables. The introduction of the mine power-plant, of washing and grading facilities, and of large coking plants favoured the joint use of such installations by more than one mineshaft. The use of electricity in the steel-mill was mainly responsible for the increase in the size of the equipment unit, since it facilitated the handling of large masses of material and large pieces of equipment. At the same time, the analysis of fuels and heat economy also served to encourage the integration of cokery and steel-mill through the development of complex systems of gas interchange and heat economy. Introduction of the mixer in the steel-mill made for easier co-ordination of the blast-furnace operation with that of the converter and open hearth, and furnished uniform materials by mixing the pig-iron from one or several blast-furnaces. In an integrated plant, the cooling of metal between stages could to a large extent be avoided. Increases in the capacity of rolling mills, permitted by improved steel in the rolls and the use of electric power, were especially notable.

A second series of changes centred about improvements in open-hearth equipment and practice. A number of special open-hearth methods were introduced after 1880 (the duplex, Bertrand-Thiel, Talbot processes); these proved of minor importance, their application being limited to certain special cost conditions. Changes in the fuel of the open hearth were of more general importance; the use of coke-oven gas permitted the elimination of the furnace's own gas-producer. Recently the use of fuel oil has been introduced. At the same time, innumerable detailed changes took place in the construction of the open hearth, in the control of its operation, and in the handling of its minerals and products. The suitability of the open hearth to produce new high-quality steels gave special significance to these changes.

Improvements of open-hearth equipment were more extensive than those in the converter or the blast furnace. After 1950, however, the use of an oxygen-enriched blast in both the blast-furnace and the converter was tried with some success and further development in this direction occurred. In the converter itself, the only notable change was an increase in size and some reduction in the time required for an average blow. In the blast-furnace plant, the most important improvement involved the cleaning and utilization of blast-furnace gas. The adoption of sintering equipment permitted the ore and coke-dust cleaned from the gas, as well as fine ores generally, to be charged. Changes in the profile of the blast-furnace were made, and even after 1900 some increases in the capacity of furnaces were achieved. With electric power, mechanical loading of the blast-furnace could be introduced. Mechanization of underground operations in mining made great progress, and above ground new equipment for washing and sorting of coal was developed and employed. In ore-mining, methods of handling large volumes of ore and earth were improved with new equipment. Some preparation of ores before shipment by crushing and concentration was introduced.

Changes and variations in practice were made first in a specific plant; information about the results of a specific change was communicated, often by an interested or ambitious plant engineer through an article in the trade or technical journals. Changes in plant layout and many changes in the design and construction of equipment had a similar origin; this was especially true where plants produced their own steel-making equipment. A steelworks, a mine, even to some extent a cokery, was a problem in construction, rather than a problem of installation of standard machinery. Not only the location, but the materials and labour involved, the cost situation of the plant, its expected markets, and the grade of product, affected the design of equipment and the operation. Controlled experiments on suggested innovations were often impossible to perform. Thus a sound basis existed for the conservatism of producers in clinging to old equipment and local practice. The conservatism of customers in their specifications was often equally great.

The effects of this process of technological change on the opportunities of production at different European locations is examined more closely elsewhere.[30] Its general effect in mines, cokeries, iron and steel plants was to reduce labour and fuel costs per ton of output. In steelworks, a reduction in capital cost per ton probably resulted from the use of larger units of equipment; however, the introduction of the mixer, and the growing advantages of the open hearth worked in the opposite direction. In mines, the changes permitted substitution of capital for labour, though some capital saving was involved where underground operations were consolidated to feed a single shaft. In all plants, the possibilities of producing products more finely graded and of higher quality increased costs – particularly the capital costs of the mine's installations above ground, the cokery's by-product plant, and the open hearth and rolling mill. In cokeries, blast-furnaces, and steel-mills, the consumption of materials other than fuel, i.e. coking coal, ore, and some combination of pig-iron and scrap, continued to be required in the same volume per ton of output as before. Here the opportunities for saving had been early exhausted, and computed on a tonnage basis the minimum input-output ratio had been achieved. However, the variety of materials – coals in the cokery, ores in the blast-furnace, ore-pig-iron–scrap combinations in the steel-furnace – which could be economically charged to produce a product of given quality was somewhat extended.

On the whole, the changes had the interesting effect of favouring a large integrated works including open-hearth furnaces, while at the same time extending the range of locations in which such a works could be

[30] N. J. G. Pounds and W. N. Parker, *Coal and Steel in Western Europe*, Ch. 10.

economically operated. The advantages of such a works using large-scale equipment and electric power, with a closely knit internal fuel economy, continued to accumulate at least until 1930, and new plants built in the 1920's could make full use of them. Even before 1930, outside of mining, the improvements which could be introduced into old plants, without extensive alterations of equipment and plant-layout, were of decidedly minor importance. After 1930 the advantages even of new installations did not grow to any large extent. Deceleration in the rate of technological change has continued in these industries throughout the world, not – it would seem – through any decline in the inventiveness of engineers, but in part through the exhaustion, in a more or less logical fashion, of the possibilities implicit in the original inventions.

STABILIZATION OF PRODUCTION OPPORTUNITIES

Minerals discoveries and technological changes after 1913 no longer permitted sharp reduction in the cost of coal or steel in relation to the cost of other products. Since the mining and steel industries were each heavy consumers of their own and of one another's products, such reductions before 1900 had had a double effect. Stabilization of techniques in mining and steel-making removed an important source of reduction in fuel and machinery costs of mines and steelworks. Opportunity for increasing output had then to depend mainly on factors outside these industries themselves – the wage rate, the rate of interest, and the level of demand. These in turn could produce mainly only such opportunities for expansion as were generally available to all industries in the economy.

The long-run movement of demand, in which chief reliance had to be placed, turned unfavourably against the mining and steel industry in general, despite certain favourable elements. Among the latter may be cited the increasing use of coke-oven gas, which widened somewhat the opportunity for coking while distorting the traditional market for coal; the improvements of quality and variety of steel also gave the demand for open-hearth steel some impetus, which was lacking in the demand for converter steel of standard specifications. In the demand for coal, the success of fuel economy generally had had an effect on requirements.[31] Electricity generated by water-power and by brown coal, and petroleum products, further cut into the coal market. The

[31]The question of fuel and steel demand has been examined recently in publications of the Economic Commission for Europe, Geneva. See *European Steel Trends in the Setting of the World Market,* Geneva, 1949 (1st revision, 1951), pp. 25–38, and especially I. Svennilson, *Growth and Stagnation in the European Economy,* Geneva, 1954, Chs. VI and VII.

export market for European steel is too complex a question to be treated in the present context; certain tendencies favouring the growth of steel-plants in importing countries had in this period already begun to manifest themselves. The principal discouragement to expansion for both the coal and steel industries in all countries was the slow recovery in the level of aggregate demand in Europe after 1919 and its collapse in 1930.

In speaking of the movement of aggregate demand, one must be careful not to reason as if producers had available, and were guided by, the data of Figure 1. In each region expectations were raised by upward movements of demand, only to be extinguished again in recession. The First World War, though stimulating to demand, raised, of course, insuperable difficulties for production from the supply side. During the long collapse of 1919–25, it was expansions and restorations of capacity that made the higher levels of the late 1920's possible. Only the German rearmament boom after 1936 restored expectations and output in a part of the area, and in the Second World War, demand was checked by rationing and controls, even where supply difficulties might have been overcome. Certain special situations induced sporadic expansions, and in the eyes of producers these expansions were as authentic as the even expansion before 1913; indeed, while they lasted they were perhaps even more encouraging. From the viewpoint of half a century, they were but incidents, temporary breaks in a narrowed margin of opportunity. Between the two wars, indeed since 1913 up to the very recent past, the significant fact is a long-run deceleration in the rate of expansion – approaching stagnation since 1929. The lack of novel opportunities to lower physical costs of production, and the absence of a level of demand that could rise strongly and steadily from decade to decade, narrowed economic opportunity to a point where any other response in these industries would have been impossible, and indeed undesirable. Whether other elements, disappearing in long-run considerations but affecting the short-run behaviour of these industries, contributed to the slowing down of innovations and to the sluggishness of demand is a question to be considered in a separate context.

4

The organization of rapid expansion

THE SIGNIFICANCE OF INDUSTRIAL ORGANIZATION

Cartels and large combines, firms and rich families, intricate chronicles of the rise and ruin of industrial empires, exercise a peculiar fascination on certain minds. The business historian – with his keen interest in the biography of personal enterprise and corporate fortune – sees in the history of the industries considered here a long procession of Krupps, Kirdorfs, Thyssens, de Wendels and Stumms, sinister or magnificent, powerful, clever and exciting. The Marxist historian, scorning to name names, finds in this same history the huge, heady symbols of his high romance – an objectification of the stages in the development of monopoly capitalism. The economic historian, examining the long-run record of output shown in the previous two chapters, also finds in industrial organization a source of interest, less spectacular than these but more subtly satisfying. For him it is the link between the impersonal opportunities for an expanded output offered to an industry (by minerals discovery, technological change, movements in costs or in demand), and the human activities and decisions of the men who carry on production.

That such a link is required is evident. In economic life, an opportunity for expansion facing a whole industry or region does not generally evoke an effective human response. The individuals who carry on economic activities can respond to prospects of personal gain or personal satisfaction only in work of narrower scope. A portion of their activity is concerned with creating the very forms of production organization within which they and others carry on their work. The process by which these forms change is in some sense a political process, since in this aspect of their activity men are concerned in large part with gaining and extending power over other men. The decisions to expand the capacity of plants, to

Adapted from N. J. G. Pounds and W. N. Parker, *Coal and Steel in Western Europe,* (London: Faber & Faber Ltd., 1957). By permission.

adopt new production techniques, to exploit new minerals deposits, to produce – or make it possible for others to produce – more output per man-hour – all such decisions with important economic consequences are taken within the framework of the industrial organizations thus established, and it is through that framework that they have their effects. The framework of industrial organization thus serves to split up and translate the opportunities facing a whole industry into opportunities for personal gain or satisfaction for individuals. Or to look at the matter the other way round, the productive energies and ambitions of individuals are channelled and combined by the organizational forms to produce the response of the industry to its opportunities, as measured by the statistics of output (and in other ways not taken up in these chapters).

The organization of production is of primary significance in interpreting industrial history when a rather wide opportunity for expansion exists. In situations where natural or economic factors are unfavourable, effective organization can do no more than efficiently maintain a stable output. Attempts at expansion then prove overly ambitious; added plant remains idle and additional output cannot cover costs. In such a situation an organization with powerfully expansionist tendencies is out of place, and its optimistic producers are quickly ruined. Chapter 3, therefore, suggests that industrial organization is of considerable interest in the interpretation of the long-run record of output before 1913 in European heavy industry, but is of much less importance when opportunity had narrowed after that date. Centering upon the earlier period, the present chapter examines the principal forms under which the expanding production was carried on – the integrated firm and the cartel. The process by which these forms originated and were transformed is not closely analysed here; some elements in the situation seen by individuals acting within these forms can be suggested. The response of individuals was, of course, strongly influenced by the qualities which they brought with them to their jobs – the supply of men of different abilities being dependent upon the operation of the social and educational system as a whole. The quality of individuals is too intimate a matter to be discussed on the basis of available information; some comparison between German and French producers in the effectiveness of their responses to economic opportunity, however, is ventured at the end of this chapter.

NUMBER, SIZE AND STRUCTURE OF FIRMS[1]

The year 1880 saw the existence in Western Europe of a number of independent industries within the range of products considered in these

[1] An illuminating comparison of British and Continental organization in firms and in the steel industry as a whole is given by D. L. Burn, *The Economic*

chapters. Coalmining was organizationally separate from iron production, and the association between smelting and ironworking was not close. Coking, it is true, was carried on largely at mines by the mining companies, and some organizations engaged in several branches or stages of the iron industry. Iron-ore mines were often connected with a local smelting-works, but already a substantial trade in purchased ore had developed. In all products intermediate in the production process sizable markets existed, and each stage of the processes was organized into a rather large number of small or moderate-sized firms, engaged in buying from or selling to one another such intermediate products as pig-iron and iron bars. This dispersion of the iron industry among separate organizations was accentuated by the relatively low degree of geographical concentration. Many local monopolies existed, in markets protected by transport costs, but each such producer was dependent upon markets, local or distant, for materials.

With the growth of production advantages centering on the main modern regions, during a period of general widening of the market and fall in costs, producers with established positions in the Saar, Lorraine, Luxembourg and the Ruhr were placed in an extremely favourable situation, requiring moderate foresight and considerable capital. Many such producers were able to adopt the new production processes, enlarging capacity and integrating as technology required or as the opportunity for profitable investment offered. Others found their organizations taken up into such expanding firms, or taken over by new capital-

History of Steelmaking, Ch. XI. Information on the history and structure of these firms is not abundant outside the archives of the firms themselves. One highly relevant source is H. Heymann, *Die gemischten Werke in deutschen Grosseisengewerbe,* Stuttgart, 1904, in the series Münchener Volkswirtschaftliche Studien (Brentano and Lotz, eds.), vol. LXV. The Saar is perhaps the best documented of the regions; apart from Capot-Rey's classic study of the region, information on the firms themselves is given in L. Born, *Die wirtschaftliche Entwicklung der Saar Grosseisenindustrie,* Berlin, 1919; Kohlmann, *Die Grossindustrie des Saargebietes,* 1911; H. Müller, *Uberzeugung im Saarländer Hüttengewerbe,* 1856–1913, in the series (A. Spietholl, ed.) Beiträge zur Erforschung der wirtschaftlichen Wechsellagen, Aufschwung, Krise, Stockung, vol. X; an interesting article in *Schmoller's Jahrbuch,* XLVI, 1922, 423–67, by E. Weigert, 'Die Grossindustrie des Saargebietes'. Useful too are the business histories of the major Saar firms – Burbach (*Die Burbacher Hütte,* 1856–1906, Saarlouis, 1906), Stumm (*Hundert Jahre Neunkirchener Eisenwerke Gebr. Stuinni,* Saarbrücken, 1906, by the publicist A. Tille), Dillingen (*250 Jahre Dillingerhütte,* 1936), Röchling (*Das Haus Röchling und seine Unternehmerungen,* and A. Nutzinger, *Karl Röchling,* Volklingen, 1927), St. Ingbert (W. Krämer, *Geschichte des Eisenwerks zu St. Ingbert,* Speyer, 1933). Less extensive material exists for the other regions. Annual reports and business histories give little or no insight into the actual decision-making processes in these organizations.

ists, either from the region itself or from outside. In the coalmining districts, such new producers generally did not come from other steel-producing regions, but represented capital often of local origin, not rooted elsewhere in the steel industry. At the Lorraine–Luxembourg ore-fields, a process of colonization was carried on by steel-producers from outside. After 1900, with increased advantages of integration, these plants in the ore-mining regions became in most cases themselves integrated establishments, though many were controlled by outside owners.

The result of this development was that in the coalmining regions the number of firms contributing to output in each branch of iron and steel production did not grow proportionately as regional output expanded, but neither did it shrink excessively as the firms grew in size. Instead the existing firms and some new entrants grew in size and complexity as firms in other, less favoured regions disappeared. Even in the ore-mining regions, the persistence of original interests was rather strong, particularly in French Lorraine (Meurthe-et-Moselle). With the growth of integrated firms in the coalmining regions, however, the total number of firms in the whole group of iron industries declined, and the proportion of iron and crude steel output passing through the market shrank greatly – being replaced by transfers between sections of the integrated firms. The size distribution of firms varied somewhat from one region to another, but the major trend in all regions was toward the growth of a group of integrated firms, in moderate number and with considerable degree of internal complexity.

This development of integrated firms was concentrated in the iron and steel industry; in the course of it, some steel firms, particularly in the Ruhr, penetrated into the coal industry. In the coalmining industry itself, however, much development came from new or existing firms without any important connections outside the mining industry, except in the ownership of cokeries. The number of firms did not drastically decline; the average size of firm remained smaller in mining than in steel-making, and the firms remained less complex enterprises.[2]

The statistical picture of the structure of the iron and steel industry at the close of the period of rapid expansion indicates the type of firm which had developed in these areas with the rise in output. It was an integrated firm, generally with several plants, and rooted in one area – in Belgium or in France, or – within German regions – either in the Ruhr

[2]This development can be approximately traced through the statistics of output by mine, given in official sources and trade association reports. The Saar mines, of course, remained state-owned throughout the entire period. See *Coal and Steel in Western Europe*, pp. 306–15, for supporting statistical tables of firms by region and type of structure.

or in the so-called 'south-west area' (Saar, Luxembourg, German Lorraine). In the German regions, it was typically larger and more complex than in France or Belgium. Alongside such firms, some firms based on a single integrated plant also existed, especially in France and Belgium, and a number of small open-hearth steel producers with rolling-mills had made their way. Complex interregional and international firms were – except for de Wendel – a relatively recent growth, and except in Luxembourg they did not overshadow the older native structure of industry.

The regional firms were themselves sufficiently complex to involve a bureaucratic structure of some proportions, particularly in Germany. Many were descendants of earlier firms, which had built up an organization and traditions as early as 1880. In some, such as Krupp and Stumm, the patriarchal spirit appears strong; in others, such as Röchling and Rheinische Stahlwerke, a less heavy hand is evident. Much more investigation into the history and the internal structure of these firms is required to discover all motive forces inducing expansions of capacity within them.

THE RELATIONS AMONG FIRMS

Although the size of firms and the scale of plants in the iron and steel industry grew greatly during the period of output expansion, the size of the market served by the producers at the most favoured locations at coal and ore deposits also grew. Among producers at these locations – particularly those selling a uniform product such as steel rails, or phosphoric pig-iron – recognition of a mutual interest in the regional market permitted the formation of more or less formal agreements as to prices, distribution of sales or even volume of total output to be sold. These agreements were generally concluded for a period of a few years, subject to renewal, and they took a variety of forms. The purpose of them all was to achieve some control over the price at which the product was sold in the regional market. To this purpose was generally added the purpose of extending the markets of the regional industry in competition with the producers of other regions or countries. Simple price agreements frequently broke down under a serious cyclical decline in demand, and did not, of course, implement the second of these purposes. Generally, a more formal control over sales, including the channelling of orders or the establishment of a common selling organization with control over members' deliveries or production, was adopted. This organization, known in Germany as the cartel or syndicate, and in France and Belgium as the comptoir or sales bureau, to some extent took on an independent existence for the duration of its established contract. Members participated in its decisions through representative assemblies, executive and supervisory committees, generally in proportion to their productive capacity or their permitted share in total sales. Day-to-day selling operations, the prices actually obtained in sales and the level of capacity utilization were in effect controlled by the organization under the supervision of the members.

In France, these organizations in each product remained separate from one another although they had many of the same members and often shared common offices. In Germany, a fusion of the separate cartels, first in pig-iron, then as between different types of fuel in the Ruhr, finally for the various products of the integrated steel-firms, occurred. These fusions, however, could not conceal the basic weaknesses of the independent structures: the relatively short duration of the cartel contracts, the difficulty of reconciling the conflicting interest of members and the impossibility of controlling the entry of new firms into the industries under cartellization. Even in Germany the cartel remained essentially a device for implementing the two objectives stated: control over price fluctuations within a monopolized market, and expansion of sales outside a monopolized market. Despite occasional exhibitions of strength on the part of the cartel organization as such, the ability of the German cartels even during the duration of the contract to accomplish these objectives depended mainly upon the recognition by the producers of their mutual interdependence. This was the more true for the formally weaker organizations in France and Belgium, and it was particularly true when any long-run objective such as the control of capacity expansion was in question.[3]

[3]Detailed tables of the regional cartels in each product are contained in *Coal and Steel in Western Europe*, 316–27. The main source of information on the German coal and steel cartels prior to 1900 is the lengthy report of the government investigation in 1903 (*Kontradiktorische Verhandlungen über deutsche Kartelle*, Berlin, 5 vols., 1906; see especially the introductory report of Dr. Völcker); the standard histories of the Roheisenverband and the Stahlwerksverband (C. Klotzbach, *Der Roheisen-Verband*, Düsseldorf, 1926, J. Kohlmann, *Der Stahlwerksverband*, 1927) and several treatments of specific questions (A. Zollner, *Die deutsche Eisenindustrie und ihre Kartelle bis zur Gründung des Stahlwerksverbandes*, 1907; Leisse, *Wandlungen in der Organisation der Eisenindustrie*, 1912; P. Sauerlander, *Der Einfluss der deutschen Eisenkartelle auf die süddeutschen weiterverarbeitenden Industrie*, 1912). The Belgian cartels have been described in detail in a little-known work of G. de Leener, *L'Organisation Syndicale des Chefs d'Industrie*, Brussels, 2 vols., 1909, Vol. 1, pp. 75–131. Compared to this careful treatment the German sources do not present a comprehensive picture of the development, except in the coal industry. (See *Die Entwickelung des niederrh.-westf. Steinkohlenbergbaues*, Berlin, 1903–5, Vol. X, Ch. 8.) For France, where the literature is very thin, the best secondary source is R. Bühler, *Die Roheisenkartelle in Frankreich*, Zürich, 1934. See also

For some of these organizations complete information is not available; this is especially true of the cartels in rolled products in both France and Germany. In Germany, the inquiry made into the cartels in 1903 showed some twenty major cartels, each covering most of the German output of a specific finished steel shape. Although the *Stahlwerksverband,* formed in 1904 to include nearly all the integrated German producers, permitted the sale of all but the heaviest rolled products through these cartels, it is likely that most of them had disappeared by 1910. Limitations of output of these products was in any case imposed on the integrated producers by the *Stahlwerksverband.* The French rolled-products cartels were probably rather numerous. Particularly in France, local agreements of an informal nature among regional coal-producers and in different branches of the iron and steel industry probably existed, but cannot be definitely traced. In France, as in Germany, the sale of all the standard types of crude and semi-finished steel was probably cartellized in 1910; in both countries cartellization of the lighter rolled products was more difficult, and was abandoned in a comprehensive way by the *Stahlwerksverband* in 1912. That the French coal market, even near the mines themselves, depended to an important extent upon imports made control over price virtually impossible for a cartel to achieve without agreement with the Ruhr coal syndicate, the Belgian and the British mines, and the weakness of cartellization in the French coal industry can be partly attributed to this fact. In Belgium, however, cartellization appears weaker than in Germany despite the large number of separate organizations. The coal cartels remained on a local basis, and a satisfactory pig-iron cartel was never organized. The steel cartel, formed in answer to the German organization, did not attempt the cartellization of finished steel products.

All the cartels had at least a regional – and generally a national – market in which they possessed a substantial monopoly. Within this market, the organizations accounted for over 75 per cent of the sales by national producers of the specific type and grade of product cartellized. A listing of these organizations, even if it were complete, measures only very roughly the extent of their power. The size of membership and the portion of the market controlled depended, in many cases very intimately, upon how the cartel organization used its powers. The actual

R. Pinot, 'L'Industrie metallurgique', in P. de Rousiers, ed. *Les grandes industries françaises,* Paris, 1913, 69–92; N. Nattan-Larrier, *La Production sidérurgique de l'Europe continentale et l'Entente internationale de l'acier,* Paris, 1921, 48–60; and the Comité des Forges volume, *La Sidérurgie française, 1868–1914,* Paris, 1920, Ch. 9, 11. A year-to-year search of the Bulletins of the Comité des Forges – not surprisingly – is productive of more information on German and Belgian than on French cartels.

power of the cartel then rested on the nature and legal enforceability of the cartel agreements, the willingness of members to abide by decisions and the strength of the potential competition in the monopolized market. Some differences among the cartels in France and Germany in respect to these points are discussed in the concluding section of this chapter.

Among these products, it would appear that pig-iron was the first in which important regional cartels were formed. In the Lorraine–Luxembourg region these may have had their impetus from the desire of producers to extend the market for the cheap, low-quality pig-iron before the discovery of the Thomas process. The French comptoir for Thomas pig-iron (*Comptoir métallurgique de Longwy*) appeared slightly earlier than its counterpart on the German side of the border, but both adapted themselves readily to the expansionary situation after 1880. The organizations in the Ruhr and Siegerland, arising from earlier short-lived agreements in both regions, worked closely together after 1897, and a common sales office for Thomas pig-iron existed, in which markets were shared with the Lorraine–Luxembourg syndicate. These German regional cartels were hampered by the existence of important non-members, and they broke down completely in 1908. In France the comptoir existed amicably alongside non-members, entering into contracts with them for the sale of their output. Its strength on the national market, however, was hampered by the lack of any arrangement with the producers of non-phosphoric iron in the Nord and Loire regions.

The pig-iron cartel agreements covered the sales of pig-iron by the members' blast-furnaces; quantities transformed into steel or into cast-iron products by the producer were not included. The syndication of steel and steel products has a complex history prior to 1904 which has never been fully explored. A German syndicate of rolling-mills existed in the 1880's, and by 1890 a large number of small cartels was functioning.[4] In Belgium and France the movement among smaller scattered producers did not proceed as far, but agreements among the large French producers for major products may have existed prior to the dates shown in the table. The Ruhr coal industry presents the classic and best documented case of cartellization. Important short-term specialized cartels which grew up during the 1880's preceding the formation of the coal syndicate in 1893. The coke and briquette syndicates remained independent until 1904. The syndicate structure of the Belgian coal industry in 1910 resembles this earlier phase of the development in the Ruhr prior to 1893.

[4]The Völcker report mentions a figure of 260 cartels in specific shapes and products of iron and steel, including machinery, in existence in 1896, indicating also that the number diminished after that time as the result of fusions. Many of these were among a few producers in a small region and they all covered only one very narrowly defined product.

Competition among cartellized groups of producers in one another's national or regional markets was limited to a moderate extent by agreements between cartels. Of these the oldest and most persistent was the International Rail Makers' Association, which was formed in 1884 and renewed at intervals of three to five years, with only short periods of suspension until the First World War. The formation of the Ruhr coal syndicate permitted several agreements between its agent in Belgium and the Belgian producers, and agreements on coke and coking coal dividing the Belgian and the Lorraine–Luxembourg markets were regularly made. After 1904, agreements between the *Stahlwerksverband* and the French and Belgian cartels were made to cover the sales in one another's countries of crude and semi-finished steel. These agreements usually lacked the formality and firmness of the national cartels; they ran for rather short periods and were subject to frequent revision. Finished steel was probably not covered by such agreements, and the French producers were particularly wary of them.

In addition to producers' agreements, firms were also often bound by close financial or personal links. The role of banks in German industrial combination has been investigated by Jeidels and others; in Belgium the *Société Générale de Belgique* was said to control in 1910 eleven companies with 25 per cent of the national output. In France certain interlocking directorates and family connections among officials of different firms were evident.[5] The whole web of these connections can probably never be uncovered, and its significance for producers' decisions can certainly never be measured. One may, however, venture a guess that such informal connections were more characteristic of the well-established firms of the 1920's than of the young and growing organizations of the turn of the century.

PRODUCTION ORGANIZATION AND EXPANSION OF OUTPUT

A moderate number of large firms joined by a cartel is not always the most suitable instrument for rapid expansion of output in a regional industry. Two dangers are present in such an industrial system:

(1) That the cartellized producers will endeavour to secure monopoly profits by agreeing to limit their own expansion, taking common action to prevent firms outside the cartel from expanding.

[5] O. Jeidels, *Das Verhältnis der deutschen Grossbanken zur Industrie,* Leipzig, 1913. J. Riesser, *Die deutschen Grossbanken und ihre Konzentration im Zusammenhang mit der Entwicklung der Gesamtwirtschaft in Deutschland,* Jena, 1905, 3rd ed. 1912 (English translation in publications of the National Monetary Commission, 61 Congress, 2nd Session. Senate Document 563, Washington, 1911). On Belgium, see de Leener, loc. cit. A simple survey of the names of officials and members of boards of directors of French coal and steel firms as given in trade association *Annuaires* shows something of these interrelationships in France.

(2) That the security of an entrenched position and the development of a bureaucratic organization in the large firm will diminish the drive toward maximizing profit by expansion, and reduce the incentive to take the risks which any expansion involves.

Why did these tendencies in such an industrial structure fail to restrain the response made to the economic opportunity for expansion in any of the Western European regions before the First World War?

With respect to the first of these tendencies, a superficial answer is suggested by the weakness of the cartel organizations. This weakness was not due to a doubtful legal position. In Germany the cartel was a legally enforceable contract, and the cartels in several instances obtained court judgments against their own members for violation of the contract. In France, the legal position was technically more doubtful, but no action was taken against the cartels at any time.[6] Still less was it due, especially in Germany, to a reluctance on the part of the cartel officials to attempt to wage war against firms outside the organization.[7] Vigorous action, including exclusive contracts with dealers and consumers, pre-emption of main sources of bank credit, buying up of unexploited coalfields or unused plants, was resorted to in the endeavour to bring outsiders under the discipline of the cartel. As instruments to check the growth of productive capacity, the cartels were hampered in the first instance rather by the short-run nature of their contracts, and the ease – especially in France – with which they could be denounced.

Given the cartels as they in fact were organized, indeed, their effect on producers ambitious to expand output was, on balance, probably an encouraging rather than a restraining one. Cartels in the coal and iron industries clearly contributed to the drive on the part of steel plants to acquire mines, cokeries and blast-furnaces. In the Ruhr, the policy of the coke syndicate, and, in the Saar, the policy of the Lorraine–Luxembourg pig-iron syndicate, may be cited as inspiring such a reaction. In these cases cartellization in the raw materials industries had probably the effect of hastening an integration backward to the sources of supply on the part of the consuming plants.[8] The cartels, however, had a similar result in accelerating a movement toward forward integration on the part of their own members. In the early stages of cartellization,

[6]The field of action in France was probably freer, but less open than in Germany, since the German government and a portion of the public took an active interest in the behaviour of the cartels.

[7]An informative, though overly general, study of this aspect of cartel policies is by F. Kestner, *Der Organisationszwang: Kampf zwischen Kartelle und Aussenseitern*, 1912, 2nd ed. 1927.

[8]This is not to say that most of this integration would not have taken place eventually.

mines could avoid a coal syndicate's quota restrictions by constructing a cokery. The blast-furnaces of Lorraine could avoid the pig-iron cartel's restrictions by adding Thomas converters, and similarly steel plants belonging to the syndicate for crude or semi-finished steel could expand their output of those products at will by adding rolling-mills to consume their surpluses.[9] Indeed, the difficulties encountered in syndicating the lighter rolled products, apart from the variety of such products and the number of works involved, may well have arisen in part from the reluctance of the steel-mills to close this last safety-valve on their expansion. The existence of the cartels also affected the psychology of the producers in more subtle ways. Power in the cartel was based on capacity, and some expansions may have been undertaken with one eye on their effects on the place of the firm in the next syndicate contract. Furthermore, by splitting off the selling functions from the firms, the cartel permitted the firm to direct its interests toward matters of production. The technical director became a more powerful person than the sales manager, where indeed the latter was left with any functions whatsoever. In a period of rapidly developing technique, it is possible that the effect of this within the firm was expansionary. Finally, producers probably believed to some extent their own claims about the syndicates: that they stabilized the market domestically and expanded foreign sales. It is likely that the supposed and much advertised security of the cartels reduced producers' estimates of the risk of new construction more than it weakened the desire to take such risk.

These incentives might have been wholly cancelled out if the cartels had produced rises in fuel and ore prices which the steel-mills could not have avoided, but the possibility of integration threw the whole effect of such price rises on other consumers. The Lorraine–Luxembourg mills, which alone failed to achieve significant integration with their source of fuel, did not generally suffer from the sales policy of the Ruhr coal syndicate, which – because of the integration of the Ruhr steel-mills with their own cokeries – was required to dispose of the output of its expanded coke industry on the edge of its monopolized market rather than in the Ruhr itself.

The weakness of the cartels was, however, in the last analysis not simply a paper weakness resulting from flaws in the contracts. It was at bottom simply the reflection of the dynamism of the firms. During this period a supply of men of all the different types required in capitalistic industrial organization was furnished by the social and educational systems of the European countries. Sufficient industrial labour was recruited – often from outside the regions; in the Ruhr from Poland and

[9] I.e. before the formation of the Stahlwerksverband.

Prussia, in Lorraine from Poland and Italy. A supply of trained engineers and foremen was made available from training schools. Investors and the institutions of finance were able to furnish funds, and were inclined to do so. A business class in each region was available to move into new and old firms where opportunities of expansion existed. For these varied kinds of human effort, required to conceive, build and operate new plants, the device of the large firm – generally now transformed from the earlier partnership to a joint-stock company – proved an appropriate instrument. Most important for the guidance and inspiration of the members of the large firm was the adaptation of the system of cost accounting and profit measurement to the new situation of the integrated enterprise. Control by close accounting not only permitted the measurement of efficiency and prevented fraud; it permitted the erection of a system of rewards within the firm in the form of raises and promotions – which animated every part of the large enterprise. The directors of the enterprises were no less under its sway, and the activity of several thousand men became guided in this way by the criterion of profit. A strong inclination existed particularly in France to use these profits in further expansion, thus diminishing reliance upon banks and the capital market.[10]

In each region then the group of firms grew up, each firm a small empire unto itself. Combinations were possible to achieve an immediate advantage, or to avoid threatening ruin. For the important decisions regarding capacity expansion – decisions in which large amounts of capital had to be invested for a long period of time – the focus of the firms appears to have been fixed on the bright prospects of the market and not on possible expansions of other firms. Even where other firms' reactions were considered, expansion was competitive once it was under way. Where combination might have been possible – as for example in the Saar – it was held back by three strong forces: the rivalries among the existing producers, the impossibility of controlling outside capital, and the competition of producers in other regions.

Further into the motivations of the producers it is not possible to go. That many individuals in these production structures were motivated by pride in their work, the desire for prestige or even by a sense of civic or national duty, cannot be doubted. The genius of the capitalist system of economic organization lies in channelling work derived from all such motives into economically useful lines, yielding an excess of revenue over cost. In all cases, loss was a criterion of failure even where profit was not the sole standard of success. Differences existed, to be sure, in

[10]See the extremely interesting series of articles by L. Vignes, 'Le Bassin de Briey et la Politique de ses Entreprises sidérurgiques ou minières', *Rèvue d'Economie Politique*, 1912–13.

the degree of risk which different production organizations were ready to assume, but with so long and wide an opportunity, there was time even for the most cautious to expand. It was in the timing rather than the fact of expansion that risk was involved, and here, in view of the uneven course of the rising demand, the more cautious were usually the more successful.[11] Even in the case of Krupp and Stumm – the industrial barons *par excellence* – decisions about capacity expansion were taken in close consultation with members of the organization. Röchling and Thyssen, who were perhaps the most independent in their decisions about new plant, are classic examples of the bold, but profit-minded entrepreneur.

ORGANIZATION AND ENTERPRISE IN FRANCE AND GERMANY

During the period of expanding output, the major producing regions probably did not differ significantly in the vigour of their response to economic opportunity. Differences cannot be measured without previous analysis of the opportunities for profit set by price and cost margins in each region. Since such analysis involves not only natural opportunities offered by geography and technology, but also the economic elements which, as it were, clothe such opportunities – wage, interest and transport rates, and the prices of products, raw materials and equipment – accurate judgment of regional response lies beyond the limits of these chapters. Output trends in the various regions, however, were similar and matched roughly the development of natural advantage. The forms of industrial organization also were not drastically different. It would be surprising, therefore, if closer analysis showed any serious deficiencies in the quality of business enterprise in any region. If such deficiencies existed, they might be expected to show up in stagnation even in a region of considerable opportunity, but in fact such stagnation did not occur. Even after 1913 – taking the period up to the present as a whole – the regions present a picture of remarkably similar response to natural opportunity. It must be realized too that capital, and, to some extent, business talent and labour, were not hopelessly confined within regional boundaries. They were able – as in Lorraine – to move into regions of high returns.

A slight difference in the adaptation of industrial forms to the temperament of industrialists, however, can perhaps be discerned between the French and German regions. Despite their essential similarity of objec-

[11] The contribution to the long-run growth of capacity made not by the successful entrepreneurs, but by those bankrupted by short-run fluctuations of demand, and overly optimistic expectations has never been fully assessed.

tive, the French comptoirs were looser and more informal organizations than the German syndicates. They generally ran for a shorter period and were more easily denounced by a member even within that period. Some of them permitted direct relations between firms and their clients, and acted simply to place orders among the firms and to maintain a common price policy. Penalties on members were almost non-existent, staffs were small and publicity was shunned. German cartels resembled a company of medieval nobles, set armoured on heavily armoured steeds and riding off to battle. Ponderously staffed, bristling with regulations and clauses, they held their members in a complicated harness and brandished noisily an array of ferocious weapons with which to attack the market. Beside them, the French comptoirs shimmered delicately like webs of light gossamer. French writers are not slow to point to this difference, and for some of them it assumes great significance. One prominent French authority, surveying the trust movement in France and abroad, delivered himself of the following comparison:

'La métallurgie française a, de son côté, donné lieu à une forme de concentration commerciale qui ne se rencontre guère ailleurs. Elle a, sinon créé, au moins largement développé le comptoir, comportant des obligations précises et peu nombreuses, moins tyrannique que le cartell allemand, poursuivant un but plus loyal que le Trust américain; organisme simple, clair et sans détour; organisme discret, qui se développe avec le besoin qui l'a fait naître ou disparait en même temps que lui, aidant sans jamais l'entraver l'évolution nécessaire.[12]

Now differences in the legal position of agreements in the two countries probably exercised some influence on the degree of formality with which these arrangements were made. Apart from that, however, certain intrinsic differences in the attitudes of producers in the two countries does make itself felt. This difference probably does not lie in the degree of 'individualism', acquisitiveness or enterprise shown by the producers; the difference is rather one of the style in which these qualities were expressed and by which very similar objectives were gained. In Germany, an awareness of mutual interdependence does not seem to have been part of the producer's deeper consciousness. Confronted with an opportunity, his first instinct was not to look around him at what others were doing, but simply and directly to grasp it. Aggressive and individualistic, he yet saw with his mind the advantages of group activity; hence his willingness to accept discipline, and his elaboration of rules and penalties. Possibly, too, in some self-contradictory way, the German producer received satisfaction, not from co-operation indeed, but from submitting himself to the rules of an organization. The French

[12]P. de Rousiers, in Comité des Forges volume, *La Sidérurgie française, 1864–1914*, 508.

producer does not appear less acquisitive, calculating or ambitious. There is probably no basis for saying that his individualism was either stronger or weaker than the German's; it was almost certainly less 'rugged' and more 'civilized'. The discipline which the German imposed with a flourish upon both himself and others was acquired by the French business man as a kind of inner discipline at some point in his education. Unprotected by laws and organizations – mistrusting these indeed in the extreme – he protected himself against other producers by a jealous secrecy, and against his own impulses by an abundance of caution. He was not for these reasons a less enterprising or less effective agent of industrial development. With respect to their effect on output, which is here the important question, the two combinations of form and spirit may have been nearly indistinguishable. Agreements requiring an elaborate code and cartel bureaucracy among the large German firms could be accomplished in France with a wink of the eye at lunch. The comparison may be made indeed between a pack of wolves, who without a leader would tear each other apart, and a school of small sharks, swimming in a different medium and comporting well with one another. But one should be careful not to attribute to a difference either in rapacity or intelligence what is in fact simply a difference between land animals and underwater creatures.[13]

[13]The action of the cartels against outsiders is indicative. In Germany outsiders were considered enemies of the cartel and vigorous war was waged to compel them to join. In France, cartels frequently made contracts with non-members, for the sale of their output, without requiring them to join the cartel. One is led to the conclusion that a higher degree of monopoly might be reached by a group of French producers with no formal arrangement than by a group of German producers heavily cartelized. Innumerable other examples might be given of the willingness of French producers to work together: the sharing of ore-mines and the co-operative operation of cokeries, and after 1920 the formation of various *consortia* to take over German property in Lorraine. In the International Rail Syndicate, for example, the Acieries de France was given a quota of 10,000 tons, although not a member. Deliveries as exports in excess of this were subtracted from the total French quota, reliance being placed on the ability of the French producers to keep the firm in hand. The extent to which the French government has traditionally depended upon groups of private individuals to manage portions of its affairs (e.g. the distribution of reparations coal) strengthened these bonds. The social cohesion of the country, particularly among these groups, arising from common education through technical schools is undoubtedly important in these attitudes.

The conclusions here do not, of course, preclude differences in the effectiveness of the French and German response to opportunities for expansion and innovation in other industries in this period. Only careful comparison of the whole position of the two national economies and the opportunities offered to enterprise by resources, technology and markets can show up any peculiar national weaknesses. Suggestions for one side of the comparison are offered in

Producers were ready in both countries to combine in minor matters, while maintaining their essential independence in the decisions about the expansion of plant capacity.

two recent articles: D. S. Landes, 'French Entrepreneurship and Industrial Growth in the Nineteenth Century', *Journal of Economic History,* IX, 1949, 45–61; J. E. Sawyer, 'Social Structure and Economic Progress: General Propositions and Some French Examples', *American Economic Review,* XLI, May 1951, 321–30. See also the interesting, if somewhat breath-taking, survey by Bert F. Hoselitz, 'Entrepreneurship and Capital Formation in France and Britain since 1700', in National Bureau of Economic Research, *Capital Formation and Economic Development,* New York, 1955, 291–337, and the discussion of the Hoselitz paper by A. Gerschenkron, pp. 373–8.

5

Law and enterprise: ore-mining on two sides of the Franco-German border

Over the past 200 years the principal Western countries have all experienced periods of rapid economic expansion. During this time they have been joined – at times more closely than at others – in a single network of trade and communication. The vivid picture drawn by Keynes in 1919 remains in our minds today because it represents an ideal with which the reality of the Western countries has never quite lost touch.[1] Capital, goods, skill, and technological knowledge did indeed move relatively readily among these countries before World War I.

Must not the common progress of this whole area be attributed to those elements whose international movement made them the common property of all? If so, differences in levels of activity and rates of growth in different portions of this area must be traceable to differing resources (relative to the prevailing industrial technology), and in lesser part to cost differentials arising from imperfect mobility of labor. From this viewpoint, the appropriate unit of study appears to be the whole international, intercommunicating region. Its long-run dynamics derive mainly from technological change and population growth, considered as independent variables to which economic life responds. The national

Originally published as "National States and National Development: French and German Ore Mining in the Late Nineteenth Century" in H. J. G. Aitken, ed., *The State and Economic Growth* (New York: Social Science Research Council, 1959), p. 201–12.

The material for this paper was gathered in connection with another project, which was carried out with the assistance of a grant-in-aid from the Social Science Research Council in 1954–55. I also wish to acknowledge the support of Resources for the Future, Inc., which has permitted this extension of my earlier work. Reprinted by permission.

[1]John M. Keynes, *The Economic Consequences of the Peace* (New York: Harcourt, Brace and Howe, 1920), Chapter 2. See also I. Svennilson, *Growth and Stagnation in the European Economy* (Geneva: United Nations Economic Commission for Europe, 1954), pp. 16–18.

economy as such then fades into nothingness; the state as an economic actor withers away. Where it has insisted on action, this appears as an embarrassment, misdirecting the stream of international investment and distorting the international price-cost system.

The view generally taken of the state's role in Western economic history does not contradict this impression. When tariffs, specific monetary and fiscal arrangements, and other examples of state interference are examined for a period predominantly laissez-faire, the impression is often confirmed. The national state is a political creature, and the fumbling fingers of many states in an international economy have generally warped the price system somewhat in directions suitable to the short-run designs of national politicians. Tax systems, tariffs, exchange controls, migration restrictions, all operating within arbitrarily defined regions, find slender and infrequent excuse as instruments for the economic development of an international area.

This is not to say that elements distinctive to national regions may not have had an important bearing on their rates of growth. Even in technology, perhaps the most communicable and international element in production, regional peculiarities impose themselves.[2] Though essentially governed by intellectual rather than economic developments, technological change is responsive to local needs and opportunities. The region where a technology originates hence often has a considerable advantage in its application. At least, every region needs a vigorous native engineering tradition to adapt foreign technology to its own uses. This holds true particularly in agriculture, mining, and smelting, which deal with natural materials in all their endless variations. A region's industrial career depends then in part on ability to train its own engineers. If this is important in technology, it is indispensable in entrepreneurship – a skill especially rooted in a particular social and geographical setting. Economic unit or not, the Western world has been splintered by language and cultural differences, and these have permitted differing responses to economic opportunity. The growth characteristic of Western nations in recent times may indeed have had a common set of causes in each. But these cannot lie exclusively in those elements of production that move freely in the international network of trade and communication. A set of immobile elements, reproduced within each

[2]For further treatment of this subject, see Norman J. G. Pounds and William N. Parker, *Coal and Steel in Western Europe* (Bloomington: Indiana University Press, 1957), Chapter 9, and the references cited therein. The adaptation of coking technology to the qualities and prices of local coals and the market for coke oven products is a particularly intriguing subject which still awaits treatment. For material on adaptation of blast furnace construction and practice, see Fred Clements, *Blast Furnace Practice*, 3 vols. (London: E. Benn, 1929–33).

national region, may account for similarities as well as for some differences in the records of Western nations. It is not essential that these separate elements be identical from one national society to another, but each society's set of elements must function together to give an effective response to economic opportunity.

In the Western world a special feature of the state is that its political organization has been roughly coterminous with the social organization imposed by the national culture. An example may suggest the general effect of this fact on the growth of the national economies. From a comparison of the operation of several social elements in production as they were combined historically within each of two national societies, the role of the national state in shaping these elements and in adjusting them to one another may become apparent.

RESPONSES OF TWO SOCIETIES TO SIMILAR ECONOMIC OPPORTUNITY

For such a comparison, a situation of similar economic opportunity in two societies must be found, and their responses to the opportunity must be measured. A similar response to similar opportunity would suggest similar effectiveness in the organization and motivation of economic life in the two societies. Comparison of the aggregate rates of growth of, for example, France and Germany would be the task of a full-scale economic history; but with a narrower focus on individual industries the two societies may be compared. Here, however, the movement of the economy outside an industry – movements of demand and factor cost rates – must be taken as given, combined with technology and the real costs of resources to provide the limits of economic opportunity for the particular industry. The record of such an industry is measurable largely in terms of its output, and of changes in inputs.[3]

Full comparison of the ore mining and smelting industries in French and German Lorraine in the period 1871–1914 would require much more detailed research than has yet been done, but there is here an unusually favorable opportunity for analysis. Differences in natural conditions on the two sides of the famous 1871 boundary[4] could be

[3]The long-run correspondence of price to production cost is also an important measure. Historical data, however, are rarely good enough to give more than an approximate output trend. Input measures are notoriously difficult, and measures of the profit rate are nearly impossible.

[4]See Richard Hartshorne, "The Franco-German Boundary of 1871," *World Politics,* 2:209–250 (January 1950); and for a brief but intriguing account of French exploration after 1871, Lucien Cayeux, *Les Minerais de Fer Oolithique de France,* Fas. II (Paris: Imprimerie Nationale, 1909–22), pp. 70–71.

compensated to a large degree by use of different types of mining equipment and different mixtures of ores in smelting. Demand for ore, and even for pig iron, was to some extent international, and the two regions had somewhat similar home markets.[5] Relative to the movement of demand, it is not unlikely that factor cost rates moved somewhat similarly for each region.

If the opportunity for development of a profitable mining and smelting industry did appear and grow in a similar manner in French and German Lorraine, then a great interest attaches to the similarity in their records of output. From 1871 to 1914 output movements of iron ore and pig iron were very close for the two regions.[6] With respect to pig iron after 1900, the movements and the absolute amounts were almost identical. A similar opportunity and a similar result would suggest an equal effectiveness of response. One who knew nothing of the organization of the two industries might suppose that he was faced with the handiwork of two national planners, equally enterprising and far-sighted, and equally constrained by considerations of cost and price. But the facts are very different. Several of the complex elements producing the response differed sharply in the two regions.

Differences in mining laws. The most striking differences were in their mining laws.[7] The mining law governing the exploration of French Lorraine was the Napoleonic law of 1810, amended in minor particulars in 1838, 1852, and 1880. Without relinquishing the state's prior claims to mineral deposits, it set up the machinery by which these rights might be conceded to private individuals. A license to explore was required even of the owner of the surface rights, whose consent was required before such a license could be given to anyone. Application for a license was

[5]The French ore and iron moved naturally west and northwest into France and Belgium, the German into the Saar and the Ruhr. In the rather smaller French market the French products had no serious competitors, whereas the German ore and iron met growing competition from imports of Swedish ore into the Ruhr. See Pounds and Parker, *op. cit.*, Chapter 10, for an analysis of the interregional balance between these areas.

[6]For data on iron ore production, see J. Raty & Cie., Societé des Hauts Fourneaux de Saulnes, *Les Mines de Fer Françaises* (Nancy, 1954), pp. 104–105; on German pig iron, *Vierteljahreshefte zur Statistik;* and on French pig iron, *Statistique de l'Industrie Minérale.*

[7]The French law, as amended, is summarized in C. Dumanet, *Traité d'Exploitation des Mines,* 2nd ed. by A. Dufrane-Dumanet, Vol. 3 (Brussels, 1898), pp. 427–438; pp. 440–444 contain a summary of the Prussian law. See also Gerhardt Boldt, *Staat und Bergbau* (Munich: Beck, 1950), pp. 1–11. For the text of the Prussian law as applied in Alsace-Lorraine, see Robert Courau, *Législation des Mines en Alsace et Lorraine,* 1871–1918 (Paris: H. Dunod & E. Pinat, 1918).

made at the local prefecture and then followed a rather long route to and in Paris for approval. Licenses were usually limited to a term of 1–2 years, and in themselves gave no title to any minerals discovered. The explorer was required to make a payment to the owner of the surface rights, whose special permission was required for drilling near and under buildings on the property. If minerals were discovered and a concession to exploit them was given to someone other than the finder, or was reserved to the state, an indemnity was paid to the finder. The exploitation of mineral deposits was a privilege conceded under a special grant from the state. Each concession was a separate arrangement, the terms of which were contained in the *cahier des charges,* but certain standard provisions were made in all such arrangements. These included the rents to be paid to the owner of the surface rights and the boundaries of the concession. In addition, the law of 1810 provided for a flat tax per hectare and a percentage tax on net revenues (not to exceed 5 percent) to be paid to the state. The operation of a mine, once begun, was subjected to close control from the *administration des mines,* which might even require it to raise its rate of output and could forbid it to shut down. Concessions and shares of stock in mining companies were of course salable, but one concession could not be combined with another, broken up, nor abandoned without permission of the state.

In sharp contrast to this restrictive policy was the system of *Bergbaufreiheit,* which was set up under the famous Prussian law of 1865 and applied with minor changes to Alsace-Lorraine in 1874. Under this law the state was required to grant a license to explore for minerals, even over the protest of the owner of the surface rights, to any applicant unless damage to the public interest was clearly involved. The sole right to exploit any minerals found was vested by the law in the finder, who might fix a field of any size and shape up to 200 hectares and up to 2,000 meters from the point of initial discovery.[8] Except for deciding what constituted a bona fide discovery the state had very little discretion; it could not decide that minerals were not exploitable nor reserve any right in them to itself. Fields might be sold, abandoned, divided, or joined. As against the surface owner, the mine owner possessed large rights. The surface owner could not object to duly authorized digging on his property, nor was he entitled to any share in the minerals found or to any other rents. The mine owner even had the right to appropriate certain materials on the property for his own use and might erect buildings on the surface, although in that case the surface owner might force him to buy the land for the purpose. The principal protection given to

[8]These limits applied only to Alsace-Lorraine. For Prussia, they were 219 hectares and 4,185 meters, respectively.

the surface owner was his power to prohibit digging under his buildings or within a radius of 62.8 meters of them.

Roles of the bureaucracy. These two mining laws imply a different role for the bureaucracy in the two countries.[9] In the operation of mines the law of 1865 gave the Prussian bureaucracy various supervisory powers, and it appears to have exercised them mainly to reduce the risks of long-term investment. Here again we must argue from examples. In the introduction of electricity into coal mines at the end of the century, the work of safety inspectors of the *Oberbergamtsbezirke* was significant.[10] No general code for electrical installations in mines was adopted until 1903, except a code governing all electrical equipment, issued by the *Verein deutscher Ingenieure.* Instead, each separate installation was made under the supervision of a government inspector. In this case the risk of an important innovation was reduced and transferred in part from the mine operator to the government. Since the German electricity industry was aggressive and the mine inspectors were not averse to exercising their authority, electrification in the German mines proceeded rapidly. In France, where the dangers of explosion were admittedly greater, the innovation was not similarly encouraged, and greater boldness on the part of a mine operator was needed to introduce it.

[9]No comment in this section should be construed as an attempt to compare French and German entrepreneurs – either bureaucratic or private. Alexander Gerschenkron has repeatedly called for such a comparison, both in the discussion of the suggestive work of John E. Sawyer and David S. Landes on the French entrepreneur and in a Comment on Bert F. Hoselitz, "Entrepreneurship and Capital Formation in France and Britain since 1700," in Universities – National Bureau Committee for Economic Research, *Capital Formation and Economic Growth,* Special Conference Series No. 6 (Princeton: Princeton University Press, 1955); see especially pp. 297–311, 373–378, 385–393.

The attempt here is simply to compare certain elements in the institutional structure within which the mining industry operated in the two countries. Until the measures of growth for the two economies – both aggregate and by sectors – are closely reviewed, it is dangerous to proceed far into explanatory elements. Comparison of certain estimates by François Perroux and associates with the estimates by Paul Jostock indicates a growth in the deflated income per capita in France not markedly inferior to that in Germany between 1870 and 1914. This represents a sharp revision of the relative movements shown by Colin Clark, and some reconciliation of the estimates seems called for. The recent studies are contained in International Association for Research in Income and Wealth, *Income and Wealth, Series III,* Milton Gilbert, ed. (Cambridge, England: Bowes & Bowes, 1953), and *Series V,* Simon Kuznets, ed. (London: Bowes & Bowes, 1955); Clark's data are in his *The Conditions of Economic Progress* (2nd ed.; London: Macmillan & Co., 1951), pp. 80, 101.

[10]H. Denis, *Étude sur la transmission et l'utilisation de la Force dans les Mines* (Paris, 1909), pp. 50–54.

Even in minute regulatory functions the German state appears rather more protective than restrictive of industrial operations. Cooperative enterprises among producers were common in exploration, research, and worker training; the trade association, the *Verein,* and the cooperative flourished – with considerable legal encouragement.[11] In France, where these forms of self-help were less common, the function of the bureaucracy as protector and adviser of producers may well have been fulfilled slightly differently. In the mining industry, at least, exploration appears to have been carried on not infrequently by state geologists and engineers, alone or in association with private companies. Whereas in Germany a private activity was protected and regulated by government officials, in France a state activity was farmed out to private producers. One must be careful not to generalize the tendency evident in mining; toward manufacturing both governments may have pursued an equally liberal policy.

Training of mining engineers. To understand how the different mining laws and their administration produced apparently equivalent results in Lorraine, it would be necessary to consider the character and motivations of the prospectors and mine operators in the two national regions. A number of these men in both countries were mining engineers, and all the major mining and metallurgical firms had such engineers in their employ. Some light is shed on this difficult subject by comparison of the French and German methods of training mining engineers during this period.[12] Both countries had state mining schools that dated back to the

[11]In Germany, for example, the *Bergbauhülfskassen* were organized originally by the state, financed by a levy on mine owners, and in 1883 turned over to the owners, to be run by them, although membership appears to have remained compulsory. The concept of the privately run organization in which membership was compulsory was applied after 1913 to the coal cartels. These *Bergbauhülfskassen* undertook numerous common projects, such as supporting training schools for miners, and contributing in the Ruhr to the construction of the Rhein-Emshäfen Canal. See Adolf Arndt, *Bergbau und Bergbaupolitik* (Leipzig: C. L. Hirschfeld, 1894), pp. 197–200.

[12]This comparison is based largely on a revealing public discussion in the *Révue de Metallurgie,* 1906 and 1907. At this time French technical education was coming under heavy criticism. The *Révue* controversy was set off by the report of an inspection trip to Germany by A. Pelleton, deputy director of the *École des Mines,* under official orders from the Minister of Public Works. Pelleton appears to have visited most of the ten *Technische Hochschulen* as well as the three *Bergakademie,* and to have been greatly impressed. His report elicited comment – largely critical of his comparisons – from the directors of several French technical schools, the president of the *Aciéries de Longwy,* a former president of the *Association des Anciens Élèves de l'École des Mines.* The spokesman of a student group at the *École* contributed to the discussion

turn of the century or earlier. In Prussia the *Bergakademie* at Clausthal had been established by Frederick the Great; the *École des Mines* in Paris was founded in the Revolutionary period. There were other *Bergakademien* in Berlin and Freiburg, and a second *École des Mines* in St. Étienne. Instruction in mining engineering was also given at the *Technische Hochschule* in Aachen.

The French and German schools differed sharply in most respects, and in ways quite upsetting to naive preconceptions of French and German "national character." Admission to the French schools was extremely difficult, depending on a competitive examination possible for most students only after two years at the *École Polytechnique* or equivalent special preparation. Five to six years of scientific training, mostly in mathematics, was the rule for the French applicant to the *École des Mines;* indeed, it was estimated that he had ten times as much mathematics as his German counterpart. In Germany, the technical schools were open to all graduates of a *Gymnasium, Realgymnasium,* or *Oberrealschule.* The result was that the successful French applicants began their special training to be mining engineers at about age 25, and were ready to take a job with the government or private industry at 28; the German student was at work well before he was 25.

Instruction and the relations of students to professors were also strikingly different. The German training was specialized almost from the start. Four alternative courses led to degrees in mine operation, topology, ferrous metallurgy, and nonferrous metallurgy in the Berlin *Bergakademie.* The *Technische Hochschulen* were equally specialized. In the first two years some general science and mathematics were required, but practical subjects predominated and some actual experience in a mine or factory was included in the program. In contrast with this specialized and practical approach, the *École des Mines* offered virtually no choice of courses, but included a long array of courses worthy of a general engineering school. To some extent it was such a school, for it trained metallurgical and industrial engineers as well as mining engineers. All were required to take essentially the same curriculum and only one kind of diploma was given. The course was encyclopedic and largely theoretical; job training as such was left until the graduates were on the job.

With the rather wide choice of courses in the German schools there was also freedom in other respects. Professors were dependent, not sim-

some complaints about courses, relations with professors, and work loads. This controversy is interesting for the critical views expressed concerning both the French and German systems. Discussions of the German system appear elsewhere, e.g., E. C. Meyer, "Industrial Education in Germany," in U. S. Department of Commerce and Labor, *Special Consular Reports,* Vols. 33 (Washington, 1905).

ply for their self-respect but also for part of their income, on the numbers of students in their classes. An established professor might double his income through his students' fees, a percentage of which he retained. At the beginning of his career a *privatdozent* received from the school nothing but a lecture room and depended for his whole livelihood on fees for his courses. Students in the *Technische Hochschulen* might move freely from professor to professor and from school to school, and some movement between these and the *Bergakademien* was also possible. The French student, on the other hand, continued to be treated as a schoolboy until graduation. Discipline was strict, relations with the faculty were even more formal than in Germany, and as choice among courses was narrow, choice among professors was inconceivable.

The French training, in short, was general, theoretical, highly mathematical, intensive, and compulsory; the German was specialized, practical, rather less intensive, and permitted rather wide choice. The French student, carefully selected and several years older, was kept under discipline in a highly academic atmosphere. The German student was free to roam, and was generally required to get some job experience before receiving his degree.

One would be foolish indeed to attribute an absolute superiority to either system of instruction. The engineers they produced almost certainly represented two rather different kinds of men. The German may have moved easily from school into a specialized job, where little direct supervision was needed to hold him to a workmanlike performance. His faults must have been those of one who specializes early, a certain lack of imagination, and an inability to move readily from one task to another. An industrial and bureaucratic organization that protected him, kept him in a secure niche in the system, and permitted him patiently to exploit a limited range of opportunity could best use the trained mind that he brought to industry. The French engineer, on the other hand, was released from 6–10 years of academic training, as from a military school. He almost certainly needed an apprenticeship before he was ready for responsible work in a plant or mine.[13] On the other hand, his mind would be more sharply and more widely trained than the German's, and over a whole career this might prove to be a considerable advantage. Men with the French engineering training, however, on entering the mining industry, might well need some guidance from trained engineers, especially since many of the best students went from the *École des Mines* into the government service. The more highly specialized abilities of the engineers of the government's *Corps des Mines*

[13]Those who supported the French system claimed, probably with some justice, that the supposedly practical training of the Germans did not in the least obviate a similar need of apprenticeship.

were available in service anywhere in France, rather than in the employ of an individual firm.

Other elements in the French and German economies. It is not possible, on the basis of such evidence, to reconstruct adequately the social and legal setting in which the exploitation of the Lorraine ore deposits took place in France and Germany. Reflected in the relation between the legal and the educational systems, however, certain elements in the French and German economies in this period became evident. France was clearly drawing on an intangible social capital in a tradition of education and administration whose elements were to some extent adjusted to one another. With the virtual termination of population growth, the phase of increasing productivity through increasing specialization of labour was largely over. The "problem" (to speak as an economist rather than a historian) for the French economy was to exploit native resources and adapt new technology to domestic use, without the advantage that growing scale and specialization would promise.[14] The "solution" to the problem lay in maintaining the hand of government, representing the maximum scale in the economy, somewhat stronger in France than in Britain or Germany, while retaining an educational system designed to prepare engineers for a varied experience. The advantage of these two elements in the system undoubtedly was felt in the settlement of the colonial empire. It cannot be imagined that it produced an industrial upsurge in France comparable to that in Germany. Perhaps a major weakness – derivable from intellectual traditions rather than economic circumstances – was that technological change in France, stemming from general science and mathematics, produced inventions of general application, which contributed less to France than to the rest of the world. It would be surprising, for example, if the failure of the automobile to gain favour in France as quickly as in the United States was a failure in French entrepreneurship.

The situation of the German economy was quite different. National administration and national technical education were in the process of formation, but local organization and the system of apprenticeship had deep roots. A nice balance could be struck between centralization and decentralization in the school system, and between freedom and control in government policy toward business. The economy at the same time

[14]The advantage of scale in a single intercommunicating society exists for native technology and technological education; but it exists also in the ability of native firms to specialize, particularly in such products as machinery. The weakness of the French electrical and chemical industries noted by John H. Clapham, *The Economic Development of France and Germany*, 1815–1914 (Cambridge, England: Cambridge University Press, 1948), pp. 256–257, might well be examined in this light.

could look to a growing population to permit important increases in productivity through specialization. At least in the heavy industries, adaptation of British and French technique was of first importance. Such adaptation required engineers with specialized training and ability to make numerous minor innovations.

The adaptation of the French and German structures of industrial organization to the different situations of the two economies is a matter for separate examination. Any superiority in German performance in this period, however, must be examined against differing opportunities offered by resources (particularly coal), population growth, and the international movement of demand and of technology. In the exploitation of Lorraine ore, where the opportunity was unusually wide, the French and German systems appear to have operated with equal success. The German system of law and education may have been unusually well-suited to the peculiar situation of other German industries. Only after such elements have been taken into account can a direct comparison of French and German entrepreneurs be made. Such a comparison would be enormously delicate and difficult, and it is not yet clear how the available materials could be made to yield meaningful results.

Such broad study may show that the role of the secular state in the West has been to form rational, economic men through public education, while shaping a legal and administrative system suitable for putting the specially trained products of that education to their maximum economic use. Only in such a way can the persistence of high rates of growth in so many Western countries in the nineteenth century be reconciled with the minor, but numerous, differences in state policy, social organization, and "national character." The alternative to such an explanation is to assume that, even taken one by one, such differences are really of no importance at all. Although attractive to an economist, such an alternative is excessively harsh and insensitive to the wonderful variety of which human nature is capable. National economies may rather be delicately compared to national cuisines. The countless examples of both these forms of social activity share three important characteristics. They satisfy hunger, they use predominantly local materials, and they are generally considered tolerable (sometimes even exciting) by those who have been brought up in them.

6

Kartelle und Konzerne: the German Coal Syndicate under the steel mills' domination

The following bit of research has two purposes, one general and one specific. Its general purpose is to suggest how the three elements in its title are linked together, and in doing this to connect more closely the work of historians, which has focused on entrepreneurship, with that of economists, which has centered around economic growth as measured in statistical aggregates. The specific purpose is to show how the organization of the German coal-mining industry in fact constituted one such connection between the economic activity of individuals and the industrial development of a nation.

The general purpose is pursued in Section I, where the need for a more sophisticated linkage between enterpreneurship and aggregative economic phenomena is exposed. This need is seen to exist particularly where, in an economic model, a system of small, competitive decision-making units is to be supplanted by complex private or public organizations of a semimonopolistic nature. Analysis of the particular example is introduced in Section II by a discussion of two alternative types of monopolistic organization, how they might be expected to develop a mining industry under the control of single-minded, profit-maximizing enterpreneurs, and how their operations might affect the fuel supply of the economy in which they operated. In Section III – rather categorically

Originally published in *The Journal of Economic History* (XIV, 4, 1954), 380–400. Reprinted by permission.

The author is indebted to the Social Science Research Council for generous assistance, which made possible a two-year residence in the Ruhr in 1949–1951, during which the material for the present study was gathered. He wishes also to acknowledge the help of numerous American, British, and German officials who gave him ready access to the records of the former Rhenish-Westphalian Coal Syndicate and several of the coal-steel combines, and to the important collection of material in the Bergbau-Bibliothek in Essen. Acknowledgement should also be made to a number of generous friends and colleagues for suggestions and advice during the preparation of this article.

because of limitations of space – some explanatory value is claimed for the model organizations of Section II for the period 1890–1915 in Germany. In the years 1925–1929, which are examined in more detail, use of a more complex model of industrial structure would seem to be required. Section IV outlines very briefly the industrial organization within which individuals worked in the Ruhr coal industry in these years and leads back to the general subject of this paper: the significance of industrial organization as a link between entrepreneurship and economic growth.

I

The study of German entrepreneurship cannot satisfactorily be conducted by examining the psychology of a few individuals or the sociology of a small elite. Instead, the concept must be defined rather widely to include any activity in the production and exchange of goods and services which is not wholly routine and automatic; in which, apart from mere manual or mental habit, an element of guesswork or judgment is involved; in which risk based on the stock of accumulated knowledge is not inappreciable. Such a definition is wider than "innovation" in Schumpeter's sense; it includes all adjustments of existing practices to new situations, and the line separating it from merely routine activity is fixed by the novelty in the situation that the individual must face. It comprehends more than command and organization of the factors of production. Including many activities that a workman faces in his daily tasks, it extends entrepreneurship down from the business elite well into the nether kingdom of labor and laboring skills.

Now any form of economic change, including economic expansion, is evidently connected, *first,* with the breadth and character of choice that individuals encounter in their daily activities as producers and sellers of goods and services, that is, with the scope for entrepreneurship as here defined, and, *second,* with their response or the skill and vigor with which they perform their many entrepreneurial functions, both great and small. One might suppose therefore that as between two economies exhibiting different rates of growth the one with the more rapid growth must either possess in the aggregate greater economic opportunities, such as better materials or a favored location with respect to world markets, or else it must be blessed with a group of unusually clever, vigorous, rational, profit-minded entrepreneurs. The economist's interests lie in examining how techniques, resources, demand, the capital market, and a little judicious government aid can be arranged to create market situations to which properly motivated entrepreneurs can respond – through the instrumentality of the business firm seeking maximum profit; the historian's interest in the entrepreneur centers in explaining how societies have produced the clever, vigorous, rational, profit-minded individuals the economist orders. Combining these, we are in danger of obtaining a study of economic growth that reduces itself to a matter of price relationships and the biographies of industrial Titans.

Such a framework of explanation is satisfactory where an economic model involving competitive, one-man firms can be utilized. In such a model, the psychology of the decision maker is all that is required for the understanding of the firm's response to opportunity. No problems of firm structure, of division of authority, of fragmentation of the entrepreneurial function among many men in a large organization need arise. The paradox of private self-interest serving the social good here also can be resolved by the mechanism of the market and the free movements of price. In the presence of other favorable factors (and even in the absence of an exact theoretical statement), it is not surprising that the clever, vigorous, rational, profit-seeking activity of the competitive entrepreneurs somehow yields a rapid rate of economic expansion.

This model of individual entrepreneurial activity in a developing economy must be made more complex and subtle to be useful in explaining economic change where large firms, combines, cartels, or government bureaucracies partially replace the market and "usurp" the entrepreneurial function. Certainly in understanding the movement of the German economy, its rapid growth, its remarkable recuperative power after disaster, a more sophisticated linkage is required. Without it, one who seeks explanations may suffer a strong propensity to flee too quickly out from the Black Forest of monopolized markets to gather brighter blossoms on loftier slopes.

To be sure, German economic development was made possible by opportunities offered by nature, by technology, and by markets, and it was carried forward by a people who adapted themselves to the industrial and commercial arts; but it depended also for its balanced success upon the framework of German business institutions. Those institutions stretched like an invisible web across the German economy, creating a division of labor within the entrepreneurial function along bureaucratic lines. Within whole industries, they served to break down the natural and market opportunities offered by the movements of demand and cost into a large number of small interdependent parts, to which each German, within the limits of his job, could make a coherent response according to his motivations, the response of each individual affecting the scope of opportunity available to others. The operation of such a system can be observed in the complex organization through which the coal of the Ruhr – Germany's principal industrial resource—was exploited, processed, priced, and distributed between 1890 and 1930.

II

The utilization of the Ruhr coal deposits involves questions central to German economic development. Even under the German Empire, when the Saar and the Silesian deposits were also available, the Ruhr deposits formed Germany's principal source of fuel.[1] At what rate should extraction take place? To what extent should the coal be processed, by briquetting or coking the fine sizes, at the mines before shipment? How should distribution be made among the various groups of German consumers, with their different types of fuel requirements? To what extent should industrial consumers be favored in the price scales at the expense of household consumers? How much of each grade and size should be exported?

Correct answers to these questions are important for a high rate of economic growth in Germany for two special reasons having to do with the characteristics of the deposits themselves: first, the location of the coal bed at the intersection of the Rhine and the principal East-West trade route in Northern Europe (the so-called "*Hellweg*"), and, second, the superior quality of the coke derived from Ruhr coal for blast furnace use.[2] For both these reasons, the Ruhr area is a favorable site for

[1]The resources available for development under the German Empire consisted mainly in a food surplus in the East, iron ore in Lorraine, the cheap North-South river transport, and the fuel deposits and timber reserves. The rate of development must be studied as the response of Germans to opportunity set by these resources on the one hand and conditions outside Germany (development of technology, markets, and supplies of materials) on the other. The Ruhr production accounted for 44 per cent of the Reich's coal output in 1871, and rose steadily to 56 per cent in 1903 and 60 per cent in 1913.—Verein für die bergbaulichen Interessen im O.B.B. Dortmund, *Die wirtschaftl. Entwickelung des niederrh.-westf. Steinkohlenbergbaues* (Berlin: J. Springer, 1904), I, 52–54; and *Statistisches Heft* (Essen, 1914).

[2]A trustworthy general description of the geography of the Ruhr area and the characteristics of Ruhr coal is given in N. J. G. Pounds, *The Ruhr* (Bloomington: Indiana University Press, 1952), chaps. 1, 2, 5. See also C. D. Harris, "The Ruhr Coal-Mining District," *The Geographical Review*, XXXVI, No. 2 (1946), 194–221. References to the German sources are given by Pounds and also in the bibliography of an unpublished doctoral dissertation, "Fuel Supply and Industrial Strength" (Harvard University, 1951) by the present writer. The following discussion draws heavily on this dissertation, cited hereafter as Parker, *Fuel Supply;* data and further references on most of the subjects treated here are given in this source. The most comprehensive bibliography of the Ruhr literature is that of H. Corsten, *Bibliographie des Ruhrgebietes, das Schriftum über Wirtschaft und Verwaltung,* 10 parts (Essen, 1941–1944), available in the United States in the Library of Congress and the New York Public Library.

steel production, and consequently for coking and for the assembly of by-product and auxiliary industries that cluster around mines, coke ovens, and steel mills. It is favorably located for the shipment of all its products, including coal, up and down the Rhine, across much of Northern and Central Germany, and overseas. Wise utilization and allocation of Ruhr coal can provide the basis of an intense industrial complex in the Ruhr area and can go far toward sustaining Germany's position in international trade. That a striking and recurrent development has persistently been achieved – under the German Empire, in the late 1920's, and once again in the last few years – is an indication that such wisdom is lodged somewhere deeply in the German industrial system.

These broad questions of national economy were never encountered by any individual, charged with any fraction of entrepreneurial responsibility in the German coal industry. Even a pipe dream such as Friedrich List produced for the German railway system was never sketched out for the development of the nation's fuel supply.[3] Within the industry itself, competition among producers, which lasted during the rapid growth of the 1860's, 1870's, and 1880's,[4] was succeeded after 1893 by a monopoly organization whose power is almost legendary and whose structure has served as a textbook model for German cartels: the *Rheinischwestfälisches Kohlen Syndikat.*[5] The influence of the large coal-steel vertical combines – Krupp, Thyssen, Gutehöffnungshütte, Hoesch, Bochumer Verein – began to grow within the Syndicate after 1900 as they purchased mining properties to supply their own fuel

[3] F. List, *Über ein sächsisches Eisenbahnsystem als Grundlage eines allgemeinen deutschen Eisenbahnsystems* (1833). Besides this famous project, the two volumes of List's *Schriften zum Verkehrswesen* (*List-Gesellschaft* edition, Berlin: Hobbing, vol. III, 1929, 1931) contain plans for other rail systems for Germany, France, Hungary, and the United States, with exhortations to all and sundry to build them. On List's estimate of the importance of coal, see *ibid.*, I *Teil*, 351–53.

[4] Description of the rings, clubs, and Vereine prior to the formation of the Coal Syndicate is given in the economic volumes of the trade association's great work: Ver. f.d. bergbaul, Interressen, *Wirtschaftl. Entwickelung* (Berlin: J. Springer, 1904), II, 87–291.

[5] The most often cited study in English of the Syndicate, F. Stockder, *Regulating an Industry: the Rhenish-Westphalian Coal Syndicate, 1893–1929* (New York: Columbia University Press, 1932), is an excellent digest of the several German monographs, mentioned in its Bibliography. A penetrating early study was prepared in 1904 by Francis A. Walker, *Monopolistic Combination in the German Coal Mining Industry,* for the American Economic Association. See also the discussion in R. K. Michels, *Cartels, Combines, and Trusts in Post-War Germany* in Columbia University Studies in History, Economics and Public Law, No. 306 (New York: Columbia University Press, 1928), pp. 67–105.

needs.[6] The German Government exercised a nominal influence through wartime measures, which made membership in the Syndicate compulsory, and finally under the Coal Act of 1919.[7] The principal result of government intervention, however, was to put the compulsory Syndicate system on a permanent basis in all mining regions, and to set up a hierarchy of semipublic bodies on top of the Syndicate structures, leaving them to effective domination by the Ruhr Syndicate itself. There is no evidence in the whole period between 1893 and 1930 that the Syndicate functioned consciously or consistently according to any plan for German industrial development.[8]

At either end of the thirty-seven-year period from 1893 to 1930, that is, in 1893–1900 and in 1925–1929, the structure of the Syndicate was such as to lend itself to some measure of formal analysis; such analysis, in terms of two model monopoly organizations, is useful in untangling the logic of the industry's operation as it actually occurred throughout the whole span of thirty-seven years. In both these two terminal periods – as indeed in the intervening years as well – the Syndicate controlled the sales of Ruhr coal.[9] Through its committees (more fully discussed in Section IV below), particularly in the latter period, it also effectively controlled the entry of new mines and the expansion of existing mines and cokeries in the area. It fixed the weekly output of the mines and determined the share of this output that could be turned into

[6]The so-called "Hüttenzechenfrage" is the subject of two monographs: A. Pilz, *Die Hüttenzechenfrage im Ruhrbezirk und Richtlinien für eine Erneuerung des Rheinisch-Westfälischen Kohlen-Syndikates* (Essen: Glückauf, 1910), also published serially in the magazine *Glückauf*, and E. Ledermann, *Die Organisation des Ruhrbergbaues unter Berücksichtigung der Beziehungen zur Eisenindustrie* (Berlin and Leipzig: de Gruzter, 1927), pp. 99–124.

[7]*Reichsgesetzblatt* 342 and 1449 (March 23 and August 23, 1919). Of the numerous commentaries on the *Kohlenwirtschaftsgesetz*, and studies of its effects, that of K. Loose, *Vorgeschichte, Gestaltung, und Auswirkung des Kohlenwirtschaftsgesetzes* (Bonn: 1930), is specially pertinent to the present study. See Parker, *Fuel Supply*, pp. 115–25, and the references there cited.

[8]Even the judicious, but essentially very favorable, studies of T. Transfeldt, *Die Preisentwicklung der Ruhrkohle, 1893–1925* (Leipzig: 1926), and H. Lüthgen, *Das Rheinisch-Westfälisches Kohlen-Syndikat in der Vorkriegs-, Kriegs-, und Nachkriegszeit und seine Hauptprobleme* (Leipzig: 1926), put forward no such claim. It seems likely that the Syndicate's policy respecting reparation shipments and deliveries to new customers during the British coal strike in 1926 was directed toward the long-run interests of the coal industry. This, however, is a different matter.

[9]The annual reports of the Syndicate show a control of between 80 and 90 per cent of the basin's output in the period between 1893 and 1914. The expansion in coal output between these years was about 300 per cent and in coke output about 550 per cent.

coke for sale.[10] The difference between the two periods lies in the fact that in the years before 1900 the independent mines wholly controlled the operations of the organization, whereas in the years after 1925 the Ruhr steel combines were in nominal control.[11] The period 1900–1913, in which the steel mills developed their own holdings but did not control the Syndicate system, lies between these two extreme situations. The years 1913 to 1925 were so chaotic that analysis of them is not helpful in the present study.[12]

For purposes of preliminary analysis, the entrepreneurial function in each of these two extreme cases may be considered as lodged in one man, or a small, well-co-ordinated group of men, intent on maximizing profit. In the first case, the profit to be maximized would be the net earnings of the coal-mining and processing industry as a whole; in the latter case, the profit would be that of the individual coal-steel combines. It may be assumed in our second case that these combines

[10]The Syndicate did not directly intervene in a company's decisions about coking. The existence of a separate coke quota, however, had the effect of controlling quantities of coking coal used for this purpose, where production was for sale. See Ledermann, *Organisation*, pp. 124–32. The system described here, however, was much simplified in the Syndicate contracts of 1926 and 1927. The collected Syndicate contracts have been published for the years 1893–1931. Rheinisch-Westfälisches Kohlen-Syndikat, *Die Syndikatsverträge des Rheinisch-Westfälischen Kohlen-Syndikates* (Essen: Glückhauf, 1933).

[11]Data given in an annual output summary of the mines, Ver. f. d. bergbaul. Interessen, *Die Bergwerke und Salinen im niederrheinisch-westfälischen Bergbaubezirk* (Essen: Glückauf), have been grouped according to mine ownership.

Percentage distribution of syndicate quota by groups of mine owners

	1913	1925	1929
Ruhr steel	42.3	53.0	53.1
Non-Ruhr steel	4.8	7.0	6.2
Other industrial	.9	5.2	6.2
Independent	52.0	34.8	34.5

In these percentages, the quota for sales through the Syndicate and consumption in the owner's works have been combined. The rise in Ruhr steel's percentage came about wholly through a rise in the *sales* quotas of the steel mills' mines, so that in 1925 their sales quotas also exceeded those of the independent mines. Furthermore, a number of mines, nominally independent, may have been under the control of the combines by that time.

[12]The analysis of these years, especially the inflation period, would provide some of the reasons for the growth of the steel combines, and for their investment program in mining and coking; these developments have been treated by D. Warriner, *Combines and Rationalisation in Germany, 1924–1928* (London: P. S. King, 1931), and P. Berkenkopf, *Die Neuorganisation der deutschen Grosseisenindustrie seit der Währungs-Stabilisierung* (Essen: Baedeker, 1928).

are competitive with one another in their steel sales but that no serious conflicts of interest arise among them in production and sale of fuel. Maximization of profits of the combines as a group in fuel sales will then be considered as also yielding maximum profits in these operations for the combines taken one by one. The details of profit maximization in the production and marketing of so complex a product as coal need not be fully elaborated; the examination of those points on which the behavior of the independent coal mines' Syndicate might be expected to differ from that of the Syndicate dominated by the steel producers, however, is of special interest.

Both monopolies would behave identically in many respects. To maximize profit, prices within an area protected by transport costs should be set with reference to the elasticity of demand, with systematic freight absorption beyond this area to meet competition up to a point at which receipts at the mine no longer covered the marginal costs of extraction. The different grades of coal would be sold simply as different products with rather limited substitutability. Within a single grade of coal, both monopolists should consider the technical possibilities for converting lump coal into fine coal and fine coking coal into coke and its by-products; the price differentials for these products in the competitive market; and the elasticity of demand for each of the different sizes and types of fuel in the monopolized market. Optimum output, the optimum extent of size transformation and coking, the optimum distribution as between monopolized and competitive markets, and the optimum price scale for the monopolized market would then be simultaneously determined.

In monopolistic behavior of this general sort, no differences between the two types of monopoly organizations are apparent. Differences do arise, however, on closer examination, for reasons that may be distinguished as relating to: (1) profit maximization in fuel sales, (2) policy considerations, (3) general outlook and attitudes. These sources of differences must now be examined.

Narrowly considered, the profit-maximizing behavior of the two monopolies would be somewhat different. The difference arises in the quantity of blast furnace coke delivered to the steel mills in the mining area. The demand for blast furnace coke by these mills is very inelastic over a wide price range; indeed the only important element of elasticity consists not in the possibilities of substitution by another fuel or even of substantial variations in the coke–pig iron ratio[13] but largely in the

[13]The coke–pig iron ratio can be varied no more than ± 20 per cent in the short run by changes in the quality of coke and in the iron content of the ore-flux mixture in the blast furnace change. Such variations are undesirable, since they may affect the quality of the pig iron. In the long run, changes in the blast furnace construction will alter the ratio somewhat. The *steel-coke ratio*

effect of the coke price on the price of the steel itself. The very high price which the independent mines' monopoly should charge would have the effect of restricting steel output to an appreciable extent. The corresponding restriction in blast furnace coke production would have the effect of reducing the output of small coke, coke oven gas, and the coke oven by-products, and the corresponding restriction in the output of coking coal would have the effect of reducing the output also of lump coal by the mines, unless either coking coal or the coke itself could be sold to customers outside the steel mills' reach.

The behavior of the Syndicate under the steel mills' control would be less restrictive. The interest of each steel mill would lie in the profits of the mill-mine combine as a unit. Particularly if the steel producers were competing with one another, and if the demand for steel were rather elastic, monopoly profits accruing to mines before their integration into the coal-steel combines might be "competed away" with accompanying increases in steel, coke, and coal output. With combination among the steel producers, the possibility of increasing profits through an increased steel output might still exist, even if this meant some reduction in the profits of the mining part of the combine for the sales through the Syndicate of the increased quantities of the other fuel types produced jointly with the additional blast furnace coke required. The expansionary policies of the steel mills might be further stimulated to the extent that their control of the Coal Syndicate permitted them to manipulate the Syndicate policies to their own advantage and to the disadvantage of the remaining independent member mines.[14]

The restrictionism of the monopoly dominated by steel producers could be expected to come about in a more roundabout manner than through direct and immediate calculations of profit. Such an organization, acting in the best interests of the dominant steel producers, might be expected to frame a policy with respect to fuel pricing and distribution with an eye to its ultimate effects in the steel market. Being interested in selling steel, the steel entrepreneurs should use the Coal Syndicate as a means of widening their steel markets, particularly if the costs of such an operation could be partly pushed off on the other, independent mines. Two ways suggest themselves: reduction in exports of blast

may be changed, however, by change-over from converters to open-hearth furnaces and by variation in the scrap–pig iron ratio in the open hearths, that is, by changing the amount of pig iron required per ton of steel.

Some data taken from the records of the Vereinigte Stahlwerke show that in the late 1920's coke formed between 30 and 35 per cent of the cost of pig iron, excluding taxes and depreciation from total costs, and using the Syndicate's coke price as a basis of assessing charges.

[14]Some means of manipulation are suggested in Section IV below.

furnace coke to rival steel producers, and distortion of the price scales in the home market to favor steel-consuming industries and to penalize household fuel consumers. The first of these policies might prove very restrictive of total fuel output; indeed, since the independent mines would have only the export market on which to sell blast furnace coke, it would require them either to shut down their coking operations or to dispose of their supplies without exporting to steel mills outside the area. The effect on the foreign steel producers might be sufficiently great to permit some expansion in the export market of the domestic steel industry provided that no retaliatory measures were taken by the foreign country.

Finally, some general differences in attitudes should exist between the two monopolies. These differences would depend on the industrial organization of the steel industry itself, on the capital invested and the financial resources available, on the accounting methods used, and on the spirit of the entrepreneurs in the two cases. A competitive organization in the steel industry would presumably be immensely stimulating to the mining industry under steel-mill domination – stimulating not only to the volume of output but to the improvement of production processes, the search for new markets, and the drive for efficient operation. Even without such an organization, however, some of the same effects might be present. Regardless of backwardness in their own mills, the steel producers might demand coke from their captive mines at the cheapest possible price, and might look upon them as a good repository of excess investment funds. This attitude could to some extent be promoted where the internal accounting system priced blast furnace coke at a residual cost after allowing for the net yields of all the other mine products; even where this was not the case, the temptation so to consider it – and to consider the whole mining-coking operation indeed as designed largely to furnish blast furnace coke – would be very great.

As for the "spirit of the entrepreneurs" – that Apple of Discord among economic historians – it is difficult to find here the reason for the observation often made that the steel industry tends to be more "progressive" or "dynamic" than the coal industry.[15] Within the same geo-

[15]This observation is probably more nearly true for the United States or Britain than for Germany. Developments in underground haulage, in washing, in processing, and in coke by-product utilization were rather rapid in Germany, especially in the early twentieth century. Nevertheless, the strongest initiative does seem in many instances to have come from entrepreneurs outside the industry: railroad, promoters, shippers, and bankers in the 1850's and 1860's, later from fuel consumers in steel, chemicals, and electricity. On the special features of German entrepreneurship, see the preliminary suggestions contained in "Entrepreneurial Opportunity and Response in the German Economy," *Explorations in Entrepreneurial History,* October 1954, and the somewhat similar conclusions of Ralph Bowen's article, "The Roles of Government and Private

graphical region one is inclined to look at the opportunities available to the entrepreneurs in each industry as expressed within the industry's structure.

III

Either of the two monopoly organizations just examined might be expected to restrict output in the German coal-mining industry. The restriction in both cases would seem to arise from a desire to limit the output of blast furnace coke available to steel producers. In the case of the "pure" mines' Syndicate, this restriction would occur on the domestic market where the demand for Ruhr blast furnace coke was very inelastic; in the case of the monopoly dominated by the Ruhr steel producers themselves, restriction would be sought with respect to exports to rival steel producers, especially in France, Luxembourg, and Belgium. The other characteristics to be expected in the behavior of these organizations are less sure and less significant than the fact that they would both be restrictive, and that the restrictions would apply to coking, taking different forms with respect to the marketing of the coke.

Restrictionist behavior directed against steel firms is evident in the history of the Coke Syndicate of the 1890s prior to and just following its merger with the Rheinisch-westfälisches Kohlen-Syndikat.[16] In the years between 1900 and 1913, the Ruhr steel firms began their purchases of mining properties partly to make themselves independent of the Syndicate's price policies on coke, although the desire to assure themselves a steady quality of coke and to find an outlet for investment funds were also reasons for this integration. By 1913, the Ruhr mills supplied virtually all of their own coke and controlled forty-five per cent of the coke output of the Ruhr.[17] The Syndicate, however, controlled the volume of sales in the market, set prices, determined the volume of exports, and remained under the domination of the independent mines.

In the period between about 1900 and 1913, the Ruhr coal industry was under a form of organization which, far from being restrictive, was in a sense doubly expansionary. The steel mills had escaped from the control of the Syndicate with respect to their supplies of blast furnace coke, while at the same time the independent mines were free to export coke to steel producers elsewhere. The effect of integration piled on top of cartelization was not to intensify the restrictionist nature of the Syn-

Enterprise in German Industrial Growth," JOURNAL OF ECONOMIC HISTORY, X (1950), 68–81.

[16] Ver. f. d. bergbaul. Interressen, *Wirtschaftl. Entwickelung,* II, 238–49. The rise in the coke price in 1900 and 1901 is especially significant.

[17] See Parker, *Fuel Supply,* Statistical Appendix, Tables C4c, CK1, and CK2.

dicate's operations; rather the coal-steel combines in a sense canceled out and frustrated monopoly restrictions in the place where they might have been most severe, and where they could have done most damage to the industrialization of the region. The result was an industrial organization that in no way obstructed the growth of a sizable coking industry in the Ruhr, producing a supply large enough to fill domestic requirements and extensive export demands. This coke was furnished to the Ruhr steel mills owning their own mines and cokeries at an effective price equal to the cost of production of the coal from which it came, less the yield from the sale of all the joint products – lump coal, small coke, gas, and chemicals.

In the period following 1925, the Ruhr steel mills acquired what would seem to have been a commanding position in the Ruhr fuel industry. This dominance was achieved largely by the merger of one of the largest coal firms with the largest combine,[18] and by some expansion of basic mining capacity on the part of the combines themselves. It is possible therefore to compare the actual results of the coal industry's operation in these years with those that might be expected from a monopoly dominated by the steel-mill consumers of blast furnace coke.

In many ways the behavior of the industry in these years corresponded to the picture of such a monopoly's behavior sketched in Section II. Certainly the most notable development was a growth in coke capacity and output sufficient to provide blast furnace coke for the additional blast furnace capacity that the industry brought into operation.[19] Pig iron output in the Ruhr mills after 1926 stood at a level about thirty per cent above the best prewar year; even with some fuel economy the rise in coke consumption was of the order of twenty per cent. To understand the reason for this rise in pig iron production would require examination of the postwar situation in the steel industry itself, the loss of some blast furnace capacity in Lorraine, the currency inflation, the formation of the International Steel Cartel, and the whole complex of factors affecting costs, markets, and the entrepreneurial structure.[20] An increased supply of coke was clearly no obstacle; indeed the advantages that expanded coke output offered – advantages for additional power in the Syndicate, for profitable outlet of investment funds – was an additional inducement to the expansion in blast furnace capacity itself.

[18] The merger of the Gelsenkirchener Bergwerks A. G. in the Vereinigte Stahlwerke in 1926.

[19] See Parker, *Fuel Supply,* Appendix 1, based on a collation of official and trade association data.

[20] On the situation in the steel industry in the late 1920's, see the report of the so-called Enquete-Ausschuss, *Die deutsche eisenerzengende Industrie* (Berlin: Mittler, 1930), pp. 11–42, 98–108.

This provision of additional coke was accompanied by the "rationalization" program in the mines and the coking establishments about which a considerable literature exists.[21] The effects in the mining industry showed themselves by a continuous rise in productivity of underground workers, utilizing improved equipment, and especially in an improvement in conditions of underground haulage. The additional coking capacity took the form of the establishment of the large central cokeries with some economy in handling and fuel costs. Most notably, the heat interchanges between cokeries and blast furnaces became more complex in several installations;[22] the additonal coke oven gas, both from the expanded coke output and from savings effected through utilization of blast furnace gas in coke ovens, was made available for sale to industrial users, municipal gas works, and household users by the erection of the extensive and consolidated network of gas distribution from the cokeries.[23] Throughout all this development, which in a sense truly created the Ruhr as we know it today, both the funds and the enterprise of the steel-mill directors is evident.

An examination of the price scales for sales of Ruhr fuel in Western Germany in this period shows a structure that might be considered favorable to steel producers. Fuels for household use were rather high-priced compared with industrial fuels, and at a number of technical points the steel mills would seem to have been advantaged.[24] There is, however, no evidence of strong steel-mill pressure for any given price

[21]D. Warriner, *Combines, and Rationalisation,* gives a general picture of this movement. The well-known study of the National Industrial Conference Board, *Rationalization of German Industry* (New York: N.I.C.B., 1931), identifies rationalization with cartelization, but see pp. 1–6 for references on technical aspects of the movement. The dissertation of R. M. Morguet, *Rationalisierung im deutschen Steinkohlenbergbau nach dem Kriege bis 1929* (Freiburg, 1936), pp. 64–83, condenses the data for the Ruhr and gives further references.

[22]The heat economy of a cokery-steel mill installation has been the subject of careful research, especially by the so-called "Wärmestelle" (*Energie-und Betriebswirtschaftsstelle*) of the Verein deutscher Eisenhüttenleute under the direction of the late Dr. Kurt Rummel. See his *Anhaltszahlen für die Wärmewirtschaft, insbesondere auf Eisenhüttenwerken* (4th ed.; Düsseldorf: Stahl und Eisen, 1947), pp. 178–91.

[23]The annual reports of this organization, *Ruhrgas A. G.* (before 1928, *A. G. für Kohlenverwertung*), give information on this development, the plans for which are sketched out in the company's published memorandum, *Deutsche Grossgasversorgung* (Essen, 1927). One dissertation by T. Runte, *Die Gasversorgung der Provinz Westfalen* (Essen, 1931), is most useful. Enquete-Ausschuss, Die deutsche Kohlenwirtschaft, pp. 26–60, also describes this development.

[24]This was true at least of the small coke produced jointly with blast furnace coke and sold largely to households. See Parker, *Fuel Supply,* pp. 136–48, 162–88, and the diagrams, showing price and yield data taken from the Syndicate records (Diagrams 4–13 to 4–37).

scale. The scale was set nominally by a semipublic body under strong influence of the Ruhr Syndicate. Considerations of monopoly pricing, plus a strong element of tradition, were the major factors setting prices in the home market.[25]

When one looks for evidences of the kind of monopoly restriction that a steel-mill-dominated Syndicate might be expected to practice, one finds virtually none at all. Here the problem revolves around the need of an expanded coke output in the first place. Why did the Ruhr mills choose the path of expansion of output rather than curtailment of exports to feed their new blast furnaces? The fact seems to be that far from interfering with exports of coke by independent mines, the mills participated in such exports themselves.[26] Given an expanded coke industry necessary to provide the fuel needs of the Ruhr furnaces, a proportionate expansion in the supplies of lump coal and of small coke was inevitable, and it is to be expected that these quantities might be sold on the export market at prices below their price in Germany. But blast furnace coke was sold abroad in large quantities at prices far below the nominal German price.[27] Moreover, there is no apparent reason why blast furnace coke sold abroad might not have been sold in smaller pieces on the German market to household and industrial users at a higher price than the foreign sales achieved.[28]

It may be argued that the expanded coke industry was itself profitable

[25]*Ibid.*, pp. 132–33.

[26]This can be established from the data on coke output and consumption by the coal-steel combines. Their output in 1929 was 20.8 million tons, of which over 16 million was certainly of blast furnace size; their consumption of blast furnace coke in that year was only 11 million tons, leaving 5 million tons or more in excess of their own requirements. Data on coke consumption are obtainable in official Statistisches Reichsamt data and in the trade association booklet: *Statistisches Jahrbuch für die Eisen-und Stahlindustrie* (Düsseldorf, 1929–1931). See Parker, *Fuel Supply,* Statistical Appendix, Table C4c. In earlier years, this surplus may have been much smaller, however. – *Ibid.*, Table 4A(5).

[27]A careful use of official German rail and waterway transport data yields better results for regional analysis than the data on foreign trade. Total coke shipments from the Ruhr to destinations outside Germany averaged 8 million tons a year in both the 1909–1913 and 1925–1929 periods. The postwar shipments were steadier in volume while the prewar shipments rose from 5.4 million tons in 1909 to 10.4 in 1913. – *Ibid.*, Table 3A(14–17). Blast furnace and small coke are not separated in these data, but records of Syndicate sales in the "competitive market" show that sales of small coke there were negligible. – *Ibid.*, Diagrams 4–39, 4–40.

[28]The average yield in Syndicate sales of small coke was over 60 per cent above that for blast furnace coke, and the differential in the accounting prices credited the delivering mines on the Syndicate's books was about 35 per cent. – *Ibid.*, Diagrams 4–17, 4–28.

to the Ruhr mills, and that the attraction of profits here was great enough to overcome any reluctance to expand. Such an argument does not answer all the puzzles involved and is in itself very dubious. There is no evidence that the fuel industry was anything but overexpanded, from the point of view of the real interests of the owners of mines and cokeries.[29] From the point of view of maximum monopoly profit, the Ruhr steel mills probably did not act wisely either in financing, and through the Syndicate in permitting, the growth of coke output, or in allowing disposal of large quantities at low prices to their competitors in the Lorraine region. It would be possible to argue that this expansion, including even the maintenance of exports, was in the best interests of the development of the German economy and the Ruhr complex as a whole. But it would be very difficult to argue that that consideration was, at least in this form, in the minds of the Ruhr steelmasters.[30]

[29]It is not possible here to substantiate these impressions except by general references. An inquiry into the financial position of the mines relative to a wage dispute, the so-called "Schmalenbach Report" (Berlin, 1928), after a reasonably impartial questionnaire, concluded that depreciation allowances were too low and stated profit figures too high. The Enquete-Ausschuss, *Die deutsche Kohlenwirtschaft* (Berlin: Mittler, 1929), pp. 125–50, 166–71, points to the conclusion that yields were excessively low. A study by a disciple of Spiethoff, C. Wilhelms, *Die Überzeugung im Ruhrkohlenbergbau, 1913 bis 1932* (Jena, 1938), based on data of 10 Ruhr mines, is of interest but not conclusive. The League of Nations Economic Committee came to a similar conclusion about the whole European coal industry in a study made in 1929 (League of Nations Publications, II. Economic and Financial. 1929, II, 19. *The Problem of the Coal Industry*, Geneva, 1929). See also the 1932 report: *The Coal Problem* (League of Nations Publications, II. Economic and Financial. 1932, II, B 4, Geneva, 1932). Finally, data available in the annual reports of the Mining Division of the Vereinigte Stahlwerke indicate a low profit figure, which fell with the output expansion between 1927 and 1929. See Parker, *Fuel Supply*, pp. 195–218, for a full treatment of these data.

[30]Rejection of a number of plausible explanations is required to establish the explanation of this behavior in terms of the industry's entrepreneurial structure. Since the central fact is the continued sale of blast furnace coke to foreign steel mills at low prices, several alternative explanations for these exports, which must be rejected, should be examined. These include the following: *(a)* reparations shipments, *(b)* degree of co-operation among national groups within International Steel Cartel, *(c)* possible differences of interest among the combines with respect to fuel output and sales, *(d)* substitutability of Northern French and Saar coke for Ruhr coke in the French market. Examination of relevant material on the first two topics indicates that they had little influence on German behavior in this period. See H. Marchese, *Le Charbon, elément de réparations* (Lorient, 1933), pp. 165–85, and Darmonnel (pseud.), *L'Office des houillières sinistrées* (Paris: Jauve, 1933), pp. 72–73. In 1927 one finds a system of import licensing for German coal established by France and protested by the Coal Syndicate. On the functioning of the International Steel Cartel see E. Hexner, *The International Steel Cartel* (Chapel Hill: University of North Caro-

IV

In explaining the behavior of the Ruhr fuel industry under what has been called steel-mill "domination," we are led back to re-examine what is meant by the word "domination" in this context. It is not possible here to reconstruct the whole picture of the combine-Syndicate

lina Press, 1943), and C. Nattan-Larrier, *La Production sidérurgique de l'Europe continentale et l'entente internationale de l'acier* (Paris: A. Rousseau, 1929), pp. 278–316. It is not apparent that the 1927–1930 steel cartel diminished the aggressiveness of the German group, although their interest was mainly directed toward expanding their internal markets. See Hexner, *International Steel Cartel,* pp. 78–79.

As among the combines themselves, the assumption of an identity of interest with respect to fuel sales would seem to be essentially accurate. Size yields and quality of coal were certainly similar; concerning cost conditions, no satisfactory statement can be made. The surplus above a combine's own requirements available for sale is the crucial point; on this the relation of a combine's consumption to its sales and coke sales quota in the Syndicate may be taken as a guide. A rough comparison between the Vereinigte Stahlwerke and the five smaller Ruhr combines is shown by the following data for 1929:

	Sales quota	Coke sales quota (millions of tons)	Consumption quota
Ver. Stahlwerke	34	11	13
5 smaller combines	33	8½	11

Differences among the five smaller combines (Mannesmann, Hoesch, Krupp, Gutehöffnungshütte, Klöckner) are not much greater than those shown above. All the combines possessed sizable sales and coke sales quotas, and so were interested in the fuel market. This does not explain, however, why such large fuel interests were acquired and whether the combine would not have been better served with coal and coke holdings that did not involve an expansion in the total output of the region. See Parker, *Fuel Supply,* Table C3a.

The final point – substitutability of Northern French for Ruhr coke – involves a question of the ability of the Ruhr Syndicate to affect foreign steel producers by raising prices and curtailing coke exports. Detailed treatment of this complex question, which involves the whole structure of the Lorraine-Luxembourg fuel market, is not possible here; in the long run, with expansion of French coal production, developments of mine or mill cokeries in France, changes in blast furnace design, and improved mixing of coals for coking, the "dependence" of Lorraine-Luxembourg producers on Ruhr fuel could be diminished. A different export policy in the Ruhr could have set such a train of events in motion; the result of such a challenge to French entrepreneurs might have been ultimately stimulating to French development. Instead, German Syndicate policy not only made coke relatively cheap but fixed a sales price for coking coal that did not system, functioning under the nominal public control of the Coal Act of 1919. Detailed descriptions of the Syndicate structure, the internal organization of the Vereinigte Stahlwerke, and the compulsory Syndicate system under the *Reichskohlenrat* have been published.[31] What has not been emphasized, however, is the exact nature and location of the decision-making function in this system.

The Coal Syndicate itself was organized under a basic contract to which all the members subscribed and which was subject to periodic renewal.[32] Even before wartime regulations and the Coal Act of 1919 made membership in this Syndicate compulsory, the pressure on dissident mines to agree to the terms of a contract proposed by the controlling group was very great. As usual in such organizations, the members' voting power and participation in total output was governed by the individual quotas they held; these quotas bore only a rough relation to the member's productive capacity.[33] The issuance of new quotas was the function of Syndicate committees under the control of the existing producers. The volume of total output to be taken from the member mines for sale through the Syndicate was set at frequent intervals through the establishment of a percentage figure based on the total quota figure, each mine sharing in this output according to the proportion which its quota bore to the total quota of all the mines. This figure was also set by a Syndicate committee in which members voted accord-

encourage foreign cokeries to buy it for coking outside the Ruhr. Such a time horizon, however, was almost certainly not available to the Ruhr steel concerns, and on a short-run basis interruption of coke exports would have seriously upset foreign producers. The continued large coke exports were the result of a large Ruhr coke and gas industry, and that was a situation not intended by anybody but simply the result of the industry's entrepreneurial structure as described in Section IV below.

A fifth objection to this line of argument—that the coke exports were necessary to the steel mills in order to obtain Lorraine ore in exchange—is based on a misconception of the economic interrelations between these two areas and is not borne out by the statistics for this period.

[31]See the sources referred to above, Notes 5, 6, 7, 8. On the Vereinigte Stahlwerke, see B. Dietrich, *Vereinigte Stahlwerke* (Berlin, 1930), and on its coal holdings, F. Didier, *Die Beteiligung der Gelsenkirchener Bergwerks A.G. an der Kartell- und Trustbildung* (Cologne, 1931), and the annual reports of the *Abteilung Bergbau* of the combine.

[32]This summary of the Syndicate structure is based on the Syndicate contracts of 1926 and 1927. (R.W.K.S., *Syndikats-verträge*) and on descriptions contained in Lüthgen, *Das R.W.K.S.*, Part I, *passim.*

[33]The coal and coke sales quotas of the whole postwar period were inflated above the mines' combined capacity. The percentage of the annual quota on which deliveries were actually called for ran between 50 per cent and 60 per cent during 1925–1929. Parker, *Fuel Supply,* Diagram 4–2, based on Syndicate data.

ing to their quotas. Coke quotas and output were set separately from coal, by the members interested in coking. Quotas for the steel mills' consumption in their own works were also established but were subjected to no percentage limitations by the Syndicate.

The mines, upon delivering coal of various grades and sizes to the Syndicate, were credited upon the books of the Syndicate at a scale of prices established by a Syndicate committee for this purpose. Actually these so-called "accounting prices" followed the price scale established for sales in the "noncompetitive" Western German market.[34] The actual sales contracts, however, were made by the Syndicate officials who were not representatives of member mines but formed an entrenched bureaucracy of their own. They in turn governed the distribution of sales between the noncompetitive and the export markets,[35] and it was their policy that fixed the final yield actually obtained. This total yield was then compared with the credits earned by the mines on the Syndicate books, and the latter were reduced by a flat per-ton levy to bring them in line with the sums actually available to be paid out by the Syndicate to its members.[36]

Under this system the opportunity for powerful entrepreneurs in the steel-coal combines to exercise vast power in their own interests was certainly very great. The acquisition of a majority of the total quota by any group meant control over the granting of new quotas, and so over any expansion of capacity in the region. The ability to fix the percentage of quotas to be delivered for sale meant a close control over output, while the exemption of the mills' own consumption quotas from any limitation gave the steel mills complete freedom in the exercise of such

[34]A good description of the internal accounting practices of the Syndicate is contained in H. Walther, *Die Entwicklung des Abrechnungsverfahrens des Rheinisch-Westfälischen Kohlen-Syndikates und seine Preispolitik* (Essen: typewritten, 1933); this work is a *Diplomarbeit,* available in the Bergbau-Bibliothek in Essen.

[35]The noncompetitive area was defined to include Germany west of the Elbe, excluding the North Sea coast where British coal could compete, and including Berlin. Nearly all the sales in the competitive area were exports to Western European countries.

[36]This levy was the source of a series of disrupting disputes within the Syndicate. It meant in effect that mines shipping mainly to the German market were subsidizing the export trade. The attempt to avoid this by splitting the accounts of sales between the two markets and imposing a separate levy on each was made in the contract of 1926, but the administrative difficulties proved impossible. More serious was the dispute over the imposition of the levy on those quantities delivered by the steel mills' mines to the combine's furnaces under the consumption quota. That the mills, after having resisted this steadily up to 1927, agreed to it in the contract of that year, is a puzzling indication of the persistent influence of the mining interests in the Syndicate. Ledermann, *Organisation,* pp. 117–21, 156–63.

power. Even more important, the ability to control the accounting price scales meant that the controlling group could, as it were, "bleed" mines producing certain types of coal at the expense of others. The steel mills, for example, could conceivably set high accounting prices for the by-product sizes of their coking operations without regard to what those sizes actually brought on the market. Finally, the Syndicate officials who controlled the actual sales policy pursued were responsible to the members, and on paper, at least, possessed no independent power. The opportunity of the directors of the coal-steel combines as a group, after providing for their own coke needs, to pursue an exaggeratedly unfair and strongly restrictionist policy in the fuel industry – penalizing the remaining independent mines and the foreign coke consumers – stands out clearly in the Syndicate contracts. Nevertheless, with exceptions on a few minor points, almost the reverse of such a policy was in fact pursued.

The reasons for the development that actually occurred are numerous and complex and can never be completely tracked down. At their heart, however, lies the fact that no steel entrepreneur or group of them saw the opportunity in such broad terms; the domination which they possessed on paper over this whole structure never existed to its full extent in their minds. The main parts of the entrepreneurial function: decisions about capacity expansion, decisions about the level of output, and decisions about pricing and sales were divided among the directors of the combines, the Syndicate committees, and the Syndicate bureaucracy. In this structure, when the coal-steel combine directors had initiated capacity expansions, the limits of their opportunity and their powers, as they saw them, seem to have been reached, and these decisions were not closely co-ordinated with market demand, which it was the job of the Syndicate officials to satisfy. To have disturbed the established scale of accounting prices would have been an even more unthinkable project, which independent mines and Syndicate and public officials would have resisted.

In Table 1 the main elements in this entrepreneurial structure are set forth, with an indication of the competence of each group, the types of decisions made, and with some guess of the possible motivations characteristic of the entrepreneurs involved.[37] Even here, the entrepreneurial opportunities are not broken down to the individual level on which they actually existed. Each group was composed of individuals who saw

[37]Table 1 is drawn from the Syndicate contracts, descriptions of the combines' organization, the histories of the Syndicate already cited, and the author's own discussions with former Syndicate and combine officials. It is not intended as a detailed and definitive organization plan of this structure but simply as a suggestion of the important elements.

Table 1. *Entrepreneurial structure of the Ruhr coal industry in the late 1920's*

Group	Limits of competence	Types of decisions made	Possible motivation
Coal Syndicate staff	Operated within Syndicate rules, decisions of syndicate committees, and state of demand on market	Destination of sales, prices actually achieved	Personal advancement in Syndicate, Syndicate strength
Coal Syndicate committees	Faced fuel market in long-run sense, syndicate structure and traditions, demands of member mines reflecting their peculiar supply conditions	Enlargement of quotas, establishment of total output and of price scales for crediting mines' deliveries	Furthering interests of member mines represented
Coal-steel combine directors and officials	Faced steel market, raw material costs, mining and coking costs, by-product market, Coal Syndicate contract and rules of operation	Investment in new capacity, output of steel, purchase of mines and cokeries, accounting methods within combine	Expansion of combine, long-term profit and incomes
Mine manager	Operated within a budget, Syndicate quotas, required deliveries, price scales, and physical condition of the mine	Day-to-day operations, choice of machinery and labor, recommendations on expansion and investment	Position in the profession

Note: These categories could be further subdivided to show positions within each group, and further extended to show the limits set by entrepreneurship in, for example, the various steel syndicates, banking houses, ore producers, labor unions, and public bodies.

their own opportunities in an even narrower and more complex way; other groups, including the mine managers as shown in Table 1, existed to set further limits to the opportunities of the combine and Syndicate officials. Table 1 and the logic of this structure would suggest that the existence of a strong entrepreneurial group from the coal industry itself, active in the coal divisions of the combines, and controlling the Syndicate bureaucracy, contributed strongly to the maintenance of the pre-1913 expansionary situation during the period of steel-mill domination after 1925.

There is no intention in this discussion to discount the significance either of cost and market conditions, which are the economist's stock in trade, or the role of the glamorous handful of entrepreneurs whom the historian loves – Stinnes, Vogeler, Thyssen, and the rest. Much less should the spirit which animated all the lesser individuals in this structure be neglected. The whole structure stood, as it were, in the great hand of the economist's god – the gap between prices and costs – and its members moved in response to their own psychological stimuli. The economic opportunity, however, was structured and subdivided as it came to be presented to individuals, and each of those individuals, motivated as he was, saw a limited area in which he could work. A final question does, however, naturally arise to which an answer may be suggested. How does a structure such as that shown in Table 1 grow up within a society?

An answer begins to be suggested when one comes to examine very closely the actual opportunity open to any individual operating within such a structure. This opportunity may be analyzed as threefold: *(a)* the individual may work wholly within the limits of his established job, taking each day's work as the opportunity for the exercise of his entrepreneurial abilities; *(b)* the individual may work to move from job to job, to find one best suited to his abilities and ambitions; *(c)* the individual may work on the limits of his job itself, operating to extend them, or passively allowing them to shrink.

To the individual German in the mining industry, all three types of activity appeared as outlets for enterprise and ambition. The first is most obviously "economic entrepreneurship" on a job, and contributed clearly to the functioning of the economy and, under other favorable conditions, to its growth. The individual's interest in the second (which may be called "social entrepreneurship") depended on the fluidity of the German social structure, the standards for advancement, and the individual's own restlessness. The economic function of this kind of activity is to get individuals into jobs where the opportunity of efficient work is greatest. But the third type of activity, which is a form of political activity, also has its economic importance. Through it, industrial structure is formed and altered to give proper place to individual abilities or ambitions. Fortunate indeed is the society in which the social structure outside the office and factory is relatively fluid, in which the number and kinds of jobs are well suited to the supply of individuals becoming available for them, and in which the structure of economic activity channels individual entrepreneurial ambitions and energies directly and efficiently into productive work. Such a society has no need for the race of entrepreneur hero-villains, although such a group, magnified by a thirsty popular imagination, may achieve a certain superficial notoriety. It needs only moderate economic opportunity and small amounts of intelligence and initiative widely diffused over its well-organized population to achieve a significant rate of economic growth. An anthill, after all, can grow at a rapid rate, but we would be hard put to it to find any ant more enterprising than another.[38]

[38]After having written this concluding statement, I made the mistake of buying a small book entitled, *The Ant World* (Penguin Books, 1953), by Derek Wragge Morley, an English "ant man." On page 161 occurs the following disturbing passage: "The time has come to enter the dangerous realms of ant psychology, to try to draw a rounder and perhaps more definite picture of the mental world in which they live. The adaptability of some ants is remarkable. The dullness, obtuseness, and seeming unchangeableness of the behavior of other ants is, in comparison, equally astonishing. This variability can be seen even within the limits of a single colony. A Chinese student by name of Chen studied the different capabilities of different workers in a colony of *Camponotus*. The particular species he studied builds its nest in the ground. All of the workers in each colony were capable of digging a nest on their own, but the rate at which they worked differed. Some individuals worked more slowly than others. Some were just bone lazy and did scarcely any work when left to fend for themselves, while others beavered away at a great pace, like a dog searching for a buried bone."

It would appear that, at least for ants, my sentence may overstate my case.

7

M. Schuman and his plan

I

When M. Schuman first presented his celebrated Plan over two years ago, American views, official and public, were divided between an easy cynicism and a careless rapture. Optimism was stirred by the promise of a unity of European peoples, achieving strength, peace and prosperity through their mutual interests in producing coal and steel. Cynicism amused itself with a vision of a new bureaucracy, exercising new controls through the monster international cartel hidden beneath M. Schuman's diplomatic dress. All groups of opinion, materialistic and democratic in outlook, would have agreed that the Plan, however conceived and dedicated, could not long endure unless it touched the popular heart through raising the standard of living. Here, as elsewhere, Americans looked for Europe's salvation in the joy, excitement, strength and sense of human kinship that is supposed to come from successfully executed achievements in engineering.

Since the Korean war began, and particularly since the Soviet's German proposals of last spring, our attitude toward Europe has grown more insistent. To many Americans the Schuman Plan now appears as a convenient self-delusion, permitting the French to cajole themselves into accepting the rearmament of Germany. That the Plan offers no immediate guarantees of security is evident; it provides for no end-use allocations of steel, no restrictions on armament production nor any international control over it. Against a fully aroused nationalist movement in Germany the agencies of the Schuman Plan would be virtually powerless; indeed as the present perils to European unity indicate, they would probably break up before they exercised any restraints whatsoever. In Germany too, the Plan has helped speed the departing American offi-

Originally published in *International Organization,* 6:3 (1952), 381–395. Reprinted by permission.

cials and their programs. It has gained from Germany concessions of "sovereignty" over her coal and steel industries greater than would now be required as the price of freeing those industries from Allied control. The conclusion from this line of reasoning would be that M. Schuman and Dr. Adenauer, like two dishonest horse-traders, had successfully swindled one another, with the main profit of the transaction accruing to the European policy of the United States. Even those most ignorant and contemptuous in their attitude toward Europe, however, can hardly remain at ease in this conclusion.

In explaining the appeal of the Schuman Plan to the European people and politicians, one is forced, therefore, further and further into vague notions about the politics and economics of the remote future. If the Plan is a success, it is said, it will lead to similar ventures in other fields; these in turn, in conjunction with the European Army and other European institutions, will so inextricably intertwine the economies and defenses of the European countries as to make war among them impossible and render them invulnerable to attack from outside. The prosperity and good-fellowship attendant upon the operation of common economic institutions will create the economic and spiritual bases of European unity.

Are these real and valid reasons for hope – even assuming that the current crisis provided by Soviet proposals for German unity is surmounted? Will these hopes stand up to a close and hard-headed examination? One may ask, for example, why a successful Schuman Plan, providing security against future wars, should lead to further ventures in other lines. The intensity of Europe's current quest for unity seems to vary inversely with American satisfaction over what has been achieved. Let us express the belief that we find Europe sufficiently united to be "worth defending", and Europe might immediately fall apart. That the European economies are already closely intertwined has acted in the past as a spur to Germany's attempts at political unification by force rather than as a barrier to it. Furthermore, to expect important improvements in European economic conditions from the Schuman Plan Agencies is probably to court serious disillusionment. The attempt must be made to understand in concrete terms how the Schuman Plan organization is likely to develop, and what changes in the economic and political scene it is likely to cause. Only then will it be possible to give to the Plan's remaining enthusiasts some real and measured reason for the hope that is in them.

II

The general purpose of the Schuman Plan, the outlines of its structure and the phrases in which it is couched, have become familiar from two years of discussion. After a brief preparatory period, its complex group of agencies – including the High Authority and the Council of the member governments – coming into full operation, are supposed to establish the "single market" in coal and steel. Within the "single market", the governing ideal is the production of coal, coke and steel at minimum physical costs and their distribution wherever the demand for them is most intense. Consequently, interferences with the free movement of these products, and all distortions of the picture of relative real costs are to be forbidden, regulated or discouraged. The member governments are obligated to abolish tariffs, quota restrictions and impediments to the free movement of workers and to attack the problem of discriminatory freight rates. Subsidies to state-owned enterprises or to private producers are forbidden. The pricing practices of producers are to be supervised to prevent discrimination in sales; maximum and minimum prices may be set after investigation by the High Authority. The most important power given the High Authority for carrying its economic ideals into operation is the right to pass on, and in some cases to veto, all new borrowing and security issues for investment purposes. It is empowered also to borrow for the purpose of initiating its own investment programs where needed.

The Schuman Plan High Authority is to accomplish its ends with a minimum of direct interference – the stated ideal being a kind of controlled competition among producers stimulated and sustained by the High Authority's "righteous, omnipotent arm". The effort is made to avoid the growth of trusts in the future, by requiring High Authority approval for mergers and similar transactions. Private cartels are abolished and all cartel-like practices forbidden to private producers. Existing public or private monopolies are subject to complete supervision and control. In a curious provision, the Schuman Plan Treaty (Art. 61, Sec. 7) states,

> "To the extent necessary, the High Authority is empowered to address to public or private enterprises which, in law or in fact, have or acquire on the market for one of the products subject to its jurisdiction a dominant position which protects them from effective competition in a substantial part of the single market, any recommendations required to prevent the use of such position for purposes contrary to those of the present Treaty. If such recommendations are not fulfilled satisfactorily within a reasonable period, the High Authority will, by decisions taken in consultation with the interested government and under the sanctions provided for in Articles 56, 58 and 59, fix the prices and conditions of sale to be applied by the enterprise in question, or establish manufacturing or delivery programs to be executed by it."

Special provision is made for drastic, cartel-like action in times of crisis: in times of shortage, supplies may be allocated as between lines of consumption and exports in each region; in crises of over-production and falling demand, output quotas can be set and enforced by fines so as to spread the work and help stabilize employment.

Finally, a five-year transitional period prior to the entering into force of the entire plan is provided; in this period certain adjustments and equalization payments may be made to cushion the shock on relatively inefficient regions and plants for whom the struggle of the single market will ultimately prove fatal.

III

What effect will the Schuman Plan have on the coal mining and processing industry and on the coal market in western Europe? How will its provisions, and the activities of its High Authority, affect the physical cost of producing coal, the wages of miners, the delivered prices paid by consumers and the quantities of coal and coke available to them? In this sphere of activity, the High Authority will face the powerful regional monopolies that now control production in France and the Saar, and the new private owners established by Allied reorganization in the Ruhr. How will its operations develop, its policies unfold, in this situation?

Organizational problems. The Schuman Plan bodies will encounter special difficulties in dealing with public monopolies. In France, for example, the *Charbonnages de France* has owned and operated the French mines since their nationalization. Investment has proceeded with the use of public funds, price scales have been set with some regard to the interest of certain consuming groups, the degree of subsidy is far from clear, the interests of the miners may have received unusually favorable consideration at the expense of consumers. Furthermore, a group of public managers has developed whose motivations and policies may be fully as incompatible with the ideal of an international single market as those of private businessmen. The managers of such a nationalized industry are likely to be "experts", "technicians", interested mainly in efficient production methods – their interest in a large French coal industry being successfully buried beneath layers of economic and bureaucratic jargon. They represent, moreover, the French government, and may, in their capacity as experts, have seats on some of the Schuman Plan agencies themselves.

In the Saar, a similar organizational problem exists. The Schuman Plan's relations with the mines in the Saar are not as closely bound up with the future political settlement there as might be supposed. Between 1919 and 1935, it will be recalled, the Saar mines were owned by the French government while the Saarland itself was an independent region governed by an international commission. A similar settlement would seem likely at present; in any case, even if the region became German again, the mines will remain state-owned. Their relation to the High Authority will almost certainly present the same problems as that of the French mines.[1]

At the time the Schuman Plan was conceived, it was not clear what sort of industrial organization would emerge from the welter of Allied proposals and German counter-proposals for the German coal and steel industry, located in the Ruhr area. German adherence to the Schuman Plan, and Allied permission for such adherence, were used by the Germans and Allies respectively as bargaining weapons in the negotiations in early 1951, in which the major questions of Ruhr reorganization were settled. The present agreement, on the basis of which reorganization in the Ruhr is now being carried out, has three major provisions:

(1) Allied reorganization of the Ruhr steel trusts and coal-steel combines is to continue, with a number of smaller independent steel and coal companies constituting the basic industrial units.

(2) The steel companies are to be permitted to own coal mines and cokeries sufficient to supply 75% of their normal needs of blast furnace coke.

(3) The famous Rhenish-Westfalian Coal Syndicate, which was renamed, continued and strengthened after 1945 under Allied control, is to be finally dissolved, and competition among the newly formed coal companies is to be the order of the new day.

The first two of these provisions seem likely to endure; the actual organization of the companies is now under way, and the omelet thus created should prove difficult to unscramble under any program short of nationalization. The elimination of the coal syndicate, however, is a thing to which virtually no group in Germany is reconciled. Is the extension of the Schuman Plan to the German coal industry likely to

[1] Can the Schuman Plan contribute to the final solution of the Saar problem? Would France's hold on the Saar's coal be relaxed if she were assured indefinitely of no discrimination in coal deliveries from either the Saar or the Ruhr? Would the Saar steel plants be permitted to escape from her control if she saw them grouped, with the Ruhr plants and her own, under a single High Authority? The answer is probably "no". The mines are profitable, and the Schuman Plan will not destroy their profitability. Control over the Saar steel mills by France of French steel interests would reduce the danger of their competition, no matter what the Schuman Plan could do. In any case, the Saar struggle is not truly economic, and even if the Schuman Plan weakened the economic motives, the political ones would remain. A solution in the Saar that kept it politically separate from Germany would not be obviated in France's eyes by the Schuman Plan, but would remain a necessary additional security requirement. It would be interesting to see the reaction to a proposal that the mines be turned over to the Schuman Plan High Authority, to be operated by it, the profits to be used for investment purposes where needed.

result in the restoration of some form of syndicated organization, and the frustration of the American plans for free competition?

The answer to this question is probably in the affirmative. Certainly in the absence of a Schuman Plan, the coal syndicate would be the part of the Ruhr's old industrial structure most likely to be revived. "Technicians" and engineers, who abound now among German business leaders, emphasize the "technical desirability" of pooling and mixing coals from different mines. Labor leaders are deeply concerned over the spreading of the work in bad times, and maintaining stability of employment in an unstable industry. Mine managers emphasize the need to maintain submarginal mines in production for periods of high demand like the present. The universal desire to revive the syndicate does not result from any conscious scheme to revive German industrial strength through the kind of subsidy to industrial users which the pricing methods of the old syndicate involved. A German, facing the uncertanties and dangers of free competition and a free market in the nation's only important natural resource, experiences a deep and acute sense of panic. The very national existence seems to him to depend upon careful, planned, "scientific" exploitation of both the coal deposits and the coal consumers.

The Schuman Plan provides the possibility of calming these fears through the revival of the syndicate under the supervision of the High Authority.[2] That the High Authority will yield to German pressure and re-create the coal syndicate seems very likely. France is known to have favored the retention of a controlled syndicate as the most convenient method of dealing with and controlling the German coal industry.[3] The High Authority, faced with the need to supervise centralized industries elsewhere, will hardly be anxious to adapt its programs and techniques to an atomistic German industry. The need to fix quotas, or make allocations, in abnormal periods will itself require some centralized organ representing the German mines. Indeed, knowing how the Europeans operate in such circumstances, one is tempted to suspect that the future of the European coal industry will prove to be an unending

[2]Section 12 of the Convention providing for the dissolution of monopolistic organizations provides for a study of the problems arising and the steps needed: "On the basis of these studies . . . the High Authority shall establish the procedures or organizations appropriate to the solution of these problems. . . . The duration of such procedures or organizations shall not be limited to the (5-year) transition period."

[3]One European veteran of international coal negotiations is said to have expressed himself to the American authorities in charge of decartellization as follows: "Very well. You must abolish the Coal Syndicate. You have your programs and policies to carry out, we know. But if you must abolish it, then I ask of you only this: *that you abolish it just as little as possible.*"

succession of periods of shortage and surplus, in which the full cartel-like powers of the High Authority will be continuously exercised. The western European coal and coke industry will enter a stage of more or less complete and comprehensive international planning. The groups of regional monopolies which, except possibly for the Ruhr, would have existed in any case, will be closely regulated and controlled by the Council and High Authority. For the European economy, is this not preferable to the British type of national-minded nationalization?

Economic prospects. The Schuman Plan's ideal for the European coal industry can be pictured by reference to a map of Europe, showing coal deposits, existing mines and coking installations and the location of the market for the different commercial grades and sizes of coal and coke.[4] According to the supposed economic ideal then, fuel should be supplied where demand is most intense from the sources whose exploitation involves minimum total physical costs of mining, processing and transport. If the Ruhr area, for example, yielded all sizes and grades of coal so abundantly and easily that every part of the entire market could be supplied by it at a lowered delivered cost than by any other area, then mining should be concentrated in this exceedingly productive region. But transport charges are so great, and the market so extensive, relative even to the Ruhr's resources, that the other deposits will in fact be mined. The French, Saar, Belgian and Dutch mining industries each has a market area of its own, protected by the costs of transporting coal from other regions into it, by the rise in mining costs elsewhere as other regions increase their output, and by the special characteristics of the coals found in different beds.[5] This latter fact means also that the different mining districts penetrate with their special grades of coal into the market areas of one another.

The market areas of the different mining regions are at present supposed to be artificially distorted from their ideal limits. One group of mines may have cost advantages over others from other than purely physical reasons. Consumers in one industry or region may enjoy lower delivered prices than other consumers similarly situated. In the former case, a region with artificially low costs is producing and selling coal which embodies a higher physical cost than coal from another region; in terms of physical resources coal is costing more than necessary to produce. In the latter case, coal is not going to those consumers who would pay most for it; it is being sold to satisfy less intense demands while more intense demands are not filled. The ideal of the Schuman

[4]For locations of mines and centers of steel production, see United Nations, Economic Commission for Europe, *European Steel Trends* (Geneva, 1950).

[5]British, Polish (and now United States) coal also have a continental market.

Plan is to eliminate all artificial cost and price differentials and enable the market to operate freely, adjusting rates of production and consumption by means of market price movements and permitting labor and investment funds to enter the regions of highest prospective yields, as envisaged in traditional economic theory.

This nominal freeing of the market, however, will probably constitute the least significant aspect of the High Authority's activity in the coal industry. Certainly, discriminatory freight rates can be abolished, though a complex revision of the entire rate structures of the French and German railways may be finally required. Government subsidies to mines can be forbidden, though provision is made to retain subsidy payments by goverments or by the High Authority where necessary. The crucial question in equalizing cost conditions, however, is the equalization of wage rates. Labor costs account for about half the cost of producing coal; including the cost of non-wage benefits, the differential in labor payments between the Ruhr mines and the French is considerable. The Schuman Plan contains provisions for free movement of mine workers between regions and provides that wage cuts for purely competitive purposes shall be restricted. These provisions are certainly insufficient to equalize wage rates among the producing areas. In mining, the wage in each area is tied to the general wage structure of the regional economy; unless the coal and steel industries were to become a kind of underground railroad through which workers in all lines were smuggled over the borders, any change in the differential between wages in mines and wages elsewhere in a region resulting from a movement of miners into or out of the region, might well be checked by a counter-movement of native workers into or out of the region's mining industry. Indeed – and this is a most significant point – so long as workers and capital do not move freely from one region to another, the engineering criterion of minimum physical cost does not apply in industrial location. The question remains not where can coal be most efficiently produced, but in what occupations can the Belgians, or the Saarlanders, most effectively work? The principle remains one of allocating national resources where there is a comparative, rather than an absolute, advantage.

So long as the market functions in a normal manner, discriminatory pricing can be prevented. The method of allocating costs among joint products, and the pricing of certain types of fuel sold only to specific customers are not covered by the Plan's provisions here; only a "dual price system" for coal and coke of the same grade is prohibited. Such discrimination requires sales by a monopolist in two separated markets, and has existed as a serious problem only with respect to domestic and export sales of German coal and coke. The German system of "dual pricing" has now been virtually abolished and the Schuman Plan Treaty insures that it will not be resumed, either in the form of "dumping" surpluses or of exacting higher prices abroad than at home in times of shortage. It does not prevent the "dumping" of by-products within a single market.

The problems of international organization of the coal mining industry can hardly be met by this simple ideal of a free market and unrestricted productive activity. The High Authority is faced on all sides with regional monopolies functioning in a chronically unstable market, with a complex product. In times of "crisis", an easy retreat into the free market mechanism is impossible; the High Authority is faced with the need to set quotas, or allocate output according to standards of judgment and the arguments of rival claimants. But even in normal times, the supervision of regional monopolies involves a kind of regulation akin to public utility regulation, where the competitive market speaks with a muffled and uncertain voice. In such a situation, standards governing the direction of investment funds in mines also are hard to come by; it is inconceivable that the choice of one region over another as the location of a new investment program should be done on a purely automatic, economic basis.

These problems of judgment facing the High Authority are brought most sharply to focus in decisions affecting the coal processing industry. A problem arises already in the supervision of price scales for coal types, particularly in the Ruhr where coal is especially suitable for coking. A small differential in the price of coke and coking coal, and no discrimination in sales as between a mine's own cokeries and a foreign cokery, would encourage the growth of cokeries outside the Ruhr in Lorraine which is a large importer of Ruhr coke. Yet coking coal and coke are each joint products of their respective production processes, and nearly any price for either one could be justified on purely "economic" grounds. The importance of a large coke industry in an industrial area is enormous. The union of coke ovens and steel mills enables substantial fuel economies to be made. Coke oven gas forms an important industrial fuel, and the by-products of the gas cleaning process furnish a basis for synthetic fuels, chemicals and fertilizers. Indeed, considering long-range development of an industrial complex, it is a case of "where MacDonald sits, there is the head of the table." Where coke ovens are located, there can grow up – in the presence of other favorable factors – a market for their products which serves to justify the original location of the coke ovens at that site. Shall the Ruhr, or the Saar-Lorraine area, be favored in future investment programs and future industrial growth? The Schuman Plan High Authority will decide, by fixing price scales, quotas and allocations in fuels, by guiding new investment in mines and cokeries, as well as in steel plants. It is a decision that will, or can, hardly be made on impersonal economic principles.

IV

The steel industry in western Europe poses special problems for the Schuman Plan; much confusion has arisen from a failure to distinguish between these problems and those presented by coal and coke.

Differences may be noted at once in the organizations with which the High Authority will have to deal. In supervising coal production, processing and distribution the High Authority will have to deal with public organizations or, in Germany, with an industry accustomed to extensive interference. Public records must be inspected, goverment bodies influenced, public policies controlled. The High Authority and the Council can expect to function as a kind of regulatory body over regional monopolies; its method of approach is direct and, with the frequent occurrence of "crises", it may have frequent recourse to the easy and drastic measures of quotas, allocations and production control. In the steel industry, the High Authority will face in each region, a fairly small number of large steel firms, with established positions and antecedents, dominating the national markets, as they have done under tariff protection and cartel arrangements for generations. Old and close-mouthed family concerns, accustomed to moving in jealous herds, can be expected to close ranks even tighter at prospects of a supra-governmental interference. Certain regional rivalries persist among them, and in some cases, the overseas export market induces some competititve struggle. But in France and Germany, national industries exist primarily for the national market, and have refrained from intruding themselves into one another's preserves. Into this jungle the High Authority is to move, set up its tents and its observation instruments like the scientists in Africa watching for the eclipse – and go to work.

The Schuman Plan as it now stands, does not contemplate a restoration of the pre-war steel cartel, even in a semi-public form. It is also unlikely that a kind of permanent crisis requiring direct cartel-like measures on the part of the Authority will be recognized to the same extent in steel as in coal. In the steel industry, the "single market" is likely to be allowed, or forced, to function with maximum freedom. The problem will be to break up the habits of collusion and cartellization.

Provisions outlawing price discrimination in raw materials – ore and scrap – are probably not of prime significance in creating and maintaining a rational production pattern in the western European steel industry. Even the elimination of the dual-pricing system for French ore shipments from Lorraine will probably not reduce Ruhr steel production cost appreciably. Even in normal times less than 25 percent of the Ruhr's iron ore came from Lorraine; furthermore, there is good reason to suppose that on purely economic principles, virtually all the Lorraine ore should be smelted *in situ*. The general impression that the elimination of restrictions on the free flow of materials – coal, coke, ore, scrap – will make the European steel industry more "economic" is based on a wholly mistaken notion of its structure. Western Europe does not constitute a single integrated and closely interdependent industrial area, particularly in the case of steel production. The Ruhr steel industry derives its economic advantage from Ruhr coal and from the transport routes to the sea which make possible the import of Swedish, Spanish and African ores. The Lorraine industry is based on Lorraine ore, and on Saar and northern French coal; the admixture of Ruhr coke in Lorraine furnace charges may well be diminished greatly by recent developments in fuel technology. Not one, but at least two, integrated steel industries exist in the Schuman Plan area; their costs will not be lowered, nor their location greatly changed by the freer movement of ore and fuel within that region, except as the result of actual investment planning which changes the site of cokeries, mills and markets.

Elimination of tariffs and cartel restrictions should improve the conditions of distribution from the great regional production centers. At present, the French and German tariffs on steel run around 15 percent for most shapes; the abolition of these tariffs might lower prices in each country by almost this much, provided that competitive conditions in national markets are achieved. Some change in the traditional market areas of the French and German industries is likely; the position of the mills in Belgium and Luxembourg is by no means clear. Under present conditions France will not be flooded with cheap German steel; modernization and expansion in the Ruhr, however, might present a serious threat.

In the steel industry, even more than in coal and coke, the ultimately important factor in the Schuman Plan is the High Authority's control over new investment. A vigorously functioning single market may, after a period, furnish some criteria as to where modernization and plant expansion should take place. Fuel pricing policies, cokery location and costs, ore prices, government tax programs, freight rate differentials, regional wage differentials, the cost of ore and fuel purchased overseas and overseas export prices of steel and steel products – these will be decisive in determining the relative economic advantages of the Ruhr and Lorraine, and of the Belgian areas, as centers for steel production. Is it likely, however, that all these complex factors will speak with so clear a voice that the question of plant modernization and location will be automatically and "economically" decided? To what extent can the studies of the High Authority replace the policies of the entrepreneurial herd, or the hunches of the maverick entrepreneur, in determining the course of economic development? Whatever the answer, the struggle will start immediately upon the formation of the High Authority with the long-delayed modernization program for the Ruhr steel industry. Will France permit the early lead she has gained, by virtue of public investment financed partly out of ECA funds, in modernization of steel plant, to be destroyed by an equally vigorous program in the Ruhr? Can Ruhr revival and French security be reconciled by the "experts", by bureaucratic economists poring over the data of costs and profits?

France has gambled her protected steel industry for a share of influence over German coal shipments and over new investment in German plants. Germany has agreed, and received in return a speedy termination of Allied restrictions, freer access to Belgian and French steel and coal markets, and the possibility of cooperating in the joint development of Africa to which M. Schuman in his original statement temptingly referred. The bitterness of internal conflict, arising when present swollen demands are reduced, may indeed be eventually relieved by common action against the outside world. In the absence of the United Kingdom – still a potential fuel supplier and competitor on world steel-markets – the inducement for joint action against foreign raw material suppliers and foreign markets will be especially great. Nothing now in the Plan points in this direction, but it would seem a logical and desirable outcome for an integrated western Europe, facing the commercial policies of the United States, the United Kingdom and the Soviet Union.

V

Examined frankly and realistically, the Schuman Plan presents certain prospects for Europe not generally realized or even suspected. The most striking of these may be summarized as follows:

(1) The Schuman Plan will probably increase competition in the European steel industry; it will probably confirm and increase the degree of international central planning in the European coal industry.

(2) Such purely negative measures as the elimination of market restrictions and price discrimination under the Schuman Plan will probably have much less economic effect, even in the steel industry, than the positive steps taken, particularly in the direction of new investment.

(3) The Schuman Plan, as it now stands, is not likely to have an important effect on the standard of living either of Europe's miners and steel workers, or of the regions where they live, or of the economies of the countries involved.

(4) The Schuman Plan Agencies could have important economic effects if they were to act as a centralized purchasing agent of ore and coal, and a

centralized sales agency of steel, in world markets. That the Plan does not offend British and American sensibilities by clearly contemplating this possibility is, from a European viewpoint, a weakness which can probably be overcome later.

(5) The Schuman Plan does not remove decisions in the coal and steel industries from the political stage into a sphere of abstract economic calculation; rather it puts these industries and the calculations and decisions concerning them directly in the middle of the Franco-German political struggle.

(6) The Plan does not guarantee to France any automatic security in the face of a revived nationalist movement in Germany, or of German rearmament.

If the economic gains of the Plan are remote, and the immediate political gains negligible, why has the Plan proved so alluring to European politicians and so generally attractive to their public? If the Plan is likely to develop into a kind of international governmental cartel of European coal- and steel-producing countries, why does it appeal almost instinctively to liberal-minded Americans interested in western integration?

The answer would seem to lie in the Plan's long-run political effects. The Plan after all has not been strongly supported by those groups most interested in the prosperity of the coal and steel industries. Labor organizations and parties have given it hesitating support, where they have not actively opposed it. The industrialists' desire to enter a new world of expanded markets, improved sources of credit, and cheaper raw materials, has in no way overcome their regret for the protections of the past and their fear of even an international bureaucracy. Nor can one say that, after the initial reaction, the Plan has been carried on by a strong and persistent popular enthusiasm. The Plan has rather received the kind of support given the United Nations organization by the American public – a kind of wistful longing for a better day, and a kindly warmth for any measures, vaguely concrete and constructive, for approaching it. It has been appreciated, rather than supported, and has aroused good will, rather than public passions.

The energy which has gone into the planning of the Treaty, and the passion which has pushed its ratification through the parliaments of the member countries, has come rather from the leading moderate politicians, and a group of extremely able supporters in official bureaucratic circles. The Plan strengthens both the domestic and the international policies of this group, and adds immeasurably to their political strength. In the first place, it secures some measure of bureaucratic control over these two industries – steel and coal – over both unions and employers, while at the same time removing responsibility for the decisions up to a higher political echelon. By a supreme act of mystification, the struggle between governments and their pressure groups has been translated into a higher sphere. The Plan has already proved a *deus ex machina* for Dr.

Adenauer, caught unhappily between Allied decartellization demands and pressure from the Ruhr industrialists who have been his supporters. M. Monnet too has clearly achieved a major victory over the French steel producers, who have consistently opposed his plans for industrial expansion in France. M. Schuman has achieved in Germany what Dr. Adenauer could not achieve and Prof. Hallstein may be able to achieve in France what M. Monnet could not achieve. These gentlemen, and their counterparts at lower levels, can come to one another's aid, and bear one another's burdens.

The Plan, furthermore, will not only relieve the moderate politicians of some of the onus of difficult decisions while they are in office, but it will help to keep them in office. Although the concrete achievements of the agencies, if compared with what would otherwise be achieved, may not be great, the fact remains that these bodies will be the means by which these achievements come into the world. Credit for engineering achievement which has hitherto redounded to the business class will now redound in part to the international "planners". Furthermore, the agencies as such, will be able to do considerable harm to the investment and production programs of the industries they deal with if they are the center of continual quarrels and bickering. They will constitute an important source of patronage which can be used to some extent by the governments represented there, provided that cooperation among the politicians is maintained. They will therefore put the greatest premium on a kind of combination of cooperation and canniness, which M. Schuman and Dr. Adenauer embody in their respective countries. They offer in short the means by which the advocates of moderate European-minded policy in all the member countries can exercise a kind of economic blackmail over the opponents of the right and left.

The attractiveness of the Schuman Plan, then, is that it strengthens the men of good will – not the servants of violent nationalism, of abstract economic doctrine, or of any special interest group in the population. It is on this intuition that moderate-minded men of good will in Europe and the United States have responded favorably to it, have wished it well, and hoped that it would lead to a wider European unity. The hope for peace and strength in Western Europe may come, not from an abstract plan, nor from an immediate popular movement, but from the cooperation first of all of a group of clever politicians. Whether they are clever enough to survive the present contest of wits with the politicians to their east remains as yet uncertain. The vague hopes of prosperity, peace and security, and the revival of Europe's importance in the world – hopes stirred by the Schuman Plan and the other European unity proposals – continue to support them in their efforts.

PART IV

Europe and the wider world: an explanation from technology

8

Europe-centered development: its natural logic

This essay is divided into three parts. In Part I, changes in techniques of communication are examined for their effects on the rate of diffusion of modern industry from Europe over the past two centuries. In Part II, changes in production and transport techniques are examined for their effects on the shifting geographical distribution of opportunities for economic development within the zone of diffusion of those techniques. In Part III, some of the reasons for the historical sequence of techniques are considered. The core of the argument is that (1) the sequence of technological change over the past two centuries has controlled both the rate of diffusion of modern industrial culture and the shifting production opportunities at specific locations within that zone of diffusion (see appendix table at end of chapter); and that (2) sequence has been governed by human capabilities in examining external nature. Together, these propositions pose a technological determinism, operating at a level of human nature beneath and beyond the influences of preexisting social environment. To the extent that this thesis is valid, the national society and the national economy lose a portion of the importance with which they are invested by much current work of historians and economists in the study of economic development.

I

Trade in commodities transmits knowledge as well as goods, and techniques may be reproduced by direct copying of the objects incorporating them. But apart from some striking cases of imitation, the diffusion of technology in the modern world has been largely limited by techniques not unfamiliar to St. Paul or Mohammed: the movement of persons and the transmittal of written documents. The latter immensely

Originally published in *Economic Development and Cultural Change,* 10:1 (1961), 1–7. Reprinted by permission.

proliferated after the invention in the fifteenth century of the printing press, and the flow has been maintained by mechanical and chemical improvements in the supply of paper and by the successive applications of steam power and electricity to the mechanism.[1] Yet the spread of technological knowledge, narrowly considered, is not a matter of mass education, but of the training of a small elite. The Greek and Arabic techniques were transmitted to the medieval world by means of scribes and manuscripts, after all, and no enormous quantity of printed paper is required to transmit modern techniques. Instructions must usually be accompanied by teachers and engineers in person and by models or examples of the equipment. Technological change has been of relatively minor importance in the movement of such persons, carrying printed materials with them and knowledge in their heads. Unlike politicians, technicians need not shuttle rapidly back and forth. The drastic reduction of travel time because of the steamship and airplane has permitted the emergency movement of technicians to trouble spots; it has also permitted a wider use of the corps of personnel available for foreign assignment. But communication is not simply, or even mainly, a matter of rapid movement of persons from place to place. Formidable barriers of language and social environment have persisted, and it is the slow erosion of these, rather than the more rapid movement of technicians, that has permitted the diffusion of modern technology.

The erosion of the barriers to utilization of new technology is itself partly the result of technological change. One must speak here of the transmission of social traits, or of certain underlying modern attitudes toward nature and human values, rather than of specific bits of knowledge about production. In the regions of European settlement, these barriers have been at a minimum. The movement of migrants on a scale large enough to reestablish fundamental ingredients of European society, in some one of its national variants, was sufficient in the eighteenth and nineteenth centuries to insure a level of receptivity to new techniques that was at least as high as that of the mother country.[2] The movement of a set of tastes and traits suitable to modern industrial and commercial activity into established tribal and peasant societies was very slow. In the nineteenth century, this movement depended almost entirely upon the work of Christian missionaries and a few merchants and colonial administrators. The techniques involved distribution of the written word – which presented formidable tasks of translation and assumed high levels of literacy – or direct personal con-

[1]Donald Coleman, *The British Paper Industry*, 1495–1860 (Oxford, 1957), Chs. 2 and 7.

[2]No higher, perhaps, in Latin America, but higher in the United States, relative to the regions in Europe from which immigrants came.

tact between persons who had overcome, at least in speech, the barrier of language.

It is not surprising that, even between the industrial and rural areas of a single nation-state of Europe or North America, separate subcultures with strongly differing characteristics persisted. The railroad, telegraph, and telephone were essentially techniques of commercial communication over long distances; except where the railroad encouraged migration, these techniques could not drastically affect popular tastes or thinking. Beyond the "Atlantic community," and to a degree even within it, substantial penetration of local cultures had to await the development of still and moving photography, radio, and television. For movies, in particular, the production of the image required a much higher level of technology than the showing of it, and remained for a long time the monopoly of a few Western countries. With these techniques, and also with the closer intermingling of peoples during the Second World War, the spread of Western tastes and attitudes has greatly accelerated. With the spread of these tastes and attitudes at the popular level, the level of receptivity to new production technology has been raised. The hearts of the heathen have been softened; in the language of the Christian missionaries, the seed is now sown on fertile rather than stony ground.

The rate of flow of Western thought, popular taste, and technology has been strongly affected by the development of these techniques of social communication. But the direction in which culture traits and knowledge have flowed over this communication network is a more puzzling and profound question. What does knowledge consist of, and why has it moved out from Europe, rather than in from Asia and Africa? Why is it that the things the Europeans have brought have been the good, the penetrating things, and why have local cultures proved so brittle before their advance? These questions cannot be answered by reference to the culturally conditioned elements in human character. Western ideas have accompanied political and military penetration, just as Islamic civilization moved with the Moorish expansion in the seventh and eighth centuries. Before the advent of mass communication techniques, techniques and styles were diffused through the conversion of a small group at the top of the existing social order. Given this sort of revolutionary overthrow of the old society, the education of a new generation may be sufficient to alter radically its character. But the spread of Western ideas is not wholly due to a combination of power and brainwashing; one must postulate instead some universal characteristics of human nature to which scientific thought and its accompanying technology, and even the curious combination of values placed on goods, enterprise, and the saving of human labor, make an irresistible appeal.

II

Under nineteenth-century techniques of communication, European society was transported to the Western hemisphere and Australia; elsewhere, the familiar phenomenon of export enclaves was thrust upon peasant and tribal societies. These regions were all bound by a network of commercial communication, by factor movements, and by flows of commodity trade. At the centers of invention in Europe, a transport and production technology was evolving, and knowledge of these techniques was, with some imperfections, diffused over the "world economy." At any point in space, the employment of these techniques depended upon factor and materials prices relative to demand – demand being affected by supplies at competing locations, and materials prices by transport costs from their points of origin. Factors moved with considerable freedom, and as between the nation-states of Western Europe, factor immobility was compensated for by the existence of alternative native sets of behavior patterns that insured adequate response to economic opportunity. This world economy, it is well known, arranged itself with heavy concentrations of industry in Northwestern Europe and the Northeastern United States. One of the most important questions for modern economic history is whether this arrangement was rooted in nature and technology, or whether it was culturally and historically determined by a relative lack of mobility of ideas, capital, and enterprise from their points of origin. It is contended here that this arrangement was essentially a natural and rational one, given the limits of diffusion of Western society as set by the feeble means of social communication.

The analysis of the shift in Europe and the United States from local industry to the concentrated pattern of the nineteenth century, on the basis of changing techniques, is familiar to most economic historians. The reasoning runs as follows:

(1) In agriculture, techniques remained land-using; rises in land yields per acre were not very great, and the main drift of technological changes was labor-saving.

(2) In transport, the railroad cheapened costs in specific directions; it produced concentrations of activity at ports and rail junctions, and it was used most cheaply where long-distance hauls of bulk commodities were possible with substantial back hauls.

(3) In manufacture, economies of scale were present to permit considerable concentration; apart from the scale of plant, imposed by the use of power-driven equipment, there were external economies arising from the scale of an industrial complex – economies in communication and in the use of social overhead capital and the overhead of a relatively immobile labor force.

(4) In the location of manufactures and their agglomerations, the substitution of coal for wood and the heavy fuel requirements of the steam engine and smelting technology made the opportunity for industry widest at coal fields.

Europe-centered development

Growth opportunities based upon the European price structure, and the sets of demand patterns, techniques, and conditions of factor supply that underlay it, were spread to specific locations in the "world economy" by movements of goods, gold, credit, people, and ideas. Beyond the regions of massive European settlement, this spread was imperfect for the reason already advanced. Some regions technically suited to industry remained undeveloped, simply because of the absence of cultural prerequisites – mass consumption patterns, disciplined labor force, strong native enterprise, a native engineering tradition, and continuing sources of capital. In these locations, European society had not been reproduced on a scale large enough to generate European production conditions. Specialization in export crops and reductions in international transport costs smothered the opportunities for industrial growth.

Improvement in communications techniques after 1920 may have brought industry within sight in a few such naturally well-endowed regions, even using nineteenth-century techniques of production and transport. But as modern industrial culture has spread, its techniques have altered. In the late eighteenth and early mid-nineteenth centuries, technical change moved in the direction of geographical concentration, and rural industry crumbled before the factory system. Since that time, the drift of technological change has been almost wholly in the other direction. The modern developments that have produced a diffusion of industrial opportunity in formerly agricultural areas are by now fairly evident. Briefly, they include the following:

(1) Improvements in per acre yields, which have undermined the comparative advantages of agricultural areas based on natural conditions of soil and climate.
(2) Reduction in transport costs at minor industrial locations, through the development of more flexible modes of transport, e.g., the truck and airplane; reduction of materials transport costs through improved economy of materials and fuels utilization.
(3) Maintenance of economies of scale in single plants; also, the breakup of economies of scale in industrial complexes, through improvements in communications, transport, and power transmission.
(4) Proliferation of usable fuels and raw materials, through utilization of oil, gas, electricity, and atomic power, and through the development of synthetic materials.

Without these developments, improvements in social communication between industrial and agricultural areas might still ultimately have equalized factor returns, but the opportunities for industrial growth at a variety of locations around the world would be narrow indeed. Since technological change does not appear likely to reverse itself in these respects in the near future, these developments offer the strongest hope that – despite the persistence of preindustrial behavior patterns and their unpredictable responses to new knowledge – the underdeveloped regions will ultimately be able to industrialize.

III

Nearly all the production of transport techniques developed between 1770 and 1870 promoted the geographical concentration of industry. Those developed since that time have, in constrast, favored deconcentration. At first sight, it appears odd that the drift of technological change should have been so strongly in one direction in one period and in the reverse in another. It suggests that some relatively simple principle may underlie the variety of changes in each period, and that a fundamental shift occurred between, say, 1870 and 1920, in the principle on which technology advanced. Our ignorance of the history of modern technology is so profound that it is not possible to work out the nature of this shift in detail from readily available materials. The most appealing hypothesis is that it involved the relative decline in purely mechanical inventions and a redirection of invention into chemistry and subatomic physics.

That such a shift would have produced the locational results observed seems likely. Mechanical invention involves the transmission of power by rigid bodies; it immensely multiplies the advantage of plants located at fairly ample power sources. The steam engine added coal beds to waterfalls as sources of power, and a few simple but drastic changes in the metallurgical industries – coke smelting and the new steel processes – were sufficient to confirm the dominance of coal sites.

In contrast, three principal bases of modern technology stand out: the internal combustion engine, the chemical breakdown and transformation of substances, and the increasing control over electrical phenomena. The internal combustion engine itself involves a chemical principle – that of an explosion – but the principle was known in the late eighteenth century, and its substitution for the steam engine as a power source involved considerable achievements in mechanical engineering. But chemical and electrical engineering involve knowledge of quite a different kind. The developments in the generation of electricity and in electronics have produced changes in communications techniques and offered alternative locations to coal beds as sources of large-scale power. Chemical technology has, by its nature, been concerned with the materials basis of economy, and its goal is unchanged from the days of the alchemists: to transform common substances into "gold."

We must now inquire why the history of technology should have proceeded from the mechanical to the chemical and the electronic. This is a problem well beyond the limits of economics or of economic history.

Economists' recent suggestions of an economic direction to the course of technological change are relevant in a narrower context.[3] Within specific established industries, need – as shaped by markets and relative factor prices – may have produced inventions with certain economic characteristics. Even as between industries, the course of invention – whether mechanical or chemical – may have been guided by prospective returns. But in the broad terms considered here, the drift of invention from mechanical into other lines must be controlled by the state of fundamental science. The processes by which scientific knowledge and interests transmit themselves to relatively unsophisticated inventors and engineers are not apparent. There are inventions in basic science, for example, in experimental apparatus, that help to shape its direction. But one must observe that the proliferation of mechanical inventions followed hard upon the formulation of Boyle's law of gases and Newtonian physics. And Edison, one recent popular biography shows,[4] was not unfamiliar with the rapid advances in the scientific understanding of electricity that were occurring in the mid-nineteenth century. The development of chemical engineering would have been impossible without a science of chemistry; and the relationship to fundamental science of the newly hatched field of nuclear engineering is so close that it is perfectly obvious.

Possibly the century long lag between the steam engine and the internal combustion engine was not due to inherent technical or scientific causes. Had petroleum been as plentiful in England as coal, or had the Arabic or the Apache culture developed a strong interest in technology, an oil-using industrial structure might have antedated a coal-using one.[5] But the whole sequence of technological development, from the mechanical to the other forms, can hardly be explained in such terms. Explanations based on local economic or cultural characteristics appear pathetically inadequate. So long as historians of science pursue Galileo and his predecessors, with an occasional excursion in the direction of Newton, the modern development remains shrouded in mystery. One suggestion may be advanced from a fragment by C. S. Peirce, written in 1891:

[3] J. Schmookler, "Changes in Industry and in the State of Knowledge as Determinants of Inventive Activity"; and W. J. Fellner, "Does the Market Direct the Relative Factor-Saving Effects of Technological Progress?" in National Bureau of Economic Research, *The Rate and Direction of Inventive Activity: Economic and Social Factors* (Princeton: Princeton University Press, 1962).

[4] Matthew Josephson, *Edison: A Biography* (New York, 1959), 25, 42, 52, 53, 61, 93, 94.

[5] R. J. Forbes had reexamined the Arabic knowledge and use of petroleum in *Studies in Early Petroleum History* (Leiden, 1958); and in *Bitumen and Petroleum in Antiquity* (Leiden, 1936), esp. viii, 28 ff.

The first step taken by modern scientific thought – and a great stride it was – was the inauguration of dynamics by Galileo. A modern physicist on examining Galileo's works is surprised to find how little experiment had to do with the establishment of the foundations of mechanics. His principal appeal is to common sense and *il lume naturale*. He always assumes that the true theory will be found to be a simple and natural one . . . the straight line appears to us simple, because, as Euclid says, it lies evenly between its extremities; that is, because viewed endwise it appears as a point. That is, again, because light moves in straight lines. Now, light moves in straight lines because of the part which the straight line plays in the laws of dynamics. Thus it is that our minds having been formed under the influence of phenomena governed by the laws of mechanics, certain conceptions entering into those laws become implanted in our minds, so that we readily guess at what the laws are. Without such a natural prompting, having no search blindfold for a law which would suit the phenomena, our chance of finding it would be as one to infinity. The further physical studies depart from phenomena which have directly influenced the growth of the mind, the less we can expect to find the laws which govern them "simple," that is, composed of a few conceptions natural to our minds.[6]

If this tantalizing hint could be pursued, it might lead to the unfolding of a history of modern science and technology based on the characteristics of the human mind and senses when facing external nature. The sequences of this history – determined simply by the inherent intellectual difficulties in unraveling the secrets of nature – have governed both the rate of diffusion of Western culture patterns and techniques and the shifting patterns of industrial opportunity within the zone in which that culture has spread. Technological determinism of this sort needs to employ preexisting cultural factors only to explain impediments to the spread of Western techniques, and how those techniques and behavior patterns originated from the preindustrial culture of the West. Once arrived in the world, they appear to have power exceeding that of a new religion, to transcend the culture of any place and time. As Western science finds universal technical applicability, so Western materialism, in its Communist or capitalist versions, appears to have a universal human appeal. Perhaps some fundamental, cross-cultural uniformities in human psychology account for this. One who shares fully in Western culture may continue to hope that these uniformities include some portions of the Western heritage beyond curiosity and greed. But a non-Westerner may possibly have valid reason to hope that cultural change will not extend too far into his existing system of values.

[6]C. S. Peirce, "The Architecture of Theories," in P. Weiner (ed.), *Values in a Universe of Chance* (New York, 1958), 145–46.

APPENDIX

Locational characteristics of advanced techniques

Period	Distant communication	Agriculture	Transport		Manufacture	
			Water	Land	Scale	Materials localization
I Pre-1750	nil	Land-using	Cheap	Costly	Small-scale	Little
II 1750–1900	Limited	Land-using	Cheap	Cheap-rigid	Large-scale	Great
III 1900–1950	Extensive	Land-using	Cheap	Cheap-flexible	Large-scale	Less
IV 1960–	Extensive	Less land-using	Cheap	Cheap-flexible	Large-scale	Little

Note: In each case, the comparison is made as between periods, except that water transport is called "cheap" in comparison with the land transport of period I.

9

Communication techniques and social organization in the world economy[1]

Werner Sombart asserted that Capitalism – and by a Parsonian extension, we may say, each type of individual and social action – exhibits an animating Spirit, a social Form, and a material Technique. Since a material technique is itself a social product, one cannot explain the movements of social life as if technology had predetermined them. Technology allows us to do what we want, but it neither compels nor impels us to do it. Indeed, as modern technology has become more complex, more involuted, but also more various, its effect has been to lift some of the constraints it previously had imposed. Where once it freed men from nature, it now partially frees men even from itself. Along its innumerable lines, it is prolific in alternatives – for energy, materials, and modes of transport and communication. Yet though technology's main thrust, since the development of electricity and chemistry, has been to widen choice, it does make some things and some lines of action easier or cheaper than others. And certain of its features and forms have been so startlingly novel, so decisively advantageous, and so general in application as to affect social life in all its manifestations and under nearly all conditions of cost, geography, and human preference.

Among these changes in techniques, those first of transportation, then overlapping them, of communication – the transport of messages – have been fundamental. It is hard to imagine the world today without them, and the access they have given to goods, services, ideas, knowledge, news, and to the means of command and persuasion has surely been the

Originally published in L. Jörberg and N. Rosenberg, eds., *Technical Change, Employment, and Investment* (Lund, Department of Economic History, Lund University, Sweden, 1982), 185–97.

[1]This paper forms one of a series on the development of American capitalism. I am indebted to the Gould Foundation of Rolling Meadows, Illinois, for support in this project.

principal contributing cause of the rapid spread of European technologies and culture forms, the forms and spirit of science, materialism, capitalism, as well as the instrument by which they are being unrecognizably altered. This whole body of technology – the application of steam and internal combustion in transport, and of electricity and light in communications – has issued out of a European capitalism that was itself expanding, feeding upon new resources and new ideas as it spread out across the globe so as to present the problems and opportunities that the railroad, telegraph, telephone, car, truck, airplane, and radio and electronic transmission were directed to solve. But that nature yielded up her secrets, let down her guard and her resistance in just this order, in these forms as science developed is still to be taken as a datum, a hard and independent fact which modern human organization and modern aspirations to power, wealth, knowledge, pleasure, and social affection could utilize and to which these have had in a degree to conform.

THE WEST BEFORE 1850

For over 300 years after the Renaissance in Italy and in Northern Europe no transport or communications invention disturbed the fundamental separateness of the world's peoples. The great discovery of the fifteenth century was an idea: that the earth was round and could be circumnavigated – that the oceans were not a one-way street. Instead of shutting off infinite horizons such an idea in a sense opened them. By fixing limits on the world's size, it released a limit on men's practical imagination and gave Europeans of the Renaissance the notion of an explorable and conquerable universe. But Renaissance cosmology had as little immediate practical effect as the theories of the universe have today. The instruments and means of wind navigation, the knowledge of coast lines and currents began to accumulate through painful trial and error, as bold voyagers, careful mapmakers, clever marine architects went about their work. Prior to the sudden thrust of steam transport by land and sea between 1830 and 1870, the European world had developed closer internal links and had expanded overseas, but at a measured, almost stately pace. Trade flourished and penetrated along new lines; ports grew and shifted in importance; trickles of migration implanted new colonies, some of which experienced rapid growth. Even agricultural regions specialized to a small extent along lines indicated by comparative advantage. The productivity of Western society's fixed equipment in knowledge, in social organization, in the use of resources, and transport routes and improvements increased through heavier use; the scale on which Renaissance capitalism could operate expanded as populations grew, trade increased, and wealth accumulated. The dynamics of the phenomenon received their clear analysis and exposition in *The Wealth of Nations*.

Recent writers – notably I. Wallerstein and A. Gunder Frank – have emphasized the degree to which this early modern capitalist economy and its modern successors have been centralized.[2] Venice, Antwerp, Florence, Genoa, Seville, Paris, Amsterdam, London, and at last New York have been centers of networks of long-distance trade and finance. But this is true, to the extent that it *is* true before 1850, because of the form taken by mercantile activity, its organization into numerous small competing enterprises. Mercantile activity had a political form: Italian, German, and Flemish cities of the Middle Ages were in effect mercantile republics, often possessed of enough military strength to defend themselves from marauders and feudal overlords, and were chartered and granted explicit rights and privileges by the King or regional lord. The Seville merchants' monopoly in the Spanish colonial trade, the Dutch, English, and French chartered companies, or the colonizing and trading companies that operated in North America and later in Africa – all were little more than political containers for independent mercantile activity. The world economy in its age of expansion was a net of small independent ventures, buying and selling in private transactions or on public markets. A little of the trading was done as barter, but nearly all took place against gold or silver or some form of mercantile credit. Money and credit then were the inventions by which the system transmitted values, and through the information about transactions, the knowledge of markets, commodities, and opportunities was spread.

The convenience and cheapness of communication at certain central places furnished the economies of scale and of proximity in this system and caused it, like a nervous system, to have a center or a head. Central markets developed for money and credit, for the shares of companies and speculations, for mercantile loans, and at length for governmental credits, even more strongly than for commodities in trade. Financial transactions clustered wherever information was best though the greatest gains and losses were made by access to privileged information and where the knowledge of the trading parties was unequal. And where such clusterings occurred, the opportunity for transient and shifting

[2] I. Wallerstein, *The Modern World System*, I (New York: Academic Press, 1974); A. Gunder Frank, *World Accumulation 1492–1789* (New York: Monthly Review Press, 1978). On Frank, see the incisive review by Quentin Skinner, *New York Review of Books* (March 22, 1979), 15–16, and Jan de Vries in *Journal of Economic History*, XXXIX (Sept. 1979), 846–7. On Wallerstein, see Jan de Vries, "Spotlight on Capitalism," *Comparative Studies in Society and History* (1979), 139–143.

monopolies, and even for manipulation by a small in-group over many years, was present. Such centers might even temporarily come under political control, but when that happened, as in the Spanish case, the market moved elsewhere to conduct its competitive business in money, bills, shares, and goods according to market principles. Such a system has its nodal points but the very need for them develops from its underlying, small-scale, fragmented structure, with many units operating under separate wills and communications along narrow lines according to standard, specific, universally understood signals and principles. The capitalist world economy developing, functioning, and extending itself through these techniques was the reverse of a monolithic, centralized, authoritarian structure, such as an ancient empire or a modern centrally planned economy.

The fragility of the world system was emphasized in the geography of commodity production. Here the huge cost of overland transport, the narrow channels of roads and rivers, the special advantages of some good harbors early combined to keep production and consumption near to one another, or where connected by trade over long distances, fixed in specific lanes and loci. News and messages travelled as slowly as goods and people, and they moved overseas as bulk cargo, arriving at a point suddenly in a rush rather than in a steady stream. These characteristics of communication added to risk, uncertainty, and profit in commerce, left price structures at different levels and prevented close synchronization of their movement. Till the mid-nineteenth century, the world, seen from Europe, was large, complex, remote, and uncertain. Trade was ventured, colonies planted, money, ships, and troops were risked, but merchants huddled together in centers and found in trade among themselves and within Europe the bulk of their business. Distant trade spread slowly and remained a thin skin, a glamorous surface covering to the body of European capitalism.

When communications techniques were combined with military technology, a further limit appeared on the speed and depth of European expansion overseas. Trade could establish itself South from Portugal and around Africa to India, and West from Spain to South America, where it could enter with considerable naval and military force. The same had been true of the Venetians in the eastern Mediterranean. Trading posts and colonial enclaves on the African and Asian coasts could sustain themselves, because Renaissance Europeans had guns and gunpowder, and required it to protect their wealth not only against dense native populations and jealous and suspicious native rulers but also against the mercantile ventures of other Europeans. The nineteenth century *pax Britannica* in world commerce was enforced by the British navy and on land by gunpowder as well as skillful diplomacy and a light hand in imperial government. The settlement of the Western Hemisphere and Australia was another matter. Here the land masses were small enough and native populations vulnerable enough to yield up whole empty continents to military force.

Before the age of electricity, then, social communication was not direct or carried on for its own sake. It was limited to writing or to direct visual or personal contact. Sheer curiosity, perhaps even sheer sociability, animated some travel, but most knowledge of social life came as the by-product of trade, warfare, or human migration and settlement. Where the resistance of native peoples was so weak as to allow these to occur in volume, European civilization, governmental forms, the Christian religion, capitalism, and European tastes and demand patterns spread, adapting themselves in new tropical environments. Where they spread – as a package – they were consequently able to remain. But they could not directly infect cultures or acquire legitimacy by rapid penetration by air, either in planes or on the waves of high-frequency transmission. This fact more than any other gave a measured slowness to European expansion in depth – an expansion which was sometimes stimulated and sometimes disrupted by competition among the European powers. It slowed down the expansion so far indeed that Africa could be carved up but not really conquered, and the Eurasian land mass, despite the czars and the British, remained socially distinct. The fascination of Britain's three hundred years in India comes in observing the dynamics of an expansion from early trading posts to the forms and shell of a political empire, and the mixing of societies and modes of thought and feeling so totally different in form and spirit. In Asia, technological history teased the Europeans by allowing them a glimpse of and a quick grab at some of the treasures, then shutting the door, almost until today, on the means to final domination of the "mind and heart." Only the Christian missionaries beginning in the age of Marco Polo made the attempt.

The peculiarly dangerous nature of history in the last hundred years, the accelerated expansion overseas of a Western society that has been increasingly disrupted at home, appears to be connected to the shape of modern technological change in production, transport, and communications. But at first in the mid-nineteenth century, the new techniques appear simply to have speeded up the old processes. The steamship is a faster, larger sailing vessel; the railroad is a fast river moving over a wider choice of terrain. These two inventions extended seventeenth- and eighteenth-century European development along its same lines into the nineteenth and early twentieth centuries. So the great migrations to North America could occur with sudden rushes over a world transport system of greater speed and capacity. Economic life could develop massively on a truly world scale, with agriculture and raw materials regions spread over continents around an industrial and commercial center in Northwestern Europe and the Northeastern United States. Wealth was piled on wealth and financial and political dominance was reinforced – though somewhat clumsily – with every extension of new techniques.

EFFECTS OF THE TELEGRAPH AND THE TELEPHONE

The first electric means of wire communication – the telegraph after 1844 and transoceanic cable after 1866 – served simply to increase the ease and speed of transmitting business and military messages, with no other disturbing social effects. Telegraph signals between market centers, especially with the laying of the cable, heightened this interdependence, and induced a tension previously absent. The nervous system of a world economy was keyed up, as it were, by the sudden openings of lanes of high-speed communication. And since messages could run in two directions over a wire, it is not logically evident that their speedier transmission might give a stronger advantage and farther-reaching control to people on the one end over those on the other.

Such a simple view, however, neglects an essential feature. In goods transport, high shipment costs had given an advantage to a scattered pattern of production. As costs fell with the steamship and the railroad, these small local monopolies, protected in their inefficiency and easy ways, were suddenly uncovered, like colonies of insects under a lifted rock. With lower transport costs, efficient producers – whether from natural advantages of soil, climate, and mineral resources, or from inclination and native energy – could compete over a wider area, employing also techniques and equipment of large scale. So the central stockyards vanquished local slaughter houses, large flour mills shut down local millers, and the huge plants and assembly lines of the twentieth century sprang rapidly into dominance.

A similar phenomenon is not less apparent in the information network as it affected mercantile and financial activities. The telegraph, and the telephone as it came in locally after 1880 and at long distance after 1900, had an effect on the relative positions of its users analogous to that of the railroad on industrial producers. Under the earlier slow and uncertain modes of message transmission, financial centers formed where a culture of financial management could accumulate. In these centers, the rapid transmission of messages by personal contact made these centers efficient within their range and gave them a certain raw aggregate direction over the world's commerce. The flexibility of electrical transmission strengthened these advantages. Local traders, small speculators, merchants, storekeepers, shippers, and warehousemen were, like their counterparts in manufacturing, no longer protected in inefficiency, in slowness or narrowness of response, in eccentricity or idleness by an environment of sluggish and uncertain price signals. The trading world economy was joined suddenly into an instantaneously reacting nervous system. The advantage went where the natural and social advantages lay – to the practical-minded and wealthy operators at the already existing centers of the webs.

The telegraph and the telephone, however, exhibited different technical characteristics in these respects.[3] The market, economists have observed, is an efficient instrument for business transactions requiring simple exchanges, where characteristics of commodities or services are homogeneous or well-known and messages can be confined to the dimensions of price, quantity, and time of delivery. But it is just such messages that a telegraph system can readily transmit. The telegraph consequently may have had the centralizing tendencies, spatially, that we have already observed, but it would seem to have favored the transaction of business through market exchanges of small traders at these locations. Stock markets and commodity markets had grown up at concentrated locations since the seventeenth century; the possibility of sending orders, offers, and price information by wire over long distances was open to these exchanges, vastly expanding their power and influence and increasing the range, uniformity, and reliability of the information with which they could operate. It increased the advantage which a naturally quick-witted trader might have over a slow one, and to that degree may have favored some concentration among the organizations at these locations.

A spatial network of branches under a single centralized control, however, is another matter. It was not unknown, of course, before the days of modern commercial communications. The bureaucracies of empires, armies, and the church functioned long and successfully, organized through the splitting of the central authority into individual cells, divisions of functions and layerings of command, and held together by written reports, the journeyings of officials, the development of exact and literal systems of law and procedure, by respect and hopes of advancement, and most dramatically by outbursts of punitive terror emanating from the central power. In banking and international mercantile organization, the Medici, the Fuggers, the Rothschilds all created multi-branch organizations, at major widely separated centers along the trade routes. Their advantage lay in the reduction of moral risk of

[3] I am much indebted to the current researches of Richard Du Boff of Bryn Mawr College on the telegraph in the nineteenth century. All this section has drawn on Du Boff and on ideas aired in discussion with my Yale colleagues M. J. Peck and R. C. Levin.

remote operations, and it was here that membership in the same family or religious group gave special advantage. The knowledge of long association, a common intimate language, and the susceptibility of pressures of affection or self-esteem made these effective economic organizations, despite the clumsiness of communications among their parts. But the advantage was not marked, and able local traders, working alone or in partnerships on smaller scale, had little to fear from such international competition.

The telegraph, or the telephone in its first phase of local exchanges, could not have much increased the advantage of command organizations operating complex activities of production over long distance. What was required here was a medium that could substitute for face-to-face contact, over which ideas could be exchanged, half-formed plans developed, and – most important – through which the qualities and complex character of individuals could come to be understood and assessed. Not until the development of the jet airplane in the 1960s could these problems of communication and control be said to have been even substantially overcome. Alfred Chandler's monumental researches on the industrial organization of those periods must be seen against this technological backdrop.[4] Between 1860 and 1920, communications technology on the whole probably did not favor industrial concentration. It made markets work better, and the rapid developments of stock exchanges, grain, and commodity markets, and particularly the futures market in dealings of all sorts, are to be attributed to the burst of speed in the transmission of simple business messages. The period then was the heyday of the fast witted financial speculator operating on such markets, with the ability to use his wits over a vastly extended terrain. Perhaps, as Chandler seems to indicate, it was easier for an industrial producer to exercise simple controls over wholesale and retail outlets, and to develop supply and advertising services. Despite Chandler's research, work remains to be done – if the evidence is available – to show exactly where the cost advantages of these centralized multi-branch firms like American Tobacco, Standard Oil, Swift, or Armour lay.

After 1920 on a national basis, and after about 1940 on an international basis, the telephone and the airplane went a long way to making such control and organization technically feasible. The transmission of complex messages made possible the national multi-branched producing firm consolidated with its own national advertising and marketing organization. The rapid national social communication which occurred via the automobile and the radio had the same effect as the telegraph had in the financial markets. Speed of messages and extension of their

[4]A. D. Chandler, *Strategy and Structure* (Cambridge: M.I.T. Press, 1962); and *The Visible Hand* (Cambridge: Harvard University Press, 1977).

range confirmed the advantages of those located at the center of style, opinion, and skills, i.e., New York. But at that point, something which might be called "the Rosenberg effect" intervened. Then, as in Rosenberg's famous case of machine tools, these organizations experienced technological convergence.[5] It became profitable to detach certain producers' services – notably advertising, but also accounting, and to a degree finance, from the firms and to place them in specialized firms located close together in a cluster, serving many producers and operating on a national market.

It is the organization of finance which has recently become of greatest interest. As we have seen, finance is an activity that pays high premiums to slight advantages in the speed of reaction time. In the 1870 to 1910 era, it was carried on in stock and bond markets, where specialized investment bankers and sharp-witted promoters played their roles. The growth of large-scale, multi-branch corporations, with ever greater opportunities for internal finance, or for exercising strong influence on banks and markets, strengthened the integration of financial considerations in the other corporate activities – investment, production, and merchandising. At the same time, development of systems of internal accounting, inventory control, and the like, possible with the improved technology of communication and information processing, has allowed financial consideration in a narrow sense to penetrate and rationalize entire structures. Financial management became a specialized producers' service, but since it deals in equities, there is a difference. In the modern conglomerate, it is the glue. It is not today a service which Chandler's dinosaur-firms buy, but by which they are bought. Thanks to the instrusiveness of modern communication techniques, financial messages and production messages are fused, and thanks to property arrangements of modern capitalism, the dealers in finance – whatever their corporate origins – can penetrate, with their quick wits, sharp eyes, hard faces, limited imaginations, and profound ignorance of all that is human or substantive in industrial production, deep into the production structure. It is, as Hamlet grimly said of Polonius's corpse, a feast, "not where he eats, but where he is eaten."

These topics carry us much beyond the range of one short essay. The point of this section's argument, however, should be clear. The technical characteristics of the transport and communications inventions were important, even decisive, in giving the advantage to one mode of industrial organization over another, and one spatial arrangement of plants and market traders over another. And the *timing* of the inventions in

[5] N. Rosenberg, "Technological Change in the Machine Tool Industry, 1846–1910," *Journal of Economic History*, XXIII (Dec. 1963), 414–446, with discussion by W. Paul Strassman.

relation to one another was fundamental in setting the sequence in which these forms and arrangements appear in the history. The world economy even today retains – one may hope – enough international mobility and competition to permit relative cost in the long run to determine how far and in what activities these forms and arrangements can extend. If so, perhaps yet the market can say to concentration, to monopoly, to regional hegemony, as God challenged Job to say to the ocean, "Thus far shalt thou go and no further, and here shall thy proud waves be stayed."

SOCIAL COMMUNICATION SINCE 1920

The period 1850 to 1920 was the apogee of a geographically centralized world financial and market system. Its central fact appears, as indicated above, to have been a technological one contained in this circumstance: while the means of long-distance shipment and long-distance transmittal of simple messages had greatly developed, the means of back and forth travel and message transmittal, of real rapid intimacy over distance, i.e., the means of social communication, lay still undeveloped. While *that* remained true, the rubes of the world remained rubes, the slickers slickers; town and country, metropolis and landscape remained as distinct in behavior, interests, values, and skills as they had in the late Middle Ages. The world, penetrated as it was by capitalism and Western weaponry, remained split; a centralized market network and centralized political states could enjoy economic relations and acquire superficial political controls over vast geographic areas and widely scattered and numerous populations. Taste, culture, knowledge, and wealth emanated only slowly from Europe outward, accumulating and adapting in pools and centers of North America and along the fringes of worlds' oceans.

It has been the transmission of social messages – not orders to move ships or to buy and sell commodities or lend money – that has changed all this. Here, as so often in history, one is astonished at how widely separated changes – in this case the gasoline engine and the wave transmission of energy – appear to combine to produce a single powerful effect. Otto, Daimler, and Diesel appear to have little in common with Helmholtz, Rutherford, and Marconi just as Morse, Bell, and Edison came from a line of invention different from that of Trevithick, Stephenson, or Westinghouse. The transportation inventions, in their two stages, were mechanical in nature, using little new science, but substituting an explosion for steam or air pressure with materials and an ignition technique made available by the developing state of technology. The communications inventions form a line in the scientific exploration of the unseen forms of energy and their transmission through space. Yet telegraph and railroad had one set of social effects, and motor car, truck, and plane along with radio, television, and wireless transmission generally had another.

These twentieth-century transport inventions moved people in person or by voice and picture as easily as goods in all directions, and gave overland and overseas movement a variety, cheapness, and speed far greater than the oceans and rivers had given to coastal communities in earlier times. The world became in a sense a giant Mediterranean; the Atlantic, even the vast Pacific, and the continents themselves became vehicles for cultural diffusion. And where people did not move, their signals, voices, and pictures filled the air, outdoors and in. In such a system, the direction in which messages flow and men move in social communication is not restricted by quick-profit consideration or military advantage. The technologies that permit the movement are not simple, but they can, nevertheless, be bought or imitated, and adapted to local use. The objectives of social life, if they can be called such – knowledge, pleasure, excitement, affection, the satisfaction of pride – are complex and ambiguous. The central question for the Renaissance West is the direction in which social communication is to occur.

To see this problem of modern culture with clarity, it is necessary to consider the very nature of communication, its internal nature and underlying assumptions – even, if you will, its dialectic. Communication has a paradoxical nature, is indeed the sort of thing a philosopher could easily prove to be impossible. For it to occur between two people, there must be differences – in experience, perception, background, and knowledge. I must know something you do not, or feel or have seen something I want to share. If we were simply clones of one another, the act would have no point. Perfect communication is possible only where it is unnecessary; it is the illusion experienced only momentarily in a moment of speechless intimacy; it produces the sensation of love (or may be indeed the experience out of which that emotion is born). It is approached beyond the fleeting second only by two humans in a lifetime of companionship, and then only rarely. Communication is then of its nature imperfect; to be lively, useful, interesting, there must be a clash, opposition, and ultimately learning. But if the communicating individuals are different, how can they communicate?

The answer of course is that any two humans have something in common, physiology if nothing else, basic capacities of brain and body, and elementary activities and instincts. Beyond those, society is simply a matter of degree. There is a sense in which the human race forms a society, splintered though it is by languages, religions, tribal affections, memory, and myth. As societies raise themselves above the universal minimum, their nature has been to exclude others, to form self-contained, internally interdependent cultures, environmental adaptations, languages, customs, structures of authority and belief, and to defend, or even to seek to extend, these against others. Between such groups no communication has been possible except peripheral and occasional trade and warfare, where the physically stronger will win and destroy what is alien to it. But modern communication is a wholly different thing from the commercial and military channels of the European age from the Renaissance through the nineteenth century. With Western explorers, missionaries, scientists, gunboats, and soldiers, there was little doubt which way power flowed, or whose ideas and values would prevail. Modern communication short circuits this whole ponderous, slow-moving process of diffusion. Superficial social communication has suddenly become instantaneous, and deeper mixings of ideas and peoples are constantly in action.

But in such an intercommunicating world, which way will the ideas move? There was no doubt at first – in the 1920s and 1940s, or even the 1950s and 1960s – as to direction. The techniques were part of Western civilization; the equipment, the skills to make use of and improve it, were of American and European export. But medium and messages are not in fact coterminous. Unlike the command systems of government and business, social communication requires a certain mutuality. As in market trade, both sides feel a benefit translated into some mutually shared standard of value or esteem.

These changes in the place of European civilization, with all its dynamism, in the world were first and most concretely experienced in the very structure of command organization, the state and business enterprises. The spread of skills and techniques, together with the changes in transport and production technology, removed from England, New England, and the North European coalfield and textile regions their monopoly of manufacture. Other centers in the American Midwest and South, in Japan, Central Europe, and ultimately in India and Southeast Asia and Latin America have grown. The diffusion of centers, however, has not necessarily meant a contraction in scale of the command and political organizations in operation.

May not germinal elements be present here to form on a worldwide basis a new Renaissance in the twenty-first century? What new value systems, motivations, animating visions may develop cannot be foreseen; no more could the bursting out of European individualism, science, capitalist enterprise, and discovery be foreseen in the plagues and wars of the fourteenth and fifteenth centuries. One great fear – that communications would Europeanize or Americanize the world, that cultures by communicating would lose vitality, variety, and survival power – appears at the moment at least to have been greatly attenuated. The opposite fear – that Western civilization like that of the Incas would be despoiled by invaders–seems far less valid than it did in 1940. The danger that rivalry joined to industrial and military power and operating still from narrow and exclusive premises and motives will blow up both East and West still haunts us.

Yet despite the laws of probability, it is by no means clear that a world with two dozen states with capacity for nuclear destruction is in greater danger than one where only two are so armed. In all of the world's societies, the survival or spread of any social or political system does not depend alone, or even principally, on communication across space, through the structures of state and business, and among peoples around the globe. There is another dimension of communication that is of particular importance to the continuity of human culture, just as the sex cells and organs are of special significance to the physical continuity of the race. This dimension consists of the institutions and messages that move between generations, and, by their linking from one generation to the next, communicate in effect through time.

The world's cultures are learned within social units by random imitation and structured precept, and no culture, as no biological species, is ever more than one generation away from potential extinction. How have the last century's communication techniques affected this vital function that is called education? In all the modern industrial cultures the means of formal transmission of knowledge and behavior models to the young has altered in only one respect. Human speech and language is still broken into its numerous languages; dual or triple language training is nowhere given as language is acquired, and the acquisition of fluency in a foreign language after the age of twelve remains an arduous and an artificial accomplishment, well beyond the reach of all but a few. Moreover, each language continues to incorporate and enshrine a body of concepts, a whole way of thought peculiar to its own vocabulary and structure. Technical knowledge in particular continues to be transmitted in books, or by personal demonstration, as it did in the Middle Ages. Telephones and planes have speeded up the communications of a few, who form an international industrial and political elite, but save for one powerful device, the training of the young remains deeply buried in the familiar neighborhoods, schools, and social groups of the innumerable small localities, within the world's numerous and distinct cultures. Religion, diet, and child-rearing appear to be almost the last elements in society to be affected by internationalizing influences.

The powerful device which constitutes the exception of all this is, of course, television. Like radio, cinema, and books, but unlike speech directly or by telephone, it permits only one-way transmission. Its hearers and viewers may think and react but they cannot talk back. Moreover, its visual transmission is, as we know, vastly more powerful in its effect on the imagination than the printed word. The greatest literary artists, with the most powerful themes of sex, violence, pathos, or suspense may induce images which return in dreams and enter deeply into the consciousness and memory of readers. But even the shallowest, cheapest television program may do the same thing. In addition, as has been often noted, television does not stimulate the creative imagination; it deadens and replaces it with its own imposed images. The readers of books can write; the viewers of television programs can simply absorb.

It is impossible, it seems to me, to overstate the vulgarizing and homogenizing power of this medium. To educate a new generation *via* the entertainment industry is not to educate it at all. To replace family and a devoted cadre of professional teachers by the shallowest, most opportunistic, and volatile minds in the population is to produce a new generation in that image. No better would be the seizure of these powerful educational devices, and of the schools themselves, by a state apparatus dominated by narrow-minded ideologues and insecure politicians. How then is a Renaissance of the twenty-first century to be brought about if those who are to communicate, and so to absorb and create a high world culture, have nothing to say or teach? That is the topic for much further serious thought as that century approaches.

10

The historians' reviews of the terrain

I have included under this title a set of reviews of eight books written during the high period of historians' interest in the economic growth of the West, i.e., the period beginning with W. W. Rostow's *Stages of Economic Growth* (1956) and ending perhaps with Rostow's *World Economy: History and Prospect* (1979). Within these Rostovian brackets, scholars of varied background and approach presented their syntheses and overviews. The multi-volumed *Cambridge Economic History,* which had started off in 1941 with a first volume on the Middle Ages, took a moment in 1966 to unload a cargo of chapters in Volume VI, *The Industrial Revolutions and After*. The notable theorist J. R. Hicks, who was later to win a Nobel Prize for his contributions to economic theory, became engaged in an effort of interpretation of the early modern period, and his book was complemented, chronologically at least, by J. R. T. Hughes's more detailed exposition of the nineteenth and early twentieth-century spread of industrialization following the English Industrial Revolution. This latter period occupied two long volumes by Alan Milward and S. B. Saul, of which only the second one, *The Development of the Economies of Continental Europe: 1850–1941,* is reviewed here.

Among all these reviews and syntheses, the principal work of original scholarship appeared in 1966 when Simon Kuznets gathered together the statistical labors of himself and his international teams of scholars in the historical national income and product estimates, and told us, with the addition of some historical generalizations, what it all meant. In retrospect, his *Modern Economic Growth: Rate, Structure and Spread* may be the only work of the period which will endure as a true advance in the state of knowledge. The review of Gunder Frank's treatment of *World Accumulation, 1492–1789* is included, though dealing with an earlier period, by contrast and because of its bearing on contemporary problems. Of course other books on these great topics appeared during these years and continue to come out from time to time. One should not overlook the much discussed work of D. C. North and R. P. Thomas, *The Rise of the Western World,* and the valuable factual and interpretive studies by Angus Maddison. But I was not asked to review these and so did not have the need to commit my thoughts to print.

These rather severe judgments on such efforts may have come with an ill grace from one who had not made the attempt himself. The authors, if they took the trouble to read the reviews, might have replied with Romeo, "He laughs at scars who never felt a wound." My reactions are presented here not to display their infallibility, despite – in the manner of academic book reviewers – their Olympian tone. I have republished them here in an attempt to make in a negative way some points which the present volume tries to make directly. I should be fortunate indeed if it will see the favors of these reviews returned by scholars as eminent and imaginative as even the least of those whom I here criticize.

W. W. Rostow. *The Stages of Economic Growth: A Non-Communist Manifesto.* Cambridge: Cambridge University Press, 1960. Pp. x, 179.

There is a peculiar, baffling charm to Professor Rostow's set of lectures. In them history is made simple. The world is a set of nations, or societies (the words are used interchangeably); each one – though a separate creature – goes through a sequence of five stages as its economy develops. The stages have oddly memorable names: traditional society, preconditions of take-off, take-off, drive to maturity, and the age of high mass-consumption. Each stage has a few general characteristics, sketched out in five brief chapters. History, it is said, fits this pattern, resembling a rather jerky horse race (in which a tragic photo finish is just now in danger of developing between the two front runners).

From economic history, the lecturer's interest shifts to the great questions of international politics. Here nations appear as the eternal, indestructible unit in human affairs. They existed in the traditional society, they thrive under the "reactive nationalism" of the transition, and they form the power blocs of the next world. The historical pattern of war and peace reflects in a complex way their relative stages of development. Most exciting is said to be the view of the future which this historical taxonomy can give. Since many great nations are moving toward economic maturity, the game of international power politics will grow more complex and competitive. In this situation, the

West must persuade Russia to abandon her pretensions to world religion and, as simply one great power, to accept international inspection of nuclear disarmament. A peaceful world of mature nations can then move on together to see what lies beyond the age of high mass-consumption. As a contribution to this great act of persuasion, Lecture 10 proposes the stages-of-growth sequence as a liberal alternative to Marxism.

Simplicity, relevance, and a high sincerity are important sources of the widespread appeal of these lectures. But there are other sources as well. There are on every page bold assertions, immense claims, sweeping insights, unsubstantiated by analysis or documentation. When a professor speaks thus to students, he excites them to look further into the material, to take more advanced courses, even to dip into that "more conventional treatise" where "the views presented here might have been elaborated . . . at greater length, in greater detail, and with greater professional refinement" (p. ix). How many times, from high-spirited undergraduate days on, must Rostow, like his more inhibited colleagues, have found that such ideas, resembling the other pleasures Burns wrote about,

> . . . are like poppies spread –
> You seize the flow'r, its bloom is shed;
> Or like the snow falls in the river –
> A moment white – then melts forever.

Surely Rostow has scattered snow liberally here upon the surface of what appears to be rather shallow water. One cannot be sure of the depth, of course, since the current is swift and the author darts like a dragon fly over the dazzling expanse. The applause of economic policy-makers and journalists to his performance betokens an important pedagogical accomplishment. And it is not enough for academic critics, themselves unmindful of the fable of the fox and the grapes, to remind Rostow of the fable of the frog and the ox.

One's chief regret is that, for all his boldness and bravado, Rostow has remained tied to an extremely conventional historical framework. One sees, gleaming up through the water a broken image of the school of Schmoller. The notion of stages is a primitive aid to thought, itself an obsolete stage in the economic historian's grasp of a complex and continuous process. And there is surely an ultimate level on which the world must be seen not as a checkerboard of national case studies, but as a single, developing international industrial society if we are ever to understand its past or to come to terms with its future.

[Originally published in *The American Economic Review*, L(5), December 1960, 1058–1059. Reprinted by permission.]

The historians' reviews of the terrain

H.J. Habakkuk and M. Postan, eds. *The Cambridge Economic History of Europe,* vol. VI. Cambridge: Cambridge University Press, 1966. Part I, pp. xii, 597; Part II, pp. xii, 437.

The publication of a new volume of the *Cambridge Economic History* is itself an historical event. Like a great freight train, bursting out from its dark tunnel, it rattles across our landscape, loaded high with gold and spices, coal and lumber – a few peasants, merchants, silk-hatted bankers, officials, and businessmen clinging to the roofs of the cars. Livestock are terrified and students astonished; but as happy economic historians we line the tracks and wave our greeting, and then, as the noise and smoke fade away, we return to our firesides to tell each other stories of what we have seen.

This time it is Volume VI, *The Industrial Revolutions and After,* that has gone by. (Volumes IV and V appear to be stuck in the tunnel, and volumes VII and VIII send out very faint whistles from over the mountain.) The cargo is the nineteenth century, and the cars stretch out as far as the eye can see. The last 437 pages (pp. 603–1040) are bound in a second part and pulled by a separate engine. The fare is $19.50. But this time I, at least, find myself looking less at the cargo than at the rolling stock. Is this the old engine from Clapham Junction? I wonder. Has the train itself, as well as its contents, been driven out of the nineteenth century? And what about the two engineers, M. M. Postan and H. J. Habakkuk, who wave to us from the cab? Are they the sure and steady hands we take them for, or do they dream secretly of dieselization and even of jets – not just of riding in the train, but of driving it somewhere?

I

For a scientific study of social change, the fundamental event is the individual human action. To explain actions we must reconstruct an environment and suggest motivations in a way that will appear plausible to other human beings who, through reading, observation, and introspection, have attained to some expectations about human behavior. Not all the actors are of equal importance in determining the environment for the actions of others. The phenomena of power, leadership, and obedience make possible a history of politics, war, and ideas through the writings and biographies of a few men. The instincts of the chroniclers and historians of aristocracy and diplomacy thus are not false; in the personal documents they examine are fixed important foci of a social environment affecting the lives and behavior of great masses of men. But even without leaders and over a wide range of individual differences in motivation, men react similarly to similar stimuli or environmental changes. It is this fact which makes possible the writing of economic and social history.

A book of history then may show in the records of human action, statistical and literary, how individual and mass responses to environmental change produce a changed environment in which new actions take place. In the effort to show this, we may endeavor not only to relate each action to its total surroundings, but also to separate strands of action over time. Actions along one strand occur more directly, we say, and are more nearly explainable, as the consequence of previous actions of the same type than of other elements in their surroundings. This appears to be true of such processes as the discovery of new lands and the invention of new techniques. In such historical sequences one act opens up knowledge from which others can proceed. To explain a sequence one must, to be sure, explain – or assume – a continuity of motivation on the part of the actors; but granted that, the lines of progress may be followed directly in the widening opportunities for action or discovery which each action or discovery opens up.

Now the growth of income and productivity can be looked on as the composite result of responses by individual men to economic opportunities appearing within their own lives. For mankind as a whole, or for any human group, these opportunities are set by certain process-histories going on in its general social history. In particular, opportunities are set by the growth of fundamental productive factors – the labor force and the knowledge of the available resources and techniques for production – taken in relation to the growth and configuration of demand. A group response to such opportunities requires the organization of individual action so that the group's opportunity apears in the lives of its members and so that their actions in responding to individual opportunities are interrelated in such a way as to utilize it. The explanation of income and productivity growth then has three parts: (1) the process-histories – of resource discovery, technological change, population growth, and the movement of demand – by which opportunity is produced; (2) the history of institutional, or organizational, evolution by which the economic activities of individuals are interrelated to produce a social response; (3) the changes and variations in the psychology of individuals both by themselves and *en masse* as members of groups.

That some such organizing scheme is at work in the minds of Professors Postan and Habakkuk in planning volumes VI, VII, and VIII of the *Cambridge Economic History* is evident from some lines in the Preface to Volume VI:

> The editors have therefore tried so to define the main themes of the separate volumes as to focus attention on topics directly relevant to the current discussions of economic growth and also to enable the authors to deal with salient

features of the modern economy treated as a whole. In accordance with this plan the first volume [i.e. Volume VI] deals with factors of economic development which are so to speak 'external' to the economic system narrowly defined, and which in economic analysis are frequently treated as social 'parameters,' or assumed conditions of the economic process: viz. population, territorial expansion, transport and, above all, technological change. The second volume will concern itself with the factors of production, the entrepreneurial and managerial functions and related topics. The third volume will be devoted mainly to economic and fiscal policies and perhaps also to the social changes involved with the economic development of the modern world.

In the opening chapters of Volume VI the chance seems high that these words will be made flesh to dwell among us.

II

Volume VI opens with a chapter on national income by Phyllis Deane and W. A. Cole stating the statistical result of the mass of economic actions to be explained: the record of income, productivity, and structural change in the industrializing countries. Ideally of course one wants to know *whose* incomes are rising as knowledge of economic opportunities is observed, responded to, and transmitted from one income receiver to another. Income accrues, after all, first to an individual or a family or an enterprise. But data on income distribution are scarce; and national or sectoral estimates are a substitute which reveals the effects of individual income growth only in certain, very artificial, aggregates. The national statistics of Chapter I are bound together by explanatory materials drawn from economic history to suggest the pattern of industrialism's spread in time and space. A strange world it is, peopled by creatures called England, Germany, Denmark, Canada, Japan – with never a footprint of merchants, peasants, manufacturers, and the laboring poor – or even of Yorkshiremen, Southerners, Bavarians, or Ukrainians. It is a world too where nations fall like lumps of snow into a growing stream of world income and where structural change means only three things: the rising share of capital in production, the relative decline of agriculture in the labor force, and the increasing importance of foreign trade. But the growth of an internationally trading economy on top of regional, local, and household economies – a growth occurring between individual trading partners across the world – is not a phenomenon which can be fully handled by comparative national economic histories imprisoned in the tight cage of national income statistics. One could ask for no better guide than Deane and Cole through the zoo of national income statistics. They teach us many curious facts about the comparative anatomy of unlike national beasts. But one should not mistake their tidy cages for the green jungle of economic history.

Chapter II on population by D. V. Glass and E. Grebenik is very heavily statistical, and a marvelous array of data and sources it is. Whereas in Chapter I national statistics are sometimes personified and paraded as live creatures, in Chapter II they are perhaps confined a bit too closely. One wishes for some speculation both into the vexed relation of economic change to fertility and mortality (the "feedbacks" from economic growth) and into the implications of population growth for the labor force, internal migration, and the structure of demand. No doubt part of the authors' restraint is due to the editors' rather strained distinction between population growth, assigned as a topic to Volume VI, and the growth of the labor force, assigned presumably to Volume VII. But it may be doubted whether population history is a process-history in the sense that the histories of land settlement and technology are. Its basis in a chain of human actions interrelated over time is not clear. No man marries early, begets more children, or dies later directly because someone before him has given him means to do so. The explanation of changes in population statistics comes then partly from the mechanism imposed by the differential incidence of births and mortality on age classes, but more fundamentally from the responses of groups to their contemporary social environment. This, of course, cannot be dealt with in a single chapter. As it stands, Chapter II is an authoritative summary of research in historical demography.

With real sensitivity and a strong sense of relevance and order, A. J. Youngson in Chapter III unfolds the process of land settlement, the drawing in of new resources to the world economy. The shadowland of frontier economics in the newly explored continents and parts of continents is exposed. It is a land shrouded in uncertainty, where knowledge of geography is the vital piece of capital, produced as a by-product to the economic enterprises – fur trade, early mining, and bonanza farming. Factors are drawn in at high risk in nearly total ignorance of probable returns until settlement spreads around mining areas and along main lines of commodity trade. Whether settlement means subsistence farming on the edge of nature or full incorporation into an international system of law and economy depends crucially in the nineteenth century on simple facts of soil, climate, and terrain. One can wish that Professor Youngson's instructions had permitted him to follow the extension of trade and the discovery of resources in the "old" regions. The discovery of minerals in Europe and the development of export enclaves in China and India show many similarities to the processes of frontier settlement and many interesting differences. In their function in world industrialization these processes are all the same, since they provide the material basis on which agricultural and industrial technology can work.

At this point Volume VI cries out for a full presentation of the process of technological change. Such a history, for the nineteenth and twentieth centuries on a world-wide basis, has never been attempted. The effort would make immense demands upon an historian's insight not only into men and society but also into nature. Technology is, like land settlement, a point where the social and material universes meet. The internal logic of its history, like that of geographical discovery, is set not only by human energy, ingenuity, enterprise, and social structure, but also by the harsh facts of nature and by the levels at which, in relation to the human mind's powers of inquiry and inspiration, nature keeps her secrets. It is not an economic history, but a piece of intellectual history, that is needed – a history that will show ideas developing from ideas and transmitted from one group to another, responding sometimes to local factor proportions, but exhibiting the continuous assault, at ever deeper levels of penetration, of the mind of man upon external nature. From the succession of events adduced in the records of population growth and migration, of land and resource discovery, and above all from technological change and its transmission, may be constructed the succession of economic opportunities for the earth's regions. Thence one might move to the materials of volumes VII and VIII, the study of the capitalistic economic and political organization by which men were molded to respond to the new technologies and new factor supplies – or to fail to do so. On a world setting of this sort, any number of studies of sectors, industries, regions, and national societies would be in order. In many matters, national cultures do present patterns, and national states pursuing military or political purposes do offer stimuli, affecting the timing and the "style" of national economic development. These peculiar facts are relevant after the main lines of opportunity and organization of the response are sketched.

But, alas! The editors have not had the courage of their convictions (or at least of what I have imagined them to be). Instead, the topic of technological change has been uncertainly diffused among chapters IV, V, and VI. Chapter IV on transport, by L. Girard, focuses mainly on transport technology, particularly on the relation of the forms of transport to one another, as the technology evolves. It argues that a new mode of transport comes as an auxiliary to the old modes – steam to sail, rail to inland navigation – then assumes dominance and overshoots its proper sphere, finally settling into a working relation as part of a complex system. In demonstrating this evolutionary thesis in a world setting the chapter exposes the similarity of the economic and organizational problems in many different locations. Like Folke Dovring's

Chapter VI on agriculture, Chapter IV hangs midway between technological and economic history – in midair with its roots cut off. But taken by itself it is an extremely interesting and ingenious piece of work. Chapter V, entitled "Technological Change and Development in Western Europe," is evidently intended as the centerpiece of this triptych on technology. What the editors must have intended was a study of industrial technology as it developed in, and spread among, the European centers of science and invention. The author, David S. Landes, has embraced this task in 330 ardent pages, attacking the tangled subject with the vigor of Hercules attacking the Hydra – and with similar initial results.

Now Professor Landes is a social – not an intellectual – historian, and it is interesting to see how, while covering material on technology, he has been able to avoid giving it any life of its own and so to avoid writing its intellectual history. Clearly, Chapter V is interested in historical explanation; the tell-tale "why" questions are everywhere present, and at times even a model pokes its bony hand through the meaty text. But what is it that is being explained? The questions asked are those to which class structures and entrepreneurial activities and motivations can give an answer. An interesting reexamination of the Industrial Revolution, for example, asks why it began in England, rather than across the Channel. And much of excitement thereafter is generated out of the race between England and Germany for industrial "leadership." But the interesting questions about this material from the viewpoint of intellectual history – and I would contend from the viewpoint of general economic history as well – are not answered by comparing the opposite banks of the English Channel. The Industrial Revolution, wherever it occurred, was, for the first time in history, a cumulative process in which one line of ideas fed into another. And as its stream of ideas spread out after 1850, it swept up branches of fundamental and previously useless science – chemistry, biology, atomic physics – in the land of Bismarck and the Hohenzollerns and everywhere else. In Landes' treatment the details of technology remain not vital but simple, separate – he speaks of them at one point as "anodyne" (an adjective not far removed from "soporific" in a druggist's vocabulary). They are never let in to the warm fireside where the old Landes circle – the families, clans, classes, and entrepreneurs – are gathered. And they are given no real home of their own. Instead all is tumbled together at last into a flood, a torrent, a tempest, an engulfing tide, boiling with detail and whirling to some undeterminedly portentous conclusion. One hears above the winds the voices of the historian's mighty gods, England, France, and Germany, and one is carried into the operatic world of Richard Wagner – a suitable and compelling evocation of late-nineteenth-century romantic art no doubt, but a bit heavy in twentieth-century ears. My preference is for Mozart; but my admiration for Landes' achievement, within the historian's modes of expression, is immense. That he has shared a 64-page bibliography with us is alone enough to put every teacher and scholar in European history deeply in his debt.

III

After Landes' digression, Folke Dovring tries in a chapter on agriculture again to pick up the original plot. The scope is confined to Europe; and the treatment touches population, internal migration, resources, techniques, and organization, showing in a useful way how these combined to permit a general rise in agriculture productivity. Trade, demands, imports, rural social organization, finance, marketing, and tariffs are expressly omitted from the treatment, and – as nearly always from this sort of ecological emphasis – some striking and fundamental facts about the opportunities offered by geography and technology are exposed. If indeed chapters IV, V, and VI had been combined into a single chapter on technology, set in relation to resources on a worldwide basis as regions were discovered and as techniques evolved spread, the scene would have been prepared for industrial or regional studies, or for the national case histories which now descend. Instead, some vital extra-European parts even of the European technological and resource base – such as the whole subject of American agriculture after Professor Youngson has got its land settlement under way – fall out between the slats. The national case histories, which begin after Dovring, have not been prepared for, and we have no understanding of what new insights are to be expected from a new division of the material along political boundaries.

National income statistics have already been handled in Chapter I, population, settlement, transport, and agriculture in chapters II, III, IV, and VI, and government policies and entrepreneurship are reserved to volumes VII and VIII. One wonders then what sort of instructions were given the authors of chapters VII through X on the U. S. A., Russia, and the Far East. The uncertainty is evident in an uneven product. In a very short Chapter VII, Douglass C. North, following the precepts of the "new" economic history, combines theory and statistics in a survey of American industrialization from 1789 to 1914. The theory is contained in the first twenty pages, on the period before 1860. Here the North cottonburning Engine of Growth is again put on exhibition; with a few new linkages added and continued lubrication with Stigler's ointment, it turns in its usual smooth performance. The statistics are contained in the eleven pages devoted to the period 1860–1914, of which nearly half are very simple statistical tables. Theory and statistics thus stand forever on opposite sides of the Civil War, and the one flees like a ghost at midnight when the other appears. Have we a built-in uncertainty principle here, one wonders, which may prevent the two from occupying the same space simultaneously? But this chapter is not a fair test of any method since, for some reason, it is written on the head of a pin. This was a difficult assignment and, as Dr. Johnson said about violin playing, one wishes that it had been impossible. In Chapter IX, Roger Portal gives an economic history of Russian industrialization; in Chapter X, G. C. Allen reviews the Japanese experience which his *Short Economic History of Japan* treated so well and adds some pages on China and India. These are interesting and useful treatments, perhaps because the authors depart from editorial constraint – as Professor North was evidently unwilling to do – and mix in subjects reserved for volumes VII and VIII. It is particularly useful to have a compact treatment of the crucial Russian decades after 1890. That Russia 1890–1914 occupies as much space as the U. S. A. 1800–1914 should trouble any person with any feeling for relative magnitudes; but then the proportions of the whole volume must have been conceived in the mind of General de Gaulle.

But there is a jewel in the head of this toad: Alexander Gerschenkron's Chapter VIII on Russian agriculture after the Emancipation. Goodness knows what it is doing here, since it explains why Russia was backward – a subject which opens the gate to full studies of China, India, and Southeast Asia. To have a chapter on Russian agriculture and hardly a word on American, seems like a backward way of explaining industrial growth. In any case, the chapter – so far as one ignorant of the subject can judge – is a masterpiece that defies brief restatement and must be read and savored in its complexity and deep irony to be appreciated.

In summary, Volume VI of the *Cambridge Economic History* is like the Scottish haggis, "full of much fine, confused feeding." It goes well beyond a chronology or a tourist's view of the terrain. It is an attempt to impose an intellectual order on this material. If volumes VII and VIII appear along the lines now scheduled, much of this order will become apparent.

But will they appear? The bold statement in the Preface is reminiscent of Glendower's boast: "I can call spirits from the vasty deep," and one is tempted to reply with Hotspur: "But will they come?" Yet the fault, if fault can be found, lies not in editors or authors, but in the stars – in the sign of the Zodiac under which all of the great multivolume Cambridge histories were conceived. The sun was in that Edwardian house, high in the heavens, when Marshall laid his hand on Clapham and inspired him to his life work. It had already moved on into the age of Edward VIII and George VI when the *Cambridge Economic History* began to appear. The present editors, Professors Postan and Habakkuk, in their own work show strong concern for economic analysis and historical explanation. Yet, modern men that they are, they have saddled themselves with the incubus of this great, antiquated, editorial labor. They have carried it on nobly and to the immense benefit of our profession. That a reviewer can yearn to reshape its materials to his heart's desire shows only how rich those materials are. This is an age of cooperative scholarship, but perhaps no composite volume can retell history on a fundamentally new and unified philosophical basis. And no doubt the task is too large for the life or mind of any one man, beset by the doubts and self-criticism of an analytical and skeptical age. If only there were a creative computer. . . .

But there is a rumor that gives hope. The *Cambridge Economic History*, it is rumored, is really all written. Its manuscripts were finished years ago by the brilliant, though now aging, young men who have been its authors. The scrolls were wrapped reverently in linen, sealed in camphor in great jars, and placed in the college vaults. Once a decade a new editor, like a fairy prince, rolls away the stone, breaks the seals, and releases a volume into the upper air. Or so the story goes. One hopes for all our sakes that it is true.

[Originally published in *The Journal of Economic History* XXVI (1), March 1966, 99–106. Reprinted by permission.]

John Hicks. *A Theory of Economic History*. New York: Oxford University Press, 1969. Pp. vii, 181.

Jonathan Hughes. *Industrialization and Economic History: Theses and Conjectures*. New York: McGraw-Hill Book Company, 1970. Pp. xii, 336.

The English Industrial Revolution is the focal point, the burning glass of modern history. Into its decades streams a diffuse light – the flickerings of capitalism from Greece through the Dutch Republic. From it pours the intense heart of modern industrial civilization. This at least is the form imposed on history by a study of economics. It is wholly congruent to the form imposed on the history of religion by a faith in the divinity of Christ. The decades of the Industrial Revolution are the decades from Christmas to the Passion in the material history of the modern world.

The two books here noticed fit together almost exactly at the point of this revolution. Both are extended essays in the grand synoptic tradition of economic history. Both betray that subject's origins in the Enlightenment and the urge to provide a rational alternative to Christian myth. In ten compelling – though hardly conclusive – chapters, J. R. Hicks turns the mind of a great economic theorist to the materials on the rise of capitalism. His theme is an old one – how the growth of trade and the culture of the trader undermined and transformed the economic organization of agrarian societies, producing at last the thoroughgoing capitalism out of which nineteenth-century industrialism could grow. J. R. T. Hughes begins with that growth and follows the nineteenth-century diaspora of elements of income growth among the nations from England to the Continent and overseas and the progressive wreckage of economic forms and ideologies, both "native" and capitalistic, that has littered the world since Marx, Mill, Marshall, and Queen Victoria.

To note their complementarity in coverage, theme, and viewpoint, however, is to give little of the flavor of the two books. Both are highly personal artifacts and derive from persons of markedly different temperaments and culture. Hicks, casting his web over the West, weaves arguments like a spider, one strand at a time. His concern at all points is to be not exhaustive but plausible and, above all, clear. One catches him on occasion in that tone of faint condescension, reminiscent of the language of *Alice in Wonderland*, that theorists must adopt in order to communicate with the academic multitude. Unfortunately, the materials of history do not readily give themselves to the devices of so cool a rhetoric. Nor can an American reviewer suppress a provincial irritation at the casualness with which an Oxonian scholar surveys the world. Of sixty-three references to other works, the frequency distribution of places of publication is as follows: Oxford 13; London 13; Cambridge 11; New York 3; Paris 2; all others, 1 each. The result of Hicks's mind working on history is not the perfect and satisfying magic of *Value and Capital* (1946), his great work in economic theory. He has produced not a theory of economic history, but a theorist's economic history – a different, but a more human and interesting thing.

Hughes's personal style is quite different – and thoroughly American. Superficially, he appears to have written a book highly usable as an undergraduate text. Written with clarity and vigor, with ample bibliography, forthright judgments, and immense coverage, the book must interest students who, however, may fail to appreciate the breadth of its learning and the subtlety of its judgments. The essays on imperialism, economic doctrines, and the interwar period are particularly original and valuable.

If economic history, then, is a religion whose theology has a certain chronological form, Hicks expounds the Old Testament in the style of an Anglican bishop and Hughes proclaims the New a bit in the manner of the Methodist minister of a large city church. Yet the message is the same – it is a message of redemption through modern capitalistic forms and industry. What is missing from it is a sensitivity to the inner logic by which economic and social life may be organized outside the market economies and directed to other ends, less individualistic and less materialistic. Yet what is interesting in the whole span covered by the two books together is the cyclical character of the evolution, from nonmarket forms through the market back to nonmarket organization again. Splitting economic evolution at the Industrial Revolution tends to obscure this huge cyclical form that the history exhibits.

And oddly enough, one other omission in both books appears: the omission of technology as an historical force. Hicks explicitly excludes it from his definition of things economic (p. 71). And Hughes having given the topic full credit in the initial English developments, loses it in a discussion of entrepreneurs, laws, thought, policies, and capital movements of the nineteenth century and thereafter. Yet Hicks presumably would not deny that it was the presence of this catalyst that distinguished the late eighteenth-century revolution from its predecessors in Greece or in early modern times. Nor could Hughes deny that the spread of modern industry occurred most easily where resources and transport conditions were best suited to the developing technology.

Hicks and Hughes then must be supplemented by David Landes, who supplies if not Christ, then at least Prometheus, as the superstar to the story. The three authors' books taken together supply an interested historian with a useful and intriguing introduction to modern history as modern economists view it. If all three get lost in their subjects to some degree, that should not be taken to show their hopeless indifference to modern economics, as some recent critics of Landes in this journal have averred (*AHR*, 76 [1971]: 467–74). It is but a sign of their baptism in the subject matter of economic history – by a sprinkling of holy water in the case of Hicks and, for Hughes and for Landes, by total immersion.

[Originally published in *The American Historical Review* 77 (4), October 1972, 1087–1088. Reprinted by permission.]

A Milward and S. B. Saul. *The Development of the Economies of Continental Europe, 1850–1914*. London: G. Allen and Unwin, and Cambridge, Mass.: Harvard University Press, 1977. Pp. 555.

When Britain really ruled the waves, things were much simpler. She experienced in succession, as Lillian Knowles told us, a commercial revolution, an agricultural revolution, and an industrial revolution. The waves which Britain ruled washed other coasts – the Low Countries, New England and the other island empire of the East, Japan. Penetration up the Seine, the Rhine and the Po brought nationalism and industrial modernization. The French Revoluton and Napoleon and the aristocratic and priestly reaction against them erected dykes, and in Eastern Europe, lords, peasants, creaky bureaucracies, armies, sultans and czars entrenched themselves. When flooded at last, as in the pressures of the deep sea, the Continent exhibited forms of bourgeois life in strange and distorted shapes, spawning at last the antediluvian monstrosities of Fascist Germany and Italy and Stalinist Russia.

This Whig view of economic history has for two decades now suffered the experience of all the other nice, clear, plausible histories that our self-confident fathers bequeathed to us. It has been submitted to torture by quantification, racked by uncertainties and relativism, crushed by stone upon stone of national case studies piled upon its chest in the effort to change its testimony. Milward and Saul in this second of their two volumes have now completed their long, exhaustive, learned, meticulous and conscientious inquisition. Following the rule that a defendant need not be put on the stand, they have done it in the most effective way possible – simply by refraining from asking England any questions. In this sense their volumes, as dust jackets are wont to say, "fill a long-felt need." Others have talked about comparative economic histories; Milward and Saul have written them. Others have promised to link the new income and output data to the literary accounts; they have provided the integration. Others have urged us to get out of the English rut in our stories of 19th century industrialization; they have taken the grand tour, beginning on the far shore. Their book travels through every country from Lapland to Sicily and the Bay of Biscay to the Urals; only Portugal, Andorra, Liechtenstein, Montenegro and Turkey in Europe have been left untouched. And this has been done by a pair of scholars, not in an edited and uneven multi-authored collection or in a huge foundation-supported series but in a single two-volume work of dimensions and price that permit use as a text. The word has been made flesh and dwells among us. Surely economic historians should not complain.

Volume 1, published five years ago, offered four topical chapters, followed by the first units of the long parade of national case studies. Now in Volume 2, Germany, France and the Low Countries march on to 1914, followed by Spain, Italy, Austria-Hungary and Southeastern Europe. Russia too, characteristically behind the procession, streams in in two long chapters to catch up. The volume concludes by returning to the all-Europe format with an excellent chapter on international trade and a struggling one on the nature of European economic development, to bring up the rear. If as after any parade, the watchers disperse, footsore both from standing still and from watching others move, a little silent and let down, the fault lies surely in the very nature of parades and in the insatiable human craving for sustained excitement.

Still it is after all Hamlet without the Prince of Denmark. Milward and Saul have given us, thoroughly, an account which must be set in the perspective of England and the lands beyond the seas. Once we have set them at the beginning and end, a definite story line can emerge. The diversity of the European national experience, proclaimed even in Milward and Saul's title, is indeed a valid observation through the lens they use. But at the most distant focus, it was not this way at all. In Kuznets' comparative national case history telescope, the view is not continental, but global in scope. Even from current income levels we know – if we did not know already – roughly what happened. Beginning in the late 16th century, some areas of Northwestern Europe began to pull away from the pack, and this motion has been transmitted successively to points around and within the Continent and to a few non-European areas, notably in North America and Japan. The industrializing experience of the Midlands, New England, the Low Countries, the Rhine Valley, north Italy marks these modernizing areas off from the rest of the 19th century world and constitutes the West's 19th century uniqueness. Even as part of crude national totalities, the total and per capita income figures of the Western European and Northeastern American regions leap from the page of 19th century history. Even the nationalisms developing so strongly along with industrialism in the 19th century appears as a general, and so a unifying, fact of modern industrial society. It really is the unity of the industrial experience that stands out; if that were not true, why would one write an economic history about Europe at all?

As honest scholars with searching minds, the authors grope in their final chapter for a design. They run through the roster of syntheses: Marx, Rostow, Gerschenkron. But what they give with one hand their honesty takes away with the other. The 'role' of agriculture, which they rightly emphasize, of demand, of income distribution, of technology and investment are all mentioned, but we are nowhere shown in just what cases and circumstances has one of these proved more 'crucial' than another. The result is that their histories seem to equivocate with their conclusions, like strong drink with lechery, as the porter told Macduff. The difficulty, I would suggest, is that so strong a focus on the comparative history of these ephemeral political units, on their relative growth rates and measurable output, has cut the European story out of world history and snipped it off even from its roots in European geography, sociology, politics and culture.

The method of Milward and Saul stands indeed at the confluence of two streams of economic historiography, the British descriptive tradition and the national income and product approach. Reading their chapters, one after another, one is tempted to cry out with Byron's pagan,

> "Thou has conquered, O Kuznets and Clapham
> The world has grown gray with thy breath!"

It is hard to imagine how a better book could be written within the limits of this method and these techniques. But will not someone, building on what Milward and Saul have done, try now to attach the continental European story to its origins in the Renaissance and in 17th century and Georgian England at one end, and to its 20th century world-wide continuation, at the other?

[Originally published in *The Journal of Economic History* 38 (3), September 1978, 799–801. Reprinted by permission.]

Simon Kuznets. *Modern Economic Growth, Structure and Spread.* New Haven and London, Yale University Press, 1966. Pp. 528. The book is Number 7 in the series, Studies in Comparative Economics, sponsored by the Inter-University Committee on Comparative Economics.

Simon Kuznets's latest book is the despair of a reviewer. Its structure is transparent. Its conclusions are fully and accurately stated. Its relevance to contemporary concerns is undeniable. Its techniques and general method are well-known. Its evidence – resting on the massive enterprise of international historical income accounting – is massive. Its limitations and qualifications are stated more clearly and scrupulously than any reviewer could possibly state them. It is in short a book by Simon Kuznets. One might as well try to write a review of the Roman Coliseum or the Great Pyramid of Cheops.

The difficulties are compounded when the reviewer is one who is a consumer rather than a producer of income accounts, and whose main concerns are with the historical rather than the contemporary evidence and conclusions. The book needs indeed a panel of reviewers: an income accountant to discuss the technique, an economic developer to discuss its policy implications, and an economic historian to discuss its framework and perspectives. At some point, too, one feels, Professor Kuznets's entire approach to economic development deserves scrutiny from a theorist who is still not too far from the cares, concerns, and data of Kuznets's version of the 'real world.' My own viewpoint is that of an economic historian who shares some of these cares and concerns and who retains still a naive urge to explain it all, with the use of a theoretical framework, broader and less well defined than a growth theorist would like, and perhaps less well based in the arithmetical evidence than Professor Kuznets would admire.

First, a word about the book. The contents of *Modern Economic Growth: Rate, Structure and Spread* are reasonably well known in other forms to most economists. Many of the estimates appear in the series of supplements to *Economic Development and Cultural Change*, and the main conclusions drawn from them have been made in those and other essays. The work rests of course upon the historical income series for the major high income countries – a number ranging from one to fourteen, depending on the detail in question and extending back from sixty-seven to two hundred and sixty-seven years. The examination of this material, supplemented by contemporary evidence of these countries, occupies Chapters 2 through 6 of the book, and the topics – as might be imagined – are: product, population, sectoral composition of product and labor force, industrial composition of sectoral product totals, factoral distribution of income, size distribution of income, distribution of output between consumption and capital formation, the distribution of consumption among classes of goods, size and type of economic units, and finally international trade and factor movements. It is useless to restate Kuznets's conclusions on all these topics. Most of them are well known, and Kuznets's own careful summary in Chapter 10 cannot be improved upon. Between Chapters 6 and 10, this historical record is compared with the data on the low and middle income countries in the last two decades, with respect to many of the same characteristics. It is thus possible crudely to compare the contemporary cross section of economic records with the historical trends, to relate change over time to scatter through space, and to make interesting comparisons between the position of the underdeveloped countries of today and the historical position of today's industrial countries at the earlier periods of their transformation.

From all this work, Kuznets concludes that a single collection of characteristics characterizes a modern developed country, notably: high income per capita (the definition of development), moderate population growth, a low share of agriculture in product, a large share of transport and government in service expenditures, a rather high share of labor in income payments, and various investment and financial ratios lying within reasonably narrow limits. Modern economic growth is then, in this view, the fairly uniform result of a process in a national economy and society which has itself many uniform characteristics from country to country. This impression in turn permits Kuznets in Chapter 1 to set the work in a larger historical frame. He defines here the concept of an economic 'epoch' as a large period over which such tendency toward uniformity prevails. The modern epoch he dates from the early eighteenth century in England, following upon the epoch of mercantile capitalism which had spread through Western Europe. Its defining characteristic in turn is a 'science-based technology,' and it is accompanied by institutional and social changes that permit that technology to take effect. Modern economic history then describes the spread of these non-economic characteristics, and of the economic structure accompanying them, from one country to another. The attitudes needed "to accommodate and foster adjustment of social institutions and practices to the exploitation of the potential provided by science-based technology" are "suggested by three terms: secularism, egalitarianism, and nationalism."

What now is an economic historian to say to all this? The practitioners of our subject have always been drawn in opposite directions – toward the minute and the mystical, the local and the universal, the documentary evidence and the overarching imaginative construct. Kuznets is pulled in these two directions too, and is able to sound like Marx or Weber in Chapter 1 and like – well, the dean of income accountants, in Chapters 4 and 5. Has he then brought it off? Has he made his concept of a modern epoch 'operational' and defined it by his statistics? Do his data show the spread of a single economic organism with somewhat uniform structural characteristics, and do they show that this has followed the spread of technological knowledge, the adaptations of institutions, and the growth beneath it all of attitudes of secularism, egalitarianism and nationalism? The verdict, I think, must be that they do not show this in any refined way, or in any way superior to the general descriptive techniques of a course in economic history. Indeed the generalizations about causes rest upon loose impressions of economic history. But on the other hand, by use of the quantitative evidence, Kuznets has established some main facts to be explained by economic historians, and – most important – has established these in a world-wide perspective. The body of the book then presents not an explanation but rather the *explicandum* of modern economic history. It gives the outline of a program in which model-builders and historians may direct their peculiar efforts to produce a useful, cumulative result.

First, one peculiarity of Kuznets's own thought must be gotten out of the way. In a truly international approach to world economic history, the national state features, not as a fundamental unit of analysis, but as one of the many institutions adjusting, affecting and regulating the great social and intellectual impulses by which productivity is increased. Kuznets – the stamp of his great work with the American data upon him – cannot quite shed its trammels. For him, today as in 1951 early in this project, the national state remains the 'fundamental unit of analysis'.

This he maintains despite the fact that his data show a very remarkable similarity in the growth rates of the fourteen industrializing states, and that all his conclusions point to similarities in their structures. The main task suggested by this work is to explain why these countries as a group showed high and similar rates of growth for a hundred years, and it is this group rather than the individual political subdivisions of it that is the fundamental unit of analysis.

Beneath the level of the developing world, the next truly fundamental level of analysis is the individual – that unreachable quantum in history, whom we can observe only here and there lonesomely in memoirs or diaries, or else in the jelly-like masses of aggregated statistics. The records of the behavior of groups of individuals are available in statistics, and in the generalizations and impressions made by observers of social conditions. The sample of evidence is poor and distorted, but it is all the history we have, and it is the material over which historians have spent their lives. Now the income statistics of countries are simply one aggregation of the records of individual economic units, as are the statistics of an industry, or a smaller political subdivision. Careful comparison of these groups may show something of the different effects of state policy or peculiarities of national character on economic reactions. Indeed, the array of national data presents a very curious puzzle. Suppose we take an area over which as a whole average per capita income grows at an average decade rate of 15% for 100 years. Now divide this area into fifteen regions of very unequal size, population and resource endowment, and of quite different income levels. Why should these fifteen regions grow at roughly the same rates themselves, preserving much the same differentials at the end of the period as at the beginning, and exhibiting – when their economies are taken as units – much the same structural characteristics? The explanation requires a set of growth models, in which very great substitution is possible among the elements and among which very special assumptions about trade and factor movement are present. To explicate this is an important and interesting task, but once done, one has solved a somewhat artificial question. Another grouping of the individual data, e.g., by industry, religion, region, race, or social status, would show other results and require a different set of explanatory variables. The fundamental question, to which the whole resources of history and the sciences of social behavior should be bent, is – why did the incomes of individuals grow in these areas and to what constellation of social and economic forces is the growth of just those incomes to be attributed? To answer this question, one must investigate the spread of modern attitudes, techniques and economic practices not just from one nation to another, but within nations and among international occupational and social classes.

To an economic historian, then, Kuznets's book represents a halfway house on the road to a full understanding of the modern epoch. No one else has gone nearly so far, or has dared to put down in numbers 'what oft was thought, but ne'er so well expressed'. There is a danger that in casting the data in the form of comparative national accounts, artificial puzzles may be created, and time used in solving them. The dangers of identifying a nation with an economy, and of seeing the world as a collection of national acounts, are as great to an economist as to a politician. We know that modern economic growth, at least for a spell, exacerbates political nationalism. The reaction is partly a unifying one, coming from an effort to overcome the localism and ruralism that hinders resource mobility and the spread of ideas. But it is also a culturally atavistic one – an effort to hold on to human values against the corrosive effects of international industrial technology and society. The nation itself is a variable in modern economic growth, and the great virtue of Kuznets's book is that in exploring and comparing national accounts he has demonstrated that except as an accounting unit, the nation is as anachronistic in the economy as in the politics of the modern world. Perhaps it is time for national income accountants themselves to look further, toward both larger and smaller groupings of their data.

[Originally published in *Review of Income and Wealth,* Journal of International Association for Research in Income and Wealth, Income and Wealth Series 13, No. 2, June 1967, 199–202. Reprinted by permission.]

André Gunder Frank. *World Accumulation, 1492–1789.* London and New York: Monthly Review Press, 1978.

History – total history – like Rumpelstiltskin, loses its power when you call it by its name. But since no one knows its true name, the game goes on. We hear noises and see lights in the fog, and we strike out wildly with the sharp swords of theory and insight, only to hear the creature calling to us from another part of the field, beckoning us to a more removed ground. When we tighten our terms and our reasoning, understanding and verisimilitude slip away like a bar of soap. We deepen and broaden our learning, adding case to case, region to region, period to period, and we reveal to ourselves only greater complexities, deeper chasms of ignorance, more unexpected forms of unpredictability. Theory and reason, learning, memory and energy, total sincerity and pressing present need – all these send us to study history, but none of our sacrifices does more than to call the goddess to the door of the temple. She passes by inside and we remain, standing without.

Gunder Frank's treatment of the early modern period of the 'world economy' is another gift laid on the altar. It seems almost to cry out for hostile reviewers to set the torch. Nothing can be more touching than the evident sincerity of his belief that history can be known and used. And perhaps this book, like his others, has a use, in the present, as a weapon in a popular struggle for socialism in underdeveloped countries. Yet one may wonder whether he is not using the polemics of the last war to fight the next. Outside of Latin America, most of the world's poor people now *are* under socialism of one form or another. Only a handful are colonial subjects of the European powers. Are the outrages of Cortez and Pizzaro, of east European lords, of British adventurers or sugar planters or slave traders the right targets today for socialist attack?

Frank's version of the early modern period, like Immanuel Wallerstein's slightly earlier and more compendious treatment, represents one variant of contemporary Marxist historiography. It follows a line laid out by Sweezy in emphasizing the corrosive influence of capitalist trade on pre-capitalist social relations, both in feudal Europe and overseas. In Frank, it is colonial exploitation rather than, as in Marx, domestic expropriation, which is emphasized as the source of original accumulation and the expansive power of capitalism. Heat, he quotes Mao as saying, may be applied to a stone or to an egg: a chicken comes from the egg, nothing comes from the stone; the difference is their internal structure. But Frank has not much to say about the structures of egg or of stone. His talk is mostly about the heat. Such an emphasis threatens to become, like Rostow's stage theories, a kind of national Marxism, with the social classes left out. It shows a world history centered around the exploitation of poor nations by rich nations, and produces a version of imperialism not much different from Schumpeter's. Frank does not go this far since he is deeply wedded to the notion that capitalist accumulation, indeed the specific thirst for gold, unleashed somehow from Europe in the 15th century, is the source of the dynamic of the world economy. But to leave the impression that this thirst is a kind of European culture-trait, the distinguishing fact which drove Europeans to enslave and exploit the world, is to give not a Marxist, but a Weberian, version of world history. A bourgeois historian may prefer it, but is it what Frank intends?

The difficulty in the end with using history for present purposes lies in the too narrow definition of those purposes. For to narrow purposes, the lessons of history have nothing to say. Can those who are sensitive to the deepest needs of the modern world, who look ahead into its future, rather than back on the battles and scars of the immediate past – whether they call themselves socialists or not – allow themselves a version of history which does such violence to the real life of the past, to its men and women, its revolutionaries and reactionaries, its artists and thinkers, its structures of belief? Is no history at all not a better guide to action than a 'total history' ringing with a shrill anti-imperialist jingoism, no matter how sincerely felt or how finely decked out in the best terminology of Marxist scholarship?

Walt W. Rostow. *The World Economy: History and Prospect.* Austin and London: University of Texas Press, 1978. Pp. xiv, 833.

Walt Rostow is known to economists as the author of *The Stages of Economic Growth,* an exciting Western about nations which gallop like riderless horses from stage to stage. But economic historians know of an earlier Rostow who emerged from the chrysalis of a National Bureau–type study of British cycles to write an even more exciting study of *Trends in the British Economy in the Nineteenth Century.* Between *Trends* and *Stages* appeared a more purely theoretical effort, *The Process of Economic Growth,* which closed before making Broadway. If the studies of British cycles represented Rostow's stay in a traditional economic historian's society, the *Process* book his uncertain formation of preconditions for his career, and the *Stages* his take-off, he has since then shown all the evidence of self-sustained growth on this drive to maturity. Between *Stages* and the book here under review came at least seven books, totalling 2600 pages, on the Communist world and American relations with it and on America's position in world politics and the world economy generally. These included *Politics and the Stages of Growth* (1971), sometimes referred to as 'Son of Stages', and the rambling *Diffusion of Power* (1972) based on his Washington years. But *The World Economy* shows the drive to maturity completed; it is a book ripe for high mass consumption. Rostow's incursions into theory and politics have troubled many of his peers, but there is no question that he is a closer approximation to an economic historian *type pur* than perhaps anyone of his generation.

In *The World Economy* then, Rostow has got his act together. He mixes history, theory, and statistics in a way that would have gladdened Schumpeter's heart. The assumptions or inductive observations underlying the organization and generalizations of the trend periods are roughly these:

(1) food, raw materials, construction and industrial goods have expanded at uneven rates in complex patterns, affected by many historical contingencies, over the past 200 years; nevertheless,

(2) largely due to lags in bringing new food and raw material sources into production, but also to some lumpiness in industrial technology and some

lagged effects of migration, population growth, and wars, the aggregate growth has proceeded with long fluctuations in output growth and composition, price levels and relationships in the classical Kondratief periods of alternating upswings and downswings: 1790–1815 (up)–1848–1873–1896–1920–1936–1950–1972.

(3) Relative price movements, especially shifts in terms of trade between industry and agriculture, and switches in investment in response to opportunities and interest rate movements have governed this process, which

(4) has been characterized in each period by certain leading sectors, which respond strongly to high demand and striking technological improvement, and diffuse their cost reduction and higher earnings through the industrial structure.

(5) Population growth and technological change are not looked on as bits of endogenous machinery in a meta-economic model, but are taken as partly independent processes, depending on social and intellectual history, only partially influenced by feedbacks from the economic history.

From such a loose reconstruction of the behavior of the economic statistics over 200 years, mixing Schumpeter, Kondratief, and Kuznets, Rostow is able to adopt a rather definite point of view toward the present and prospective situation of the world economy. In particular, it might be inferred, though he does not explicitly state it, that the 'downswing' from 1950 to 1972 was a definite break in the previous pattern. As in the 'downswing' of the 1880's and early 1890's, there was growth in real output with relatively falling agricultural prices. But any alternations between agricultural and industrial expansion may now not occur, since agricultural expansion is based no longer on empty lands or simple technical changes but on a major branch of an essentially industrial chemical, or bio-chemical, technology. The accumulating supply problems that broke in 1972 and may produce slower growth rates for some time before a real upturn could occur, have been based on relative supply constriction in agriculture and raw materials as well perhaps as on a period of consolidation in industrial technology. Perhaps we are moving out of the world of the 19th century Kondratief altogether, and even drifting away from noticeable secular growth. Rostow's view of history is sufficiently deterministic to suggest that governments cannot alter these underlying technological and social controls on world economic expansion, but he is much too much of an optimist to exclude a role for what he calls public policy. Governments, particularly on an international basis, can do something, to redistribute gains, to smooth out kinks, prevent short-run fluctuations, even perhaps to control population.

Rostow's book then does not contain a model, but it is a plausible account of some elements he observes in the economic statistics since the 1780's, where regularities and contingencies are both observable and where several model mechanisms surface like Loch Ness monsters at enough points to show signs of some continuing presence. This is not statistical testing, but it is statistical description, in the historian's mode, animating just enough theoretical generalization to keep it interesting. Moreover, without claiming to uncover the "law of motion of capitalism", its statements about the course of recent history and the problems of coming decades are informed and carry a weight derived from the historical survey.

It is said that economic historians do their best work in their sixties – at least economic historians in their fifties claim this. This is clearly Rostow's best book, the highest development of the art form he has made his own. No one has ever accused its creator of undue modesty in his claims; yet this time there is a certain temperateness in the book. No longer is he billing the work as an alternative to Marx, or the definitive theory of economic dynamics. He states his limits, brings out his familiar themes – leading sectors, terms of trade, technology à la Schumpeter, the automobile revolution, etc. – and weaves them together. What worlds then are left for the Rostow of the late 1970's to conquer as he continues through his seventh decade? One thread in the present study is, I suggest, left hanging. There is need for a tighter stitching into the fabric of the twenty national case studies, in the section on Stages (pp. 363–569). Even adopting both parts of Rostow's model, or myth, ('parable' would be a word with a precedent in such a usage) – stages and trends – how do they fit together? How would a cross-tabulation of the countries, by stages and by the position of the world trend when they entered them, look? Do countries which enter the take-off in an upswing of the Kondratief differ from those whose entry occurs in downswing? Of course the flaw in the garments which Rostow throws over the nakedness of history is that when you pull at loose threads, things start to unravel. This scandalizes some economists, but historians surely will understand the problem and sympathize with the tailor. And the older, wiser, and more secure scholar that Rostow shows himself to be in this book may even overcome the difficulty. One way to integrate national stages and world trends would be, of course, simply to drop altogether the idea of stages and the unit of the nation-state in which the economic history is expressed. But that Rostow is unlikely to do.

[Originally published in *Journal of Economic History*, XXXVIII (4), December 1978, 1041–1043. Reprinted by permission.]

PART V

European capitalism: a synthetic view

11

Opportunity sequences in European history

All history-writing, whether Ranke's or Rostow's, is a stylization of the infinity of facts, and all theorizing on history is a stylization of the infinity of relationships among them. Over the past twenty-five years, in teaching the economic history of Europe to graduate students in economics, I have selected three stylized relationships as the core around which to assemble the record. (It is well-known that three, being the number of observable dimensions in our human world, is the largest number which people can hold simultaneously in their minds; a science which rests on three factors of production should appreciate the point.)

The groups of relations around which I assemble each year the facts of European economic history each bear the name of a notable economic theorist: Malthus, Smith, and Schumpeter. Malthus is taken to symbolize the evident truth: that a population, reproducing geometrically, has the potential of outrunning its food supply. Smith symbolizes the notion that the extent of the market limits the division of labor, and that over history the extension of the market raises the limits of the division of labor, producing through scale economies and specialization higher levels of productivity. Schumpeter is a name for capitalist expansion deriving from continuous, though fluctuating, technological change and innovation, financed by the extension of credit.

It should be noted at once that these three expansionary processes are not conceived wholly as stages, and do not follow each other in linear sequence over the historical record. All three are tendencies, continuously active. Nevertheless, it is apparent that in the period before 1750,

Originally published in C. P. Kindleberger and G. DiTella, *Economics in the Long View, Essays in Honour of W. W. Rostow* (London: Macmillan, 1982, Vol. II), pp. 1–24. Reprinted by permission.

the Malthusian tendency is very strong—before 1500, probably dominant. Between 1500 and 1900, it is overlaid by the Smithian tendency yielding productivity growth with growth of trade. And after 1770 or thereabouts, Schumpeter's cast of characters steps forward on the stage and the ceaseless transformation of production functions, with its accompanying "creative destruction," takes over the leading role. The three processes then are themes of the complex opera of history, each dominating a successive Act, but on stage throughout, swelling up together in a happy nineteenth-century trio, and moving together in the world today into—who knows what grand finale?

A sketch of the operation of these processes over history, then demands not only a simple statement of their essential character, but also an analysis of:

(1) How each came to dominate history in certain periods and to be subordinate in others
(2) How the transitions from a Malthusian to a Smithian to a Schumpeterian dominance occurred
(3) What exogenous forces, or processes from political or intellectual history – not readily interpreted in economic or even social terms – impinged to release or to restrict their movement
(4) What feedbacks occurred from the later Smithian and Schumpeterian processes to the Malthusian population phenomena, and from the Schumpeterian technological change to Smithian trade expansion and market growth

This essay can offer no more than the merest sketch of the history conceived in these terms. An appendix outlines some of the feedbacks among the three processes in more detail. Rostow may see in my three-process schema three stages of his five-stage schema – the Malthusian traditional society, the Smithian preconditions, and the Schumpeterian drive to maturity. But perhaps none of us in European economic history does much more than warm over the three revolutions, agricultural, commercial, industrial – as Lillian Knowles and Paul Mantoux presented them, sixty years ago – with a little modern spicing.[1] But my schema moves into the present and future, I think, in a rather different direction from the others and the present paper, moving sketchily over the terrain, tries to follow it there.

[1]See L. C. A. Knowles, *The Industrial and Commercial Revolutions in Great Britain During the Nineteenth Century*, London, 1926. Knowles does not deal with the agricultural revolution, but Mantoux devotes an important chapter to it. See P. Mantoux, *The Industrial Revolution of the Eighteenth Century*, 2nd ed., London, 1961.

MALTHUSIAN PROCESSES IN HISTORY[2]

Malthus and his poor we have always with us. Human society, like that of every other species, runs continuously the danger of excessive population growth, and a history, if not a social policy, can be organized around "escapes" from it. In Western Europe, there is some historical evidence that widespread population growth occurred, initially stimulating and ultimately dangerous, in the thirteenth and early fourteenth centuries and again in the sixteenth, with the modern rise beginning in the mid- to late eighteenth century. As a mnemonic, one might accept a rough dating of every third century – the thirteenth, the sixteenth, and the nineteenth – as periods of general population rise in the West and the intervening centuries as periods either of disaster (the fourteenth and in Germany the early seventeenth) or of stagnation or merely localized rise (the fifteenth, seventeenth, and parts of the eighteenth and the twentieth).

There are two problems in such a dating, or in using population trends as a basis of much economic change in these periods. One is that the data on the periods of growth are not very good. The estimates still rest – I believe – largely on the 1900 work of Beloch for 1600 as the centerpoint, on Levasseur's equally early collection of contemporary French estimates, on Russell's researches based on the English poll tax of 1377, and on the early nineteenth century census benchmarks summarized in Reinhard, Armengaud, and Dupâquier (1968). Recently local studies of parish records back into the seventeenth century and archaeological evidence of the extent of city walls and margins of cultivation have given the tale some local color.[3] To use the evidence of

[2]An interesting starting point for the study of modern population growth is the brief and bold sketch in B. H. Slicher van Bath, the *The Agrarian History of Western Europe, 500–1850*, London and New York, 1963, 77–98, which collates M. K. Bennett's estimates with those of Russell and Abel. See M. K. Bennett, *The World's Food*, New York, 1954; J. C. Russell, *British Medieval Population*, Albuquerque, 1948; and W. Abel, *Die Wüstungen des ausgehenden Mittelalters*, 2nd ed., 1955. Bennett is based, it appears, on Beloch ["Die bevolkerung Europas," *Zeitschrift für Sozialwissenschaft*, 1900, 3, 405–33 (im Mittelalter); 765–86 (zur Zeit der Renaissance)], while Russell and Abel cover less than all of Europe. The movement of the series is very roughly the same, but obscurity surrounding the movement of the French population, which exceeds Germany and England combined, gives rise to doubts. The most recent survey appears to be the third (1968) edition of M. Reinhard, A. Armengand, and J. Dupaquier, *Histoire Générale de la Population Mondiale*, 3rd ed., Paris, 1968. The same trends are observable in the regional and provincial data. See also the rather brief sampling in C. Wilson and G. Parker (eds.), *An Introduction to the Sources of European Economic History, I, Western Europe*, London, 1977.

[3]The work of the Cambridge group in England has done somewhat more than this, thanks to a sampling of 404 parish records from 1540 to 1840. The gap between baptisms and burials indicates population growth from 1560 to 1660,

rising relative prices of food as evidence for population growth in the thirteenth and sixteenth centuries, and then to attribute that price behavior solely to population growth is too immediately circular a mode of reasoning to be immediately persuasive. But surely it is fair to feel – as Postan has – that those price movements help to confirm other evidence of a rising trend.

But is the limit – if there is one – in the intervening centuries indeed "Malthusian"? Is it overpopulation in some meaningful sense which produces the catastrophe of the fourteenth century and the stagnation (or worse) of the seventeenth, and is it an agricultural restraint which Northwest Europe bursts through, or wriggles out of, after 1750? Unquestionably there is short-run sensitivity to local harvest failures. And it does seem inherently plausible that a thicker population is weakened as it presses on food supplies, and is carried off disproportionately more readily by communicable disease and military depradations. But one must admit that it is far from totally clear that the checks that appear are a result of excessive human fecundity rather than wars, climate changes, or the random incidence of disease. Perhaps that is all we know and all we need to know.[4]

A MECHANISM FOR THE TRANSITION

An interpretation of economic change from 1300 to 1700 need not rest in any case strongly on strictly Malthusian assumptions. If the mere rough dating of the population rises is accepted, some interesting questions form; i.e., why the difference in the population's economic and social behavior in the three periods? Why did not the expansion of the sixteenth century follow on the thirteenth-century peak of medieval expansion? Why was Europe condemned to 150 years of plagues and wars before the Renaissance and the Discoveries? And why then did the industrial and agrarian changes of the post-1770 years not come at once, without the intervening wretchedness, ferment, and wars of the seventeenth and early eighteenth centuries? The answer to all such questions is of course that history takes time. In a world of instantaneous adjustment, the modern

then stability to 1740 (with some moderate rise from 1700), then a noticeable rise in baptisms with relatively stable numbers of deaths on to 1840. See the summary in C. Wilson and G. Parker (eds.), op. cit., 1977, 115–119.

[4]This flippant literary dismissal of the problem will do perhaps for the moment. But the problem is somewhat different from Keats's in trying to distinguish between truth and beauty. Obviously if nature, or political events rather than "internal dynamic" produce population "cycles," the history requires a much broader model, as wide as the whole creation, for its explanatory structure.

world – indeed the future itself – would have sprung full blown from the Garden of Eden. Time is required for the parts of the total historical process to unfold, to follow their separate paths, and to come together in just the concatenation that produces a particular historical event.

A population on the land can increase at increasing returns, even without trade and specialization and more intensive cultivation techniques, if movement is into better new areas rather than on to poorer land, as Ricardo had assumed. But it is fairly clear that such a spread of an agricultural population in Europe, which occurred after about 5000 B.C., had come to an end by 1200 A.D. In Western Europe there were no surprises in store – only the cutting down of more woodland, movement into highlands, and the draining of marshes. The evidence of pollen samples, dated from soundings in marginal areas, as interpreted by Slicher van Bath (1963, p. 117), seems to show periods when the margin of cultivation of the grains moved back and forth over the poorer land – presumably in response to changing population pressure. It is sufficient, moreover, for a transition from a Malthusian to a Smithian dynamic that the population growth be accompanied by an increase in the total volume of agricultural production above subsistence, i.e., in *absolute,* if not the *per capita* size of the real, or potential agricultural "surplus."[5] If this increase occurs without any pressure on agricultural producers to create and give up – in rents, taxes, or trade – their surplus above subsistence, then the population growth increases the absolute amount of idle rural labor, i.e., a surplus not exploited either by lords or by the market, but potentially available nonetheless, either to be worked in more intensive cultivation on the land or to move into employment off the land, depending on the returns and opportunities for employment.

Now if a political or economic mechanism for extracting agricultural goods and labor is available, the supplies added or realizable, by a growing population above its subsistence are available to enter into trade or production outside agriculture and so to increase the absolute

[5]Henry Palairet and Rosalind Mitchison (Edinburgh) in discussion of this paper reminded me of the limitations on the concept of a "surplus above subsistence." They pointed out that: (1) food intake varies with activity and vice versa, and (2) over time a population adjusts physiologically to a surprising degree to the size and nutritional content of its standard diet. "Subsistence" then consists not of a single physical daily intake of each nutrient, but a zone within which more or less activity can be carried on with limits which can change over time as the size and build of individuals in a population responds to conditions of food supply. These functional relationships between "subsistence," physical activity, and body size must be taken into account if the size of the potential agricultural "surplus" over and above such limits is to be measured. But they do not, it seems to me, invalidate the concept of such a surplus.

volume of trade and nonagricultural output. Or if the agricultural population retains title to and control over its labor and the fruits thereof, this "surplus" is available as a broadly based market for nonfarm output. Population growth under conditions of not too sharply diminishing returns, i.e., with marginal product in excess of subsistence greater than zero, increases the total incomes of the class of receivers of rents, tithes, taxes, and the like (though individual incomes in their class depend upon *its* rate of increases as well – since Malthusian fecundity knows no class boundaries) and with it, the market for their "luxuries," as well as the potential market for the cruder goods consumed in peasant households. Whether this latter market demand is realized and becomes effective depends on how hard the lords and tax gatherers press on the peasantry and on whether merchants can penetrate into the countryside to bring to life latent patterns of peasant demand.

If then trade and nonagricultural production can occur in this situation under conditions of increasing returns (the Smithian dynamic) or in some sort of built-in sequence of endogenous technological change (the Schumpeterian dynamic), population growth induces productivity growth and possibly, depending on the net result of the movements in agricultural and nonagricultural productivity, higher total per capita incomes in the economy as a whole. And if the growth of trade and the availability of industrial or imported products occurs in products and places that can call out the "potential surplus," i.e., tempt peasants to work harder, then a mechanism to produce a rising output is operative, to be checked only as the effects of diminishing returns in agriculture (or of some exogenous factor) slows down or reverses the population growth.

INCREASING RETURNS IN TRADE

Is it possible that the expansion of local and overseas trade in the sixteenth and seventeenth centuries, and the industrial growth accompanying this expansion, met with increasing returns? Why should this occur?

Several sources may be conceived of. First, there is the standard source of increasing returns: the spreading of fixed costs. River ports and harbors, docks and ships, warehouses, and the knowledge of sea lanes are large items of fixed capital. As their use expanded in Italy in the sixteenth century, in the United Provinces in the seventeenth century, and in England in the late seventeenth and eighteenth centuries, per unit costs presumably fell. Douglass North and Ralph Davis have well detailed the fall in shipping costs that accompanied the expansion of shipping in the eighteenth and early nineteenth centuries, the elimination of overcapacity and empty backhauls that accompanied the increased complexity of shipping routes, and the greater variety of products to be shipped. The advent of navies, the elimination of piracy, the greater capacity of merchant vessels which could forego the need for armament – these effects of large scale in mercantile activity were all present in the expansion of the late eighteenth and early to mid-nineteenth centuries. May they not also to a degree have been present in the sixteenth? Still it must be admitted that the whole scale of trade in the sixteenth and seventeenth centuries relative to the mass of local agricultural production was minuscule, except for the shipment of Eastern European grain through the Sound to the Netherlands and beyond. De Vries indicates that these shipments probably furnished the bulk of the Dutch urban grain requirements – not as much as the world furnished England after 1850, but still a lot. Apart from grain, textiles, and timber, the trade – to Spain, France, England, and the East – was a trade in "luxuries."

Nevertheless, such a trade is not to be despised by historians, infected though they may be by the sensitivity of a democratic and egalitarian age. It is through the trade in luxuries that capitalism enters European agrarian society. The ferment that began with the Crusades and was checked by the crises of the fourteenth and fifteenth centuries bubbled up again in the Renaissance. The commodities available through trade – fine textiles, spices, precious metals, and metal wares – fitted well the structure of demand in a Europe where, despite gains made by the French peasantry through the labor shortage of the fifteenth century, the rate of exploitation by lords, church, and royal courts was high.

Before the growth of "plantations," and the sugar, tobacco, and slave trades of the late seventeenth and eighteenth centuries, the discoveries and overseas trade produced increasing returns in European trade more through their effect in establishing capitalist institutions and practices and supporting centralized state power than directly through the cheapening of luxury goods. Here the scale of state demand may have brought Adam Smith's celebrated principles of organization into play. The luxury demand, the demand of courts and states was hardly a standardized demand for mass manufactures; a large part of it was a demand for rather simple labor – soldiers, seamen, servants, and construction workers – and above these for "officials" – tax gatherers, estate managers, and overseas and military officers. But a demand for artisan labor in fairly standard categories accompanied this – for cloth workers, masons, carpenters, toolmakers, metal workers, clockmakers, mint masters, bookmakers, and copiers. And there was a demand for services more properly labeled "bourgeois," i.e., the skilled trades –

entertainers, academics, artists, actors, doctors, lawyers, and at last businesspeople (or at least people of business), bankers, notaries, money changers, enterprisers of all sorts, and merchants.[6]

None of these trades was new. Trevor-Roper emphasized the growth of a market in courts and administrative centers as well as in the medieval cities – now somewhat eclipsed. The important fact was the new *scale* on which they all functioned and were demanded. That scale brought division of labor in trades and business services, and it made the provision of overhead capital and institutions – universities, law courts, a civil bureaucracy, and army – worthwhile. Centralization made governments stronger – in Philip II's Spain, Henry VIII's England, the France of Richelieu and Mazarin, even in the "United" Provinces. Did it make them all richer? Did it make for a more efficient utilization of the surplus extracted from a growing population on the land?[7] In addition to economies of scale in the spreading of fixed physical and institutional (or transactional) costs, the phenomenon of diffusion also occurs – the spreading of arts and knowledge, the imitation at one point of what has always been done and known at another. A third source of growth is regional specialization on a pan-European scale. Outside of agriculture, can this have been important? Wallerstein for one, has recently emphasized the economies of centralization and localization in financial markets.[8]

The price movements of the late sixteenth and early seventeenth centuries are the salient feature of this history. Once again as in the fourteenth century, the terms of trade turned against industry – and in the midst of a general price inflation. There is indicated here both a growing population pressure and a relatively rapid growth in productivity outside of agriculture. The shift is usually interpreted as rising agricultural prices; but it is also a case of relatively falling industrial prices. And indeed if the surplus from the land is being extracted and commercialized more effectively, peasants might go hungry, but why should supplies on commercial markets be short? And how could the vast new

[6]Two interesting recent pieces of research suggest how the market had developed by the late seventeenth century. See P. H. Lindert, *English Occupations, 1670–1811*, Working Paper 14, University of California, Davis, 1980, where a sizable sample of burial records and scattered early urban occupational censuses is examined, and R. M. Berger, "The Development of Retail Trade in Provincial England, ca. 1550–1700," *Journal of Economic History*, 1980, *40*, 123–128; this study of retail trade in three towns and scattered places in Central and Southern England.

[7]See the balanced and suggestive concluding chapter 7 in J. de Vries, *The Dutch Rural Economy in the Golden Age*, 1500–1700, New Haven, 1974.

[8]See J. R. Hicks, *A Theory of Economic History*, Oxford, 1969; these essays on the subjects of this paragraph provide many valuable and plausible insights.

demand for nonagricultural products be satisfied at falling prices, except by appreciable productivity improvements?[9]

This brings us to the final question of technological change in Nef's Industrial Revolution of the sixteenth century.[10] It is evident that some stirrings of technical change were felt – in mining and metallurgy, and these were responding to a growing demand for metals, and in England for coal. The waterwheel was put to more intensive use in milling, fulling, and iron working, and with the ribbon loom and the stocking frame, even textile operations were touched, according to Usher, at two very specialized points. The increase in minting, with royal coinages, utilized the stamping and pressing operations on which Gutenberg drew. So industrial techniques – in ships, firearms, clocks, scientific instruments – improved, but the body of improvement, lacking a new power source or any appreciable cheapening in raw materials, did not create a wholly new technology or set in motion a self-propelling sequence of technological change.

AGRICULTURAL IMPROVEMENT

To produce a sustained dynamic, it is not enough that the Smithian process of trade expansion should produce growing productivity in trade and industry, a growing middle-class demand for large-scale industrial products, or laws and behavior patterns that facilitate business activity. The Malthusian demon is not yet laid to rest; that requires either "moral restraint," or increases in agricultural supplies, or both in some combination. I indicated above how some increases in agricultural productivity could occur simply *via* the expansion of distant trade. Surely the major effect was by regional specialization such that agricultural regions best suited to grow a crop were put in touch with its markets. The trouble with this is that in times of high transport costs and uneven distribution of factors, the cost differentials between different regions due to natural causes are smothered under transport cost differentials and interregional differences in factor proportions. This effect of trade carried on into the nineteenth century, when the world's agricultural regions took their current shape. It increased the world's food supplies after land and ocean transport costs had fallen and capital and labor had spread into new areas, which could outcompete the old.

[9] C. Wilson and G. Parker (eds.) op. cit., 1977, pp. 103–105, 139, 181, 216–218 give an all too brief, up-to-date review of the price history.

[10] D. C. Coleman's incisive critique of the various 'industrial revolutions' of modern history, and especially of Nef, is an essential reference here. See D. C. Coleman, "Industrial Growth and Industrial Revolutions," *Economica, 523, 1956, 1–22.*

The second effect of trade on agriculture was the diffusion of seeds, stock, and techniques. Here the New World's corn and potatoes come into play after the mid-eighteenth century, but in the earlier centuries, nothing of importance is evident.

Trade and urbanization in the seventeenth and eighteenth centuries do appear to have made inroads on rural underemployment by fostering the growth of rural industries, inducing peasants to work harder and farm more intensively, giving incentive for improvement and specialization of livestock breeds, and stimulating some steps in the so-called agricultural revolution, i.e., the conversion of the three-field system rotation to a system of continuous cropping with sowing or planting of the fallow in cover or root crops. This increased the productivity of land both directly and by the additional fertilizer supplies provided, and the latter at least increased the productivity of the labor in tasks which are fixed per acre. Slicher van Bath shows that in England and the Netherlands yield–seed ratios rose, and on the Continent, a technique of immense reserve capacity was made known and readied for use in the real population expansion of the nineteenth century.

More important still, the improvements – at least those related to livestock – seem not to have been forced out of the system by population pressure from below – as the well-known Boserup model suggests – but to have been *pulled* out by an urban and middle-class demand of high income elasticity. Here then is the "breather" which Arthur John and Eric Jones found that population growth may have given at least to England in the decades around 1700 to have allowed incomes and living standards to rise to levels sufficient to form a broader demand for the industrial goods of the Industrial Revolution.

Some final elements that distinguished the trade and overseas markets of the eighteenth century from their still-medieval composition in the age of the Discoveries were of course the trade in slaves and in the products of colonial "plantations," the early exploitation of the surplus, the supplies and the vast peasant demand of India, and the reproduction of a whole new urban trading society in the West of England ports – Southampton, Bristol, and finally Liverpool – as sugar, tobacco, and colonial cotton entered as the staples, along with New England's fish and timber. I have not seen the weighting of this in England's total trade before 1800, but from 1720 on it is clearly important in its own right as a market as well as a source of movable merchandise and liquid wealth for a mercantile class.[11]

[11]As the reader will observe, the comments in the preceding and following section are a kind of home brew, made up of bits of a Dobb, a Sweezy, a

THE TRANSITION TO ECO-TECHNIC CHANGE

At this point, i.e., about 1750, a truly new element enters the scene. It must appear if we are to furnish an answer to the question: Why did the collection of iron, machinery, and power inventions that we call the Industrial Revolution not come into existence in the upswing of the sixteenth and early seventeenth centuries, at the time of Nef's Industrial Revolution? The answer, I think, is in two parts, and both go deeply into the attitudes and organization that underlie economic change. The first is signified, though much too simply, by what historians call the growth of science; the second, again, by economies of scale and communication. Let me elaborate each a little more fully to indicate the point at which they fused into the single phenomenon, the Industrial Revolution.

Every freshman survey of European history identifies the late sixteenth and the seventeenth centuries with the real beginnings of experimental science and that joint development of empiricism and rationalism that together have provided Western man's understanding of nature and his ephemeral illusion of control over nature which made possible nineteenth- and twentieth-century expansion and destruction. Rationalism, model-building, exact reasoning from assumed premises, has been present as an element in Western thought at least since Euclid. It is a

Hobsbawm, a Trevor-Roper, and their associated controversialists, as well as information and impressions gleaned from 'bourgeois' historians (Trevor-Roper rates as an aristocratic, rather than a bourgeois, writer in this context), insofar as these writers seem to me to to provide evidence of the *economic* processes at work in the period. See H. R. Trevor-Roper, "The General Crisis of the Seventeenth Century," in T. Aston (ed.), *Crisis in Europe, 1560–1660*, New York, 1967, reprinted from *Past and Present,* II (1959); and H. R. Trevor-Roper, "Religion, Reformation and Social Change," *Historical Studies*, 4, 1963. That the controversies over the interpretation of this period remain unsettled, and incapable even of being reviewed, as in the recent work of I. Wallerstein, *The Modern World-System*, New York, 1974, and A. Gunder Frank, *World Accumulation, 1492–1789*, New York, 1978, is partly due to ideological differences, but also to lack of a thoroughly quantitative attack on the data, though much has been done by individual scholars. Dr. P. K. O'Brien, St. Antony's College, Oxford, for example, has made an effort to quantify the extent of the overseas trade in British trade, and to relate the volume of profits to British net investment. An outside estimate of volume would place it at not more than 10 to 15 percent of British foreign trade in the mid-eighteenth century. Figures on profits are too uncertain as yet to give a good indication of their size relative to net investment. However, the profit and savings rates would have had to be fantastically high to have permitted a body of mercantile capital accounting for so small a fraction of national product to have generated any large proportion of net savings.

human propensity that expressed itself in the sixteenth-century theology no less than in mathematics. What is sometimes forgotten is that empiricism – fumbling trial and error with a vague goal in mind, observation sharpened by keen perception of needs, or simply random mutation selected for survival by a cruel physical or social environment – these activities of the mind and senses have been around even longer. No defined theory of mechanics guided the shaping of the first stone axe. It came, we must conceive, as an intuitive extension of the use of an unshaped or accidentally axe-shaped natural stone. Altogether the neolithic revolution took at least five-thousand years to work out the basic techniques in agriculture and the industrial arts accompanying farming – ceramics, weaving, and metallurgy. And another four thousand years were required for these arts and techniques to spread over the globe from their one or several sources of origin. But only the three centuries that included Newton, Lavoisier, Priestley, Faraday, Liebig, and Mendel *et hoc genus omne* were needed to develop techniques that allowed scientists to analyze these processes in the laboratory, and mental constructs that gave predictable control over them. The reasons are clear: (1) Experiment done consciously in the presence of statistical controls and interlaced with a continuing effort to frame valid theory is a vastly more powerful tool than random discovery; (2) the application of science not only to basic discovery but to communication of the results, in a world society directed consciously toward similar goals of material progress, produces a vastly enlarged *scale* on which even random trial and error takes place. The result is a greatly accelerated rate of useful, or dangerous, discoveries about nature.

Why the rationalistic and the experimental impulses of human thought and behavior began to join in the seventeenth century into a method that, despite vagueness and ridiculous extremes in its early stages, grew into nineteenth- and twentieth-century scientific and engineering research is a subject, I would insist, in intellectual history, not to be reduced to a socio-economic explanation except by a really crude and insensitive mind. Both the scientific impulse and the impulse to modern capitalism derive from, or were immensely strengthened by, the materialism and the individualistic humanism that we see displayed in Renaissance literature and art – the element that distinguishes fifteenth-century culture so startlingly from the twelfth and the thirteenth. But since early history is full of examples of capitalism without science and of science without capitalism, it is impossible to call one the cause of the other. Instead one must translate both back to some higher or deeper human source from which they appeared jointly in the Renaissance – and partially Protestant – culture of Northern Europe. And apart from the coincidence of timing (which in the loftier heaven of the history of the intellect and the spirit may be no coincidence), there is the matter of the scale and variety in which scientific thought flourished across Europe, from Warsaw to Amsterdam, Paris, and London. For in science as in nature hybridization within the range of acceptable cross-fertilization can produce a range of breeds adaptable to a variety of environments. Here the growth of trade and commercial communication as well as war and the interrelations among royal courts no doubt can claim credit. This scale phenomenon is even more important, however, at just a little later point in this story.[12]

We come then to the argument often made, particularly by those economic historians who like Mr. Gradgrind pride themselves in dealing in "facts," that the inventors of the Industrial Revolution were not scientists but humble men – "tinkerers" is the usual denomination given them. The hard facts are hard enough in the cases of Darby, Highs, Kay, Arkwright, and Hargreaves. The scientific training, even perhaps the mathematical aptitude, of the American inventors – Whitney, Fitch, Fulton, McCormick, and Goodyear – was low, even zero. The facts are a little squishier in the case of Watt, as the research by Musson and Robinson has shown. And French inventors even this early had perhaps a better connection with the speculations of natural philosophers.[13] But

[12]The relations among humanism, capitalism, science, and the Reformation form still a lively and fundamental issue in the historical understanding of all these linked phenomena. In recent literature, I have found the controversy in *Past and Present,* 27, (April 1964) originating out of Christopher Hill's article "William Harvey and the Idea of Monarchy," and contributions by various authors contained in nos. 29 (December 1964) and 31 (July 1965) most helpful in getting my bearings. See also R. Mandrou, *From Humanism to Science,* The Pelican History of European Thought, III, Harmondsworth (UK), 1978, and the earlier articles by Trevor-Roper, op. cit., 1963, and H. Lüthy, "Once Again: Calvinism and Capitalism," *Encounter,* 22, 1964, 26–38. With respect to both science and capitalism, it seems now possible to argue that it was not Protestant doctrine as such that offered a more receptive atmosphere to modern thought or business practice, but rather that its individualism and its lack of social and political control allowed "modern culture," or "bourgeois society" to grow strong in Northern Europe and North America.

[13]The work of Musson and Robinson has greatly clarified the relationship of science and technology in the Industrial Revolution. See A. E. Musson and E. Robinson, *Science and Technology in the Industrial Revolution,* Manchester, 1969; A. E. Musson (ed.), *Science, technology and Economic Growth in the Eighteenth Century,* London, 1972, esp. chapters 1 (P. Mathias), and 2 (by A. E. Musson). An interesting statement of the relationship in France is offered by C. G. Gillespie in chapter 4 of the same collection, reprinted from *Isis, 48,* 1957, 398–407. Gillespie's views, based on research into the origins of industrial chemistry, give support, I feel, to the impressions voiced here and in my earlier article (W. N. Parker, "Technology, Resources and Economic Change in

does the fact that Shakespeare knew "little Latin and Less Greek," according to Ben Jonson, who knew an abundance of both, make him less of a Renaissance man? He was a working inventor saturated with what a sociologist would limply call the "value system" of his times. Could the eighteenth-century inventors have been equally well sixteenth-century men? And if a few of them could have been so (and indeed they were – hence the stocking frame and the ribbon loom that stand out like sore thumbs in the early history of textile technology), could so large a body of "simple tinkerers" have been at work simply tinkering, along so many different and interconnected lines and in such close touch with the economy three hundred years earlier?

We come here to the second feature of the eighteenth-century invention – again to the phenomenon of *scale* – not the scale of science indeed, but of the economy. The articulation of a single price system across Europe – detailed by Braudel and Spooner – the accession of England, with its better world trading location, resource base, and more complex society, to world leadership in trade and commerce – the whole involvement of a major nation-state in all its branches in commercial economy – this in the presence (unlike the case of ancient Rome) of a body of already developing technology – all this was built for the first time into the economy itself and into its production structure an invention industry, or to put it more grandly, an eco-technic process.

I like to put the matter to economics students in this way. Mantoux in his great book explains the sequence of the textile inventions in terms of successive bottlenecks – the flying shuttle created a demand for yarn, which induced the development of – or focused inventors' efforts on – spinning inventions, and these in turn overshooting the mark created bottlenecks in weaving that induced the power loom. It is all very simple and neat. It seems to be built on some impressionistic evidence of yarn shortages in the 1770s, but we have no measure of the actual

the West," in A. J. Youngson (ed.), *Economic Development in the Long Run,* London, 1972, 62–78).

See also Rostow's able survey of this aspect of the early modern history (W. W. Rostow, *How It All Began,* New York, 1975, Ch. 1, 4). While allowing "science" an independent causative role in the formation of modern industrial society, Rostow also emphasizes mercantilist politics and trade. Like Usher and most of us in the Anglo-American tradition in economic history, he has little to say about social structure, social and group psychology, intellectual and religious doctrines and values that created the "Renaissance" man, in the arts, religion, government, science, and commerce. I wonder if he is as uneasy as I am about this neglect. The treatments by J. R. Hicks, op. cit. 1969, and D. C. North and R. P. Thomas, *The Rise of the Western World,* Cambridge, 1973, powerful and searching as they are in some of their insights, leave one with a similar sense that we have not yet gotten to the bottom of all these matters.

diffusion of the flying shuttle among weavers. Moreover, as Usher insisted, the development of a power loom continued to be held up by purely technical difficulties. Evidently the supply side of an invention industry also must be taken into account. But there is a more fundamental problem: How does such an explanation square with the purely competitive model which ought to have worked, if anywhere, in the England of the Industrial Revolution? If yarn was in short and weavers in surplus supply, why did not some weavers become spinners, and later on, vice versa? The answer, of course, is "labor immobility," "noncompeting groups." *Some* immobility then must be good for invention if a society has available a body of eager, ingenious, inventive tinkerers with a good eye to what is practical and economic.

Here then, I think, we come to the essential element in the transition from the purely Smithian to the Schumpeterian dynamic of the world economy. Capitalistic economic organization had come to exist on a large enough scale, with penetration of its price system deeply enough into the production structure in agriculture as well as in the market for family labor, so that the opportunities for immediate profit became evident in invention as well as in trade, exploration, and resource discovery. These opportunities altered industrial organization so that invention moved in to resolve bottlenecks even faster than capitalists and laborers could do so themselves. Moreover, this was occurring on a large enough scale, and over a wide enough industrial terrain, with sufficient communication among inventors and with sufficient knowledge of investment opportunities that a self-reinforcing process of technical change was set in motion. One small gap was closed and that in turn made other gaps smaller. Improved iron was used in improved steam engines, which powered the improved and more finely calibrated machinery.

CONTROLS ON SCHUMPETERIAN GROWTH

It is, as Marxists like to say, no accident, that these inventions appeared first most strongly as substitutions of natural resources – fuels, water power, and iron – for human or animal labor. One observes here the delicate balance of factor proportions and types of market demand required for the Industrial Revolution to get under way. Some population growth appears to have been desirable to increase the absolute size of the potential agricultural surplus and to bring scale economies in trade and industry into play. This the population growth of the sixteenth century appears to have been able to do, especially in conjunction with the centralization of the state administrative systems and the mini-industrial revolution and technical changes of the Renaissance.

The suspension of population growth still left underemployed agricultural labor in the eighteenth and even nineteenth centuries available to be drawn into factories and mines, and the resumption of population growth in the centers of rural industry in the eighteenth and early nineteenth centuries added to the pool. But labor did not become abundant as in some Asian or some Latin American countries today, and in any case it remained sufficiently immobilized to give the incentive to labor-saving inventions in regions where water power and coal were cheap.

The more important determinant of the path of technical change came from the supply side of inventions: the relatively easy access to a knowledge of mechanics, i.e., of that part of engineering involved in economizing on power. I have argued elsewhere, though not with much elaboration, that the order of progression of scientific and engineering discovery must be traced back to fundamental structural conditions of the human mind in approaching nature through the medium of scientific method. That method – with its theories, laboratory techniques, mathematics, and instrumentation – was not much more than one hundred years old by the start of the major technical changes in England, and it was obviously most directly applicable – and was so applied by scientists and inventors from Galileo through Newton and by tinkerers and inventors from Newcomen through Stephenson – to problems of mechanics, most of which had been defined by Archimedes. The electrochemical revolution came later because its secrets lay more deeply hidden, were less apparent to the naked eye. The real agricultural revolution waited until recent decades because of the enormous complexity of life processes and perhaps because of some human fears about direct experimentation with the sources of life.

A track of invention then can be traced in the nineteenth and twentieth centuries out of the difficulties from the supply side, which progressively yielded to increasingly more powerful applications of scientific method. As a branch of knowledge grew to the point of direct applicability to useful invention, the choice among lines to pursue was no doubt strongly affected by markets, bottlenecks, and factor costs, as well as by the many random accidents that dot the biographies of the inventors.

Now there are, it seems to me, two sorts of error that are injurious to the health of a reasonable study of nineteenth-century technological history. One – deriving from the side of the history of science since Thomas Kuhn – emphasizes that science is a series of "paradigms," separate and discrete, like pearls on a strand, each with a delicate and internally supportive structure, spun, like a pearl, around a single irritant, a single grain of sand, a single problem which has crept into the shell of a single social oyster.[14] Kuhn's theory is not a Marxian theory, since it interprets scientific change almost wholly in terms internal to scientific thought itself. A new paradigm is created by an act of insight, as a growing body of observation becomes increasingly hard to accommodate within the categories and logic of its predecessor. Nevertheless, this way of looking at the history of science has an intellectual affinity to the Marxian theory of history, with its stages and its revolutions from stage to stage. It contains a truth, and a truth which may be well fitted to an age that seems, like the sixteenth century, to be in a revolutionary psychological and spiritual upheaval. Any notion of economic history as a string of stages or paradigms, the logic of whose shifts and revolutionary displacements is derived either from internal "slippage" or from events outside the activity, i.e., from society, technology, the logic of the superstructure, techniques of warfare, or whatnot – any such notion is itself a paradigm, emphasizing one truth whose relevance (to use that demonic word of ten years ago) – may already have seen its best days. Scientific revolutions, like political or industrial revolutions, furnish a problem for historical explanation. The mind is driven back to Tennyson's verses learned in high school:

> "Our little systems have their day;
> They have their day and cease to be.
> They are but broken lights of Thee:
> And Thou, O Lord art more than they!"

Such lines, supportive of the paradigm mongers can yet be turned against them. Scientific revolutions are themselves incidents in scientific evolution; just as political and industrial revolutions are parts of total history. We know (or fondly believe) there is a great historical totality in which all is compounded, even Marx, or Braudel – even what I am saying here. The growth of modern science – many of us still believe – is a cumulative process whose correct model is not the pearl in the oyster but the successively more stately mansions of the chambered nautilus. But if this is so, and if this succession of what I would persist in calling "advances" has been in a major way guided by some internal intellectual and structural logic of its own, then one has here a potent exogenous variable in the structure of explanation of the modern economic world.

[14]Brown gives a good survey of the state of the discussion of Kuhn's much-discussed "paradigm model" and makes many telling points of his own, by reference to Kuhn's earlier writings in the history of science. I do not quite feel that he fully states the point which bothers me, i.e., the question of a standard against which the succession of paradigms is measured. No doubt I am being naive. See F. M. Brown, "Putting Paradigms Into History," *Marxist Perspectives,* 3:1 (Spring, 1980), 34–63.

In the understanding of so profound and majestic an historical movement, a further obstacle is presented by modern economists' delicate theorizings over the trivia on the demand side of applied science. They have an unquestionable value in contemporary studies of problems of allocation of research resources. And the observations of the value of "focusing," and the subtle effects of factor scarcities in shaping technological change in the small are original and essential insights in understanding the biographies of specific inventions or lines of invention. But taken as a vessel to hold the history of technology, these have about as much use as a little boy's effort to scoop out the ocean with a teacup. To understand the history of technology in the large, one must unfortunately know something about technology in all its branches, and that is a dark and thorny terrain into which none of us with training in the humanities or social sciences has been brave enough to enter.[15]

THE NEXT TRANSITION?

With the Industrial Revolution, an interactive process between technology and the economy was built into the structure of modern capitalist development. In marrying technological change, the economy and the entrepreneurs who were its guiding force, delivered society into the hands of science, which has moved where it listeth. There is, it seems to me, no controlling its internal development. The efforts of socialist or fascist societies to place science directly, obviously, and totally in the service of the state have been catastrophic for the development of knowledge and for the innocence of the state. No large political and bureaucratic power structure – whether of public officials or of private capitalist lackeys – can be trusted not to blow itself up in the pursuit of more power. This is *its* internal logic, the dynamic of capitalist or socialist imperialism. Under the capitalism of large-scale organizations, power goes disguised under the name of profit, because these organizations still live in a world of accounting, of money and markets. Under socialism, these organizations move under the name of social welfare. But the naked thrust for political dominance and the paranoic drive to destroy everything in the name of security for a system, are the same.

The fourteenth century and to a degree the seventeenth and early eighteenth in Europe are understandable by Malthus; the sixteenth and much of the eighteenth and early nineteenth by Smith. The nineteenth and early twentieth require that a Schumpeterian insight be added to the Malthusian and the Smithian to account for the complexity of the growth, and for its variety as it extended beyond the Atlantic, the Mediterranean, and

[15] I refrain from footnoting these rather bad-tempered comments. References will be furnished by correspondence to scholars presenting proper credentials.

the Urals. But where is to be found the figure for the period that is now perhaps already thirty years into its development?

Clearly, it seems to me, the uncontrolled and evidently uncontrollable development of natural science, pure and applied, is the deepest problem of the modern world. This is hardly a novel observation. First atomic physics and now modern biochemistry are causing us all to shudder. Yet our fears get buried constantly, first under the glamor and science fiction of space exploration, and then under the much more immediate power struggles of international politics. It is ironic that at the same time as our fears of science are growing, we find ourselves pressed by the obsolescence of the nineteenth-century power-using technologies to turn toward science in a kind of desperate hope. The problem is epitomized in the dilemma of nuclear power. But – and here is the grain of truth in the paradigm about paradigms – society appears in history to have an ability to breed around its intellectual and social problems, though often only after catastrophe and at a frightful human cost. Somewhere in that ability, the ability simply to grow in a different direction, intellectually, spiritually, and materially, may lie salvation.

I am reminded of the experience I had once on a jury, after we had retired to the jury room to deliberate on our verdict. It was not too serious a case, except to the defendant, but the jurors took it seriously, conscientiously to the point of self importance, and came at it with very different perspectives, perceptions, value systems, and bodies of experience and prejudice. They also were acting under different degrees of stress with respect to how long they were willing to remain locked in the jury room with one another. For some the discussion was a positive good, and they behaved like academics. One or two others wanted quick dominance and instant discovery of the truth so apparent to themselves. Most wanted simply to fight their way through to agreement to give themselves the feeling they had done a decent job the judge would respect so he would release them to their families. As we discussed the case, going back over the testimony, expressing assessments of the credibility of the policemen, the witnesses, and the defendant, we would come to points of absolute disagreement around which no accommodation seemed possible. I noted that at such times the discussion drifted. People began to talk about things other than the case, to make personal inquiries, to voice complaints, to discuss the hat and makeup of a woman in the front row of the courtroom. After perhaps five or ten minutes of such talk someone would begin to steer the discussions back toward the case, the various small group discussions would consolidate, and it would seem that the evidence had taken on a different cast. Sometimes it seemed that the previous opinion leaders had suffered, as a result of the inconsequential discussions, a certain loss of respect, found themselves less listened to, felt their replacement by others whom the group appeared to deem more reliable. In this way, not by direct argument over the points, though that occurred too, but partly by the development of a reliable leadership, a leadership which seemed in human terms to be worthy of trust, or to express best the consensus of value, a group opinion emerged powerful enough to face down and embarrass holdouts into acquiescence.

Do societies – which are but broken parts of the whole society of mankind – do the same thing as history is lived out? Is there any possibility of a global consensus on what is worthwhile in life, a consensus in which comfort, knowledge, art, individual achievement, and the thrill of group endeavor, personal "fulfillment" – that last refuge of the Renaissance value system – and a joyous social intercourse do not at last contradict one another? In such a utopia, what is the model for economic behavior and economic change? The Malthusian model was based on the joy of unlimited procreation, and as the population experience of the tropical world shows, it is a hard model to put down. The Smithian model was based on the excitement of spectacular wealth from trade and the comforts derived from a rational, natural, and orderly organization of the work process through trade. The Schumpeterian model took its dynamic from the thirsty incorporation of the results of scientific and engineering discovery into an expanding array of synthetic materials and machinery for both production and destruction. The corporate and state power derivable from the domination of this process has become the dominant motivation of twentieth-century economic activity. Uncertainty remains, as strong as in the nineteenth century, though afflicting larger-scale units than the small farms and manufacturing enterprises of that period.

The temptation is present to try to dominate the uncertainty by extending economic power not only over individual actors, but over the development of scientific activity itself. Before that happens – if it has not happened already – is it possible that societies will simply grow away from the whole rationalistic and scientific way of looking at the world, that science and the exploration of the material universe will simply wither away out of disinterest? That seems hardly possible, and if it were to happen as the passions and excitements of a new generation develop – for one must remember that extinction or savagery are always for society only one generation away – is it possible that present levels of "good" technology, in agriculture, medicine, and communication can be sustained? Will a race of people develop which, like some primitive tribe, knows how to do traditional things but has no interest in the bases of its power or in extending it? The arts came to civilization before science, presumably out of the perpetuation of random useful accidents. Perhaps they will remain, even revive, when the Faustian pact that Western man sealed with the devil of total knowledge has been paid in suffering and fear. Still when one considers that science and the use of the mind is in fact also a kind of art, perhaps that is not what can or should happen. Perhaps the prophet, or the theorist, of the twenty-first century will be not an Anglican parson, or a dour Scottish bachelor, or a Viennese intellectual, but a figure who better expresses the inherent sense of balance which, along with passions and excesses, also characterizes the movements of human society as a whole over its history. Marx, Weber, Parsons, Toynbee, Mao – have all been candidates for the job – yet history seems to have outrun them all. And perhaps it is too much to ask that a new phase of socio-economic organization should furnish its analyst before it is full born. The owl of Minerva, Hegelians love to remind us, flies abroad not at dawn, but at dusk. Still after the owl has flown about all night, the rooster (or the Rostow) may wake to crow again, causing the sun to rise.

APPENDIX: AN OUTLINE OF THE ARGUMENT AND ITS EXTENSION IN FEEDBACK MECHANISMS

I. *Transitions in Europe's sequences of opportunities*
From Malthusian to Smithian requires:

1. An agricultural surplus above subsistence, growing absolutely with population expansion
2. Increasing returns in industry and trade, permitting expansion of industrial production
3. Relief from Malthusian pressures in some combination produced by:
   - (a) Birth and death-rate movements, within a class structure with differential birth rates and death rates
   - (b) Increases in agricultural resource supply through
     - (1) Trade and specialization in agricultural and resource products
     - (2) Out-migration and creation of new centers of trade
     - (3) Diffusion of known agricultural techniques and materials within expanding trading area
     - (4) Fall in diets, absorption of rural underemployment, and increases in work load in agriculture.
4. Formation of Smithian (capitalist) response mechanism, i.e., institutions of money, credit, capital accumulation, financial management, and enterprise within the state
5. Some transformation of political and social institutions: church, state, locality, family

From Smithian to Schumpeterian requires:

1. Smithian scale large enough and activities specialized enough to focus invention and produce continuous sequences of invention
2. Science-based engineering forming as a social, professional institution extending knowledge of material world and its application
*3. Diffusion of Smithian response mechanism (capitalist business forms and markets) to industrial organization, and its transformation to a scale compatible with technology utilization and advance
4. The appropriate sequence and timing, so that trade discoveries, individualistic character structures, population checks, market formation within Smithian period, and resulting economic expansion produce pressures on technology just as invention and engineering become equipped intellectually to begin to deal with them.

Feed-backs

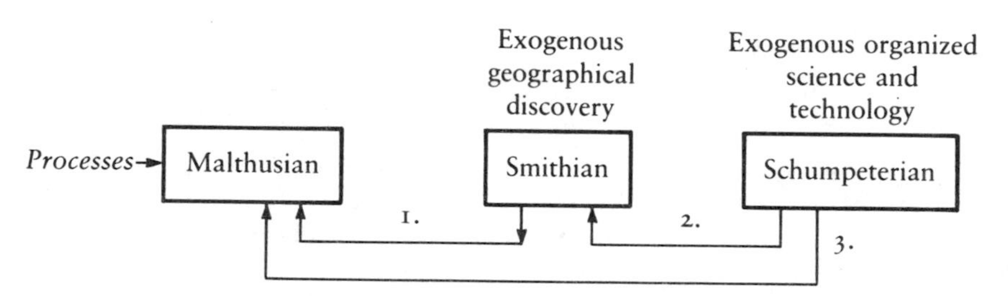

1. Growth of trade affects population-resource (Malthusian) balance *via*
   (a) Specialization in agricultural regions with trade in agricultural products
   (b) Enlargement of inventory of available agricultural techniques and genetic materials by geographic discoveries
   (c) Diffusion of knowledge of methods and materials to meet commercial demands
   (d) Extension of money economy and semicapitalistic organization in agriculture

   Growth of trade and of rural and urban industry affects population response *via*
   (a) Effects on death rates (spread of new diseases but also of new drugs and medical knowledge)

*Parts of the response mechanism.

   (b) Effect of urbanization and of a rural manufacturing working class on birth and death rates
   (c) Opening up of knowledge and routes of migration
2. Growth of scientific technology and large-scale organization affects trade patterns *via*
   (a) Effects on industrial location and optimal specialization patterns, (product cycles in world economy)
   (b) Contribution to flows of capital, capital goods, technology, and organization of trade and international enterprise and investment
   (c) Replacement of small-scale organizations and markets by large-scale multi-branch firms
3. Growth of scientific technology and large-scale organization affects population-resource balance *via*
   (a) Development of chemical and biochemical science and invention to increase resource base
   (b) Lowering of death rates through medical science and public health measures
   (c) Flow of investment from large firms and governments into agriculture and resource industries
   (d) Effects of location and population distribution patterns on death rates
   (e) Ecological effects of modern technology with negative externalities
   (f) Improvement in knowledge and dissemination of birth control techniques
   (g) Changes in role and social position of women and of family structure

12

The response mechanism in the twentieth century

SOCIAL DYNAMICS IN THE AGE OF SCHUMPETER

In the twenty years between its two great twentieth-century wars, the capitalist West did not enjoy peace. Its economies, and with them the economies of its trading and financial partners in overseas areas, experienced every sort of economic calamity – violent inflation, deep depression, an excessive boom, a worldwide collapse of trade, fluctuating prices and employment, and in places, after a partial revival, a second recession prior to the outbreak of World War II. The individual national economies of Germany, France, England, and the United States experienced these catastrophes in different combinations and to different degrees. But all experienced several violent price fluctuations, long periods of heavy unemployment, and a relatively low rate of overall economic growth. If an equilibrium growth path is that which all men seek, then the West in these decades had surely lost the way.

Today, however, one cannot explain the breakdown of capitalism so confidently in the apocalyptic terms of the 1930s. In the twenty-five years following 1948, France, Germany, and Italy all grew rather steadily at rates almost without precedent for so long a stretch. And any explanation of this revival must be further tested in turn against the drastic slow down since 1973, although even in this last decade nothing, not even the special problems of internal and external adjustment that Britain has faced, resembles the chaos of the 1920s and 1930s. Certainly the United States and the European nations handled the oil shock rather better than they handled the problem of war debts and German reparations after World War I. Both the domestic and the international institutions seemed more buoyant and more flexible in the 1970s than in the period between the wars, and this despite an inflation

Originally published in the *Journal of Economic Behavior and Organization*, v (1) March 1984. Reprinted by permission.

as serious and continuous as any that a peacetime Europe had seen. Whether credit is to be given to innovations in international economic arrangements taken within the framework of the existing capitalism, for example, multinational corporations, Euro-dollars, the EEC, collaboration on tariffs and exchange rates, or to semisocialist measures: nationalizations, codetermination, state subsidies and insurance, wage guarantees, and the like, remains to be examined by historians – perhaps twenty years hence.

The purpose of this essay then is simply to explore from the widest of perspectives the setting against which the interwar break occurred. The problem is to account for the chaotic and uneven record of Western Europe between the wars in such a way as to leave room for an understanding of the postwar growth and the post-OPEC slowdown. It would be surprising if an investigation of scope and historical depth did not involve the investigator in an effect also to develop social theory. Although that effort is not formalized here, the vision of a theory lies at the center of this paper. That vision borrows ideas from three bodies of thought, Veblenian institutionalism, Parsonian sociology, and the "structural-functionalist" thinking of Radcliffe-Brown and others in anthropology, systems all much out of fashion at present these days.[1] Historians must take their theory where they can find it, and they must use it where it helps them derive a sense of synthesis and intellectual catharsis from their evidence. In doing so, the historian does not become a theorist, but his effort may contribute to the validity, relevance, and scope of the social and organizational theorist's formulations. If economics is not to become a branch of mechanical engineering strangling itself in its own logic and narrow assumptions, it too, one may feel, must break out in these directions.

I

An explanation might begin by looking at the real prospects which the European economies may have faced in the 1920s – the jobs to be done and the opportunities to be seized. Compared to the problem after World War II, the tasks of postwar physical reconstruction, except in

[1] See in particular: Thorstein Veblen, *The Instinct of Workmanship* (New York: Macmillan, 1914) for the notion of "drives" or instincts, now long outmoded in psychology; A. R. Radcliffe-Brown, *Structure and Function in Primitive Society* (Glencoe: The Free Press, 1952), especially Ch. 9 and 10 for a modified statement of "structural-functionalism" in social organization; Talcott Parsons and Neil Smelser, *Economy and Society*, (Glencoe: The Free Press, 1956) for the concepts of social "roles," and subsystems built around them. I have developed my schema a bit further, with the aid of some "plumber's nightmare" diagrams, in Chapter 13, below.

certain devastated French and Belgian regions, do not seem inordinate. It is fatuous to suppose that economic recovery would have been faster or steadier if the destruction had been worse, if that is, it had been given a stronger boost by the need to reconstruct new physical capital; certainly the immediate demand conditions following World War II were more favorable to a quick start-up. But what concerns us here is not the immediate postwar years in the two cases but the longer run – not the early 1920s and the late 1940s, but the instability and semistagnation of 1925–1939 set against the continuous growth of 1950–1968.

Now for any economy, real opportunities derive from three characteristic historical sequences which in an earlier essay I have labeled "Malthusian," "Smithian," and "Schumpeterian," attaching them to each of three overlapping periods of *longue durée* in European and American history.[2] These are simply an historian's quaint names for three elements in a growth model: population (creating a labor force), resources (including conditions of trade and availability of external markets), and technological change (including knowledge which can render both physical and "human" capital more productive). Given suitable behavioral and institutional responses, the history of growth opportunities, I contend in the earlier essay, is the story of movement of the European economies, by reason of an inbuilt logic, from one set of opportunities to another.

The first, because in a sense the original and most persistent, of these forces – population growth – is, as is well-known, a double-edged sword. In the West since the late Middle Ages, periods of population growth have also been periods of economic growth up to a point, but much was also gained by the breathers offered by lower population growth, for example in the late seventeenth and early eighteenth centuries. The reason is a modified Malthusian one: The population growth must be accompanied by an expansion of the resource base or by improved trading conditions, or in the Schumpeterian era, by technological changes offering the opportunity for scale economies or a finer division of labor.

Did the downward movement of the birth rate, on which the deceleration of population growth depended, have some connection with the decline in the simple land- and resource-oriented investment opportunity of the nineteenth century? Demographers, mired in parish records of the seventeenth and eighteenth centuries or swamped by the pressing problems of population control in poor countries, have not trained their

[2] "European Development in Millennial Perspective," in C. P. Kindleberger and G. di Tella, *Economics in the Long View*, Vol. II (London: The Macmillan Press, 1982), pp. 1–24. Reprinted as "Opportunity Sequences in European history," Ch. 11 above.

arsenal of techniques very fully on this problem. The fertility decline was partly a reaction to the earlier mortality decline which created the bulge in populations that sent Europeans to the cities and overseas. It occurred in the countryside especially as rural industry withered and peasants were obliged to keep families within the available land. Here the decline in New World migration opportunities may have had an effect, but it must be remembered that except for the Ukrainians and Scandinavians the great peasant migrations to North America had largely sought industrial jobs in cities, or taken them *faute de mieux*. And in cities, the improvement in health conditions and the falls especially in infant mortality threatened to produce larger families.

But the fall went beyond a mere reaction to improved mortality conditions, as is shown by the fact that completed family size itself decreased. It may be that North European society was optimally poised to encourage efforts at upward mobility through family restriction. Such an effort undertaken by a large segment of a society requires the society have a structure of wealth, breeding, respectability, through which movement is seen as desirable. An egalitarian society has no such structure and hence no such stimulus. Yet, it must not be so structured as to be frozen by criteria of inherited rank or race, and it may be perceived that what one cannot one's self attain may be attained by one's children if they are properly provided for, both through training and inheritance. Moreover, in matters of family limitation, the relative power and views of the man and woman in a marriage are controlling. The sharp break from the large family system in Britain, Germany, and the United States to the small family system of the 1910s and 1920s must mean a change in attitudes and perhaps in the relative power of the partners in deciding the matter. The early 1900s are too early to show the effects of women's liberation but already young urban women were beginning to find clerical jobs and to delay marriage. Urban living conditions, in flats and apartments, must also have had an effect. Perhaps too the Victorian age's division of labor, which left the woman so fully in charge of the household realm, may have given her the moral authority to decide how large that realm would be, what resources would be devoted to child-raising, and how those resources would be divided among children. The whole matter is a great mystery, but the fall in fertility is an incontrovertible fact and it came at a time when a rapidly growing population might have produced a threat rather than a stimulus to the growth in per capita incomes.

It may have been merely luck that both population growth and overseas expansion decelerated simultaneously in the period 1910–1950. The reasons for the two trends appear to be quite different and remote from one another. The famous end of the West's frontier occurred because exploration finally penetrated up the rivers and across the plains of Africa and into the inner reaches of Central Asia and of the Western Hemisphere. With the settlement of the plains of North America and Argentina, the taking up of lands in Australia, the thickening of peasant populations in Asia, the eastward migrations from Russia, the great movement of farmers and herders, begun in neolithic times, reached its natural limits. The great mineral bonanzas were over, too, except in oil. And except for the Chinese, whose continued population growth had brought levels of farm productivity allowing little room for trade, no new peasant populations appeared in the orbit of the world economy to exchange agricultural surpluses, traded or extorted, for the products of Western industry.

Moreover what I fancy calling a "biological dialectic" had already appeared in the diffusion of Western industrialism. As people, products, and techniques moved out from Europe, financed and encouraged by exports of European enterprise, organizational skills, and money, new and competing centers of industry appeared. Textile industries arose with exports of English machinery and machinists, first on the Continent, then in America, then in India and Japan. In iron and steel, the second basis of England's industrial dominance, huge industries arose at coal and ore deposits in America and Germany. Notable progress was made in Russia and India as well. The movement of the product cycle, so prominent a feature of the international economy since 1950, was clearly visible in Britain's trade patterns especially after 1890.

We come then in the catalogue of economic opportunities to technological change. It had not at all run its course by 1920. Behind lay the mechanical revolution, the chemical and metallurgical discoveries, the internal combustion engine, with its accompaniments – airplane and motor car. The discoveries in electricity and long-distance wave transmission were still in progress. Ahead lay all that we have known since, in electronics, biochemistry, and nuclear energy. A clustering of inventions came in the 1940s and 1950s and thereafter, partly surely under the stimulus of wartime research and the postwar boom, themselves stimulated by Korea and Vietnam. Certainly in atomic energy, for good or for ill, a great breakthrough reaching deep into fundamental science was required. The effort might have required half a century at the pace of privately financed peacetime research. Was there then a slowdown in the rate of growth of new technical knowledge between the wars? If so, did it derive from what the economist's parochial vocabulary calls the "supply side" of the process – fundamental impediments, sticking places which required time, work, the construction of theories, mathematical tools, and experimental equipment to overcome? There is surely no inherent reason that the course of technology any more than that of true love should run smooth. Or, if there were a temporary dearth of inventions, was this the result of "demand failure"; of enterprise, slack and confused; of expectations, uncertain; of resources diverted from long-run to shorter-run investment and speculation? And did not the bad times, whenever and wherever they appeared, feed back on the supply side as well, depriving research of needed funds and private inventors of needed freedom? These are the questions that need to be answered by a close scrutiny of the history of invention and of noninvention, of the conditions surrounding invention and scientific and technical progress.

We have no real evidence that scientific progress and the supply of ideas for new technology slowed down in this period; indeed some of the growth after 1948 represents the catching up in the utilization of prewar technology, for example, in automobiles and consumer appliances. The growth of other industrial countries on the earth's surface offered competition, indeed, along certain lines, but they also offered markets. And if a slowdown in growth had to occur, consistent with diminished real opportunities, why could it not have been easier, more gentle and gradual, and more evenly spread? In the end, it is hard to believe that well-functioning capitalistic institutions connecting a group of countries of relatively high wealth and advanced technology could not have handled the adjustments incidental to "the end of the frontier," the changing comparative advantage of various regions in world trade, or a possibly arid stretch in technological change. Perhaps the most that should be said is that an adjustment problem was present and that it had to be tackled within this group of nations by economic institutions which were themselves disordered and weak. If one must apportion responsibility between opportunities and the organization responsible for the response, one might feel that most of the blame must go to the fact that the European nations were still in a sense at war with one another, that there was pervasive bitterness, resentment, and fear which poisoned both domestic political life and international economic arrangements.

II

The fact of an institutional breakdown is not in dispute; contemporaries and later historians have all agreed on that. In the international economy, the Treaty of Versailles, pressed on defeated Germany by the national politicians of the Allied and Associated Powers, jealously, fearfully, vindictively, was pointed out as the chief culprit. Its territorial provisions, Keynes said, broke up a natural integration of industrial resources existing within the former German Empire. (This was not wholly true.) In Eastern Europe it created half a dozen new national boundaries in the name of national self-determination. But observe here how nationalist impulses and the old international economy of capitalism were at odds with one another. While severing Germany from some important resources and trade connections, the treaty loaded her with heavy reparations payments, both in kind (coal) and in gold or foreign exchange. This in turn strained the German government's capacity to tax and also placed on the international financial system the intolerable burden of transferring such heavy payments abroad, largely to France, in some acceptable form of payment. France's efforts to compel the coal deliveries by occupation of the Ruhr in 1923 in turn closed the German mines, while the support payments made by the German government to the miners during their strike were a major contributing cause to the huge budget deficit. This deficit was financed by paper currency, obliterated the value of the mark, impoverished German owners of financial assets, abolished much of the debt structure, and redistributed wealth to entrepreneurs and speculators. To these very unevenly distributed financial windfalls were added the inflows of American loans, for which the domestic proceeds were used for reconstruction and expansion while the dollars themselves went not to finance imports of capital goods but as payments into the reparations account. The result in Germany was the overheated and very uneven expansion of 1925–1928 instead of a better balanced and more gradual response to the opportunities for restoration and development. The credit expansion and the levels of new capacity generated, greatly in excess of what could be immediately sustained, were the domestic conditions under which the country after 1929 plunged to levels of collapse and unemployment deeper than those of any other country in Europe, and at least as deep as those reached in the United States. The treaty, it was claimed, made the German economy the sick man of Europe, and since it was sick, the economies of its neighbors could not be healthy.

Apart from the strain of the German transfer problem, the international system of payments, it has been argued, was strained after 1920 by the reimposition of the gold standard and the British efforts to maintain the pound sterling at prewar parity. Keynes, it is well-known, disagreed about the level at which the pound should be fixed, but no one in Britain, Keynes perhaps least of all, seriously questioned the need or the possibility of restoring the British position as the financial center of a world economy. The foreign exchange gains from that position, the payments for British shipping, insurance, and banking services, along with the return of interest, dividends, and principal on foreign loans and shares had become increasingly more important to Britain during the several decades preceding World War I.

Only a very severe historical judge, armed in advance with the deep wisdom of retrospection, could have assessed the likelihood that a restoration might not succeed. Yet on the face of it, two circumstances militated against it. One was the shrinkage in overseas investment opportunities of the sort which British international finance had been developed to serve. This was occurring not simply because of the "end of the frontier" but also through the "biologic dialectic," the growth of the United States as banker to the Western Hemisphere, of Japan to a degree as a provisioner in Britain's Southeast Asian sphere, and of France, as a colonizing power in North Africa. Egypt, South Africa, even India – the great support of the economic empire – were all beginning to be troubled by domestic unrest. In the great age before these developments, British prosperity had been identified with the international expansion of a liberal, free trade capitalism. The spillover effects from British lending and monetary management to the rest of the world were beneficial and of significant proportions. Now the effort to restore that central position would have benefited chiefly Britain alone, whatever her leaders might have imagined. Related to this was Britain's growing relative industrial and financial weakness, derived from those flaws in her own industrial structure which have been much studied of late, and from the wartime transfer of her foreign assets into American ownership to pay the costs of food and *matériel*.

As if all this were not enough, the United States during the 1920s continued to insist on the repayment of the enormous "war debts." "They hired the money, didn't they?" was President Coolidge's Yankee response to the protests. The unreadiness of the American bankers and Federal Reserve authorities to assume the central position in the system of international exchanges is a major theme of Kindleberger's recent valuable reexamination of this experience. Yet here again the reasons are understandable. The American banking system had developed to service the United States, an area of a manufacturing and agricultural capacity equal to that of Western Europe, including Britain. That economy and its rate of development had been significantly affected during the whole nineteenth century by "shocks" from abroad. Despite America's dominant position in the 1920s, its bankers were used to the defensive posture. Moreover the dilemma created by the volatility of short-term capital movements in 1927–1929, the so-called hot money phenomenon, was one Britain had never had to meet in so direct a form. Perhaps on the scale of international cooperativeness, the Federal Reserve authorities were a little ahead of the Bank of France, whose behavior was notoriously disruptive and independent. Efforts to harness all the wild horses loose in the international markets through conferences, culminating with the catastrophic London Conference of 1933 – came to very little. It is now generally agreed that such stability as existed depended largely on the personal ties and realization of mutual interdependence and accommodation among the three leaders or the systems in their respective countries – Moreau in France, Norman in Britain, and Strong in the United States. Friedman and Schwartz, with their strong and elaborate framework of theory and statistics, come close to crediting the entire collapse of 1931, and its decade-long aftermath, to the death of Benjamin Strong.[3]

At the same time that the four great Western European powers, along with the United States, followed narrowly nationalistic economic policies in their international economic relations (the persistently high American tariffs are a further instance of this), they were without the means of following effective – much less, coordinated – policies toward their domestic economies. Unlike the conditions in the liberal period, the British economy and, to a lesser degree, that of the United States were beginning to feel the constriction from interests and groups whose self-protective reactions impeded ready economic adjustment through price change. We have no good measures of this and can speak only impressionistically. In the marketplace, labor unions were beginning to have some voice; large firms and employers' associations, much more. At the ballot box, in legislative chambers and in the halls of state bureaucracies, influences and lobbies from farmers and local and regional interests to obstruct and bypass market adjustments were even stronger.

France and Germany, of course, had never experienced total market freedom. Those societies had long abolished the forms, but never wholly the emotional burden, of manorialism in the countryside. They had eliminated most of the craft guild restrictions on industrial development, but mercantilism in state policy was still much alive. There were many points of liaison and mutual understanding and support between the state bureaucracies and the representatives of the large private interests: church, landowners (great and small), importers, exporters, industrialists with their cartels and syndicates, the mining interests, the trades, and professions. To these influences after 1900, and particularly after 1920, must be added those of the labor unions and the labor parliamentary parties. Their voices had not been stilled, but rather strengthened, with the adoption of welfare and pension legislation and

[3]Milton Friedman and Anna Schwartz, *A Monetary History of the United States, 1867–1960* (Princeton: Princeton University Press, 1964), 411–419. They write, "Because no great strength would be required to hold back the rock that starts a landslide, it does not follow that the landslide will not be of major proportion." But the fundamental cause of a landslide is not the rock whose fall precipitates it, but the whole positioning of the masses behind the rock, such that whether one rock or another gives way first is a matter of purely anecdotal significance.

the income and estate taxes imposed during and following the World War I.

All this is history, descriptive fact, or impression. It pushes explanation of the interwar period back one level deeper into the recesses of historical circumstance, into economic and political organization and social response. Why, one must now ask, did all this mutually destructive group spirit appear, issuing at the highest level in inextinguishable national rivalries and hatred?

Explanation is most often framed in political terms indicated by frequent appeals to the "if only . . ." formula. The biggest "if only" is that deriving from the failures of the League of Nations. "If only" the United States had joined the League, "if only" Wilson could have brought greater political skill to the service of his idealism, then, it is said, the gropings toward international amity and coordinated political and economic policies might have been formalized, the Weimar Republic might have become viable, and the pre-1914 development of capitalism might have picked up where it had left off, under a somewhat different and better contrived organizational structure. In economic relations, the candidate for "if only" is the financial orthodoxy of the British Treasury and the Bank. To this has been added recently the series of evidently ill-timed lowerings and rises of the New York discount rate by reserve authorities, torn by the need to restrain domestic speculation without at the same time attracting huge inflows of funds from abroad. But could the thirty-five-year hiatus between 1915 and 1950 have been dropped out of European history like a piece of leaky pipe, and the label of "miracle growth" for the 1950s and 1960s been placed on the 1920s and 1930s? Wrong actions were taken and wrong policies adopted, in response to situations created by a structure in which such dilemmas were recurrent. In 1910 the European nations had been set in an international political system of shaky alliances and poised power balance which needed only a tiny incident to set off the chain reactive explosion. In 1929, the European economies were in a similar position. To say, "If only Benjamin Strong had been alive" is equivalent to saying, "If only the Archduke Franz Ferdinand had not been shot." It is to confuse incidents of short-run and proximate significance with the structural and substructural conditions which permitted them to have such staggering effects.

Capitalism was an international phenomenon, an international system. Even its problems as they appeared within the shell of the various national economies seemed to be everywhere much the same. Why then were international policies, or an internationally coordinated set of national policies and structural changes, permitting a readier adjustment to new conditions and opportunities, evidently impossible to achieve?

Why was it that Wilson, Clemenceau, Lloyd George – or later McDonald, Baldwin, Blum, Roosevelt, and Schacht – were what they were? Was it impossible that the political cultures from which they emanated could have produced differently? Explanation is pushed back to the state of European society before World War I, to the national mercantilism, domestically and in foreign relations, that was growing after 1890.

Historians observing the troubled surface of the waters cannot simply point to one wave as the cause of the next. They must try to peer beneath the surface to look for disturbed currents and upheavals of the ocean's floor. We turn now to an immodest but fundamental and necessary effort of this sort.

III

The explanation of the interwar breakdown in competitive capitalist institutions and liberal economic policy forms a long and winding trail. By a strictly economic criterion, the system had had notable success in accommodating the growth opportunities in the five decades after 1870. These opportunities were of the two sorts suggested above: (1) those derived from trade and the division of labor unfolding over ever-extending geographic regions and encompassing populations growing through international migration so that new resources were brought into the network of exchange while the geography of production was rearranged to put those resources – land, minerals, and populations – to specialized use; and (2) those derived from technological change as it continued to unwind in many directions, offering continuously changing production functions and expanding openings for economies through the large-scale and systematic operation of industrial systems.

In exploiting these opportunities, the merchant capitalism of the century before 1870, with its organization around small-scale, market-linked industrial operations, proved itself remarkably able to expand and to innovate. In international finance, new types of credit instruments and new banking institutions made their appearance to facilitate trade and the transfer of capital. In the organization of capital to permit the construction of infrastructure and fixed equipment embodying new technology, and to help sponsor the development of that technology, other new or modified organizational forms appeared. The chartered corporation – an ancient device of the Crown to create monopolies – was transformed to serve industrial expansion. Industrial credit banks, stock exchanges, markets in bonds and securities, and financial intermediaries of all sorts were vigorously developed. Even international migration, though largely a matter of communication between family groups, was sometimes organized by steamship lines, railroads, manufacturers, and government agents. European governments followed surprisingly liberal policies toward emigration while governments in newly settled countries worked actively to attract white settlers.

In the pressures for economic development, legal institutions, especially concepts of property, changed, as did the concepts of appropriate state participation. Institutions, private or public, arose to supply specialized needs – small firms, large combinations, or, as in agricultural research, the agencies of the state. In the large firms, some service activities, especially distribution, were integrated into the firm; others, such as advertising, were split off to form separate professions. Along with large-scale techniques of production, capital and cost accountancy and a "science" of management constituted ingenious responses by owners to profit opportunities. As Alfred Chandler appears to imply in his recent work, much of this growth in scale and complexity of integration in large firms served socially useful, cost-saving purposes, permitting steady flows of materials and product from origin to markets.[4] Both in international trade and in large-scale production and distribution, capitalism showed itself to be ingenious and imaginative in devising structures to utilize available and abundant opportunity.

Yet in response to both these types of growth opportunity, an inner "dialectic" manifested itself. In overseas expansion the "biological dialectic" produced international rivalry and competition as the European exports of goods, money, and technology created centers of industrial capitalism elsewhere. This has been commented on above. In the growth of the large enterprises, the second, more famous dialectic, well-known to socialist thought, was at work. Capitalist enterprises bent on profit maximization and capital accumulation had no reason to stop their institutional innovations at the point where their contributions to the social good were exhausted. Larger-scale organizations developed market power and encouraged monopoly in order to maximize profits, going even beyond "pure" profit motivations to acquire power for its own sake of the marketplace. But similar impulses motivated other political elements: labor, peasants, landowners, small manufacturers, and shopkeepers. It also resulted in a strengthening, as we shall see, of the national state.

Here a curious contradiction is apparent between the two lines of

[4]See Alfred D. Chandler Jr., *Strategy and Structure* (Cambridge, Mass.: M.I.T. Press, 1962) and *The Visible Hand* (Cambridge, Mass.: Harvard University Press, 1977). A good summary of Chandler's historical findings is contained in his chapter in P. Mathias and M. M. Postan, eds., *Cambridge Economic History of Europe*, Vol. VII, Part II. Ch. II (Cambridge: Cambridge University Press, 1978).

new capitalist organization which emerged – and one which was to prove of fundamental importance in the breakdown. The new capitalist organizations in trade and finance did business internationally; a few of the largest were worldwide in range. The cutting edge of nineteenth-century finance, like that of the Renaissance, knew no nation. When threatened, capitalists ran for cover behind their national states, but in times of expansion, they seemed ready to outgrow their protection. And this expansion occurred under the phenomenon of British "hegemony," as political scientists call the centralization of the world's financial markets in London, the British control of the seas, and the large, though shrinking, British preponderance in manufactures. With free trade and free markets in gold and money, accompanied by the large British, French, and even German capital movements within Europe and into overseas spheres of influence, the system revolving around Britain *did* pass for a world system, in which tariffs and restrictions, and even other nations' attempts at empire, appeared as violations and intrusions rather than merely as the mercantilism of rival states.

Interestingly enough, as already noted, socialist labor movements of the later nineteenth century also professed internationalism. The goal of the Second and the Third Internationals was to unite the workers in every country to join the struggle against their international oppressors. *Proletarier aller Länder, vereinigt euch!* Why, then, we may ask, did the growth of a working class within capitalist society – the Marxian dialectic – lead not to internationalism, but away from it? One immediate answer is, of course, that victory in such a struggle requires control of the means to violence, and violence was contained within national armies and police. Simply put, except for the British navy, there was no international police force. If working-class movements had erupted simultaneously in many places, as liberal revolutions had erupted in 1848, capitalists could have resorted only to the separate national governments for repression. Politically, then, international capitalism was wholly dependent upon the monopoly of force lodged in the national state.

Now the nineteenth-century European national state was a peculiar animal, inherited from a mercantilist past.[5] It encompassed not simply laws, property rights, police, and armies, but the whole assortment of "precapitalist" social groups. National states were based in a funda-

[5]An objection to the various schemata for nineteenth- and twentieth-century economic history – notably those of Gerschenkron and Rostow – lies just here. By taking the nations as given entities, the history is turned into a mechanical dog race; if the policies, extent, and strength of the state itself are not included as a variable, political analysis has no way of blending with the economic, so as to allow each to share in the explanation of the other's phenomena.

mental way on national cultures, on linguistic groups, and on the sentiments and myths of national identity. There were reasons for unrest in the liberal order that lay deep in the unsatisfactory nature of the capitalist culture of Western Europe, for capitalists and socialists alike, which cannot be overlooked, even by a determined economic determinist. At this point, then, it is necessary to look outside the economy in order to explain the breakdown of the interwar economy. One must look to the state of European society, of which the nation or the national state was one manifestation.

IV

This is not the place for an elaborate methodological excursus. I hope to explain someday more clearly what I have in mind in abstract terms in a separate paper, if I can bring off anything at so high a level of abstraction. Briefly put, society may be defined as a human group which communicates well within itself and is able to reproduce itself with a certain continuity over time on the basis of values held in common and on individual behavior patterns which command mutual respect or tolerance.

Defined in this way, it is apparent that society is a matter of degree. A family, neighborhood, professional group, club, corporate organization geographic region, and nation all are societies or partial societies of varying extension, organized around different impulses or interests. There is a sense in which the human race forms a single society, held together by very weak links and without the social agencies required for reproducing itself in its entirety. A nation is one such social grouping, a rather large one, and when such a social group – often, though not always, facilitated by a common language – is coterminous with the area over which the control of force and violence is centralized, the nation-state so identified acquires great stability and force.

In order to reproduce themselves, societies must maintain institutions, organizations, and structures of rules, which allow for adjustment to their environments. But environment in this context has three components. First, the external environment must be managed in order to obtain the means of life and to defend a society against other groups. This involves (1) an economic organization and (2) an organization which can avail itself of physical force. Second, in its internal environment, a society must control members who, having not internalized the shared values, threaten to disrupt it. This requires (3) a civil government and police. But along with repression a society must also have (4) sets of institutions which permit the individual to have the means of self-expression and pleasurable social intercourse. This internal environment

– the interface of society with human nature itself – is perhaps the most pressing and the most difficult for a society to handle. Finally, to reproduce itself physically and behaviorally, a society must have (5) institutions which channel sexual and emotional drives (forms of self-expression and of love) into reproduction and care of the next generation, and it must also have (6) institutions to form this generation, i.e., child-begetting and child-training institutions.

These sets of institutions together give expression to such elements in human nature as may be considered basic. I suggest that these elements are: (1) an economic or acquisitive drive even beyond subsistence, a drive for the acquisition of materials goods or, put shortly, the satisfaction of *need* and *greed;* (2) a drive to *power* over others, whether to gain a sense of security or for the pleasure of exercising power and (3) a drive to self-expression which is based both on an internal need of the ego and on *love*. On the latter, familial, religious, artistic, intellectual, and sportive endeavor is based and organized. The drives work through one another – certainly acquisitiveness and power are closely allied, as also are power and love. In any role set, since whole persons and not disjointed "economic" persons or political animals are involved, all the motivations are to a degree present. Perhaps they are all in turn forms of a single "pleasure principle" or utility, but whether as unconscious instincts or objects of rational maximizing procedures, they function to produce individual action, and by interrelation with the actions of other individuals, the action of the social group. At its basis a society can achieve the highest degree of strength, stability, and durability if it can integrate all the institutions based on these drives into a unified and peacefully functioning whole.[6]

[6]This, I realize, is an "equilibrium" concept. It requires, indeed, a concept of the "complete person," in whom the drives are balanced, and for whom society has provided both the limits, or forms, and the opportunities for expression. Obviously in the human personality there is the possibility of a great deal of substitutability – to use an economist's term – among the drives, depending on how an individual has been formed, and also among alternative roles in which the drives can be expressed.

But if one cannot imagine the "complete man or woman," is it perhaps possible still to imagine (i.e., model) the "complete society," in which the range of roles and the range of personalities are well suited to one another, and reproduction goes on at a steady rate and composition? Obviously such an equilibrium (the traditional society?) may be disturbed by shocks from the external environments it must accommodate – natural catastrophe or war – and it may be continually altered from within by "slippage," a lack of fit of roles and individuals and inadequacy of the role sets to satisfy and express the drives motivating the whole population. Moreover, complex interconnections exist between the role sets in that each produces materials and ideas which individuals face in other compartments of social life. (For example, a labor force created

There is need for a consistency between institutions and the character structures which underlie them. The institutions shaping behavior and controlling it may succeed in producing a balance among individual personalities which throws a weight in one direction or another among the basic drives. But social theory, I suggest, must be based on the idea that there is something structural, something inborn, something "pre-wired" in the human individual which, taken over a group of individuals, requires some degree of expression in a set of social institutions.[7]

within the family is taken up in the economy, or technical and scientific ideas, created partly for their own sake, become available to alter production functions.) Evolution in the society over time occurs as sets change in their internal structures, pushed by the elemental dynamism of the basic "drives" and in response to environmental changes (opportunities) occurring through action in the other sets.

[7]On this, as on so much, scholars seem to fall into two camps. Economists who reject, or have remained untouched by, Marxian thought hypothesize a universal, fairly simple human nature in which an entrepreneur is latent. Such a creature is capable of both calculation and risk-taking, and is willing to devote most of his activity to trade or to organizing others for production for trade – working beyond reasonable hedonistic limits of comfort and welfare, simply for the joy of wealth accumulation and the outlet for the creative energies which produce, even as a by-product, that accumulation. Such a creature is assumed to be latent, if not in every individual, at least in some uniform frequency distribution among every population. This individual does not create the opportunities that make him and his society rich – these are created for him by nature, by consumers' "tastes," by the growth of geographical and technological knowledge, and by the development of social instruments – laws, monetary arrangements and the availability of supplies of labor and skills – all of which, lying within his range of vision, show him an opportunity which can be seized.

The whole thrust of a culture then as it reproduces its behavior traits in one generation after another may be slanted toward supplying relatively more such economic creatures, but the main social influence on their numbers comes from the favorable set of arrangements – the opportunities – by which such behavior is rewarded. In this view of things, the opportunities deriving from the Renaissance explosion of knowledge and social and intellectual freedom are seen as the activating cause of the expansion of modern capitalism.

In its extreme form, the alternative view of human nature makes it the creation of society itself. But as one follows out this view, one becomes mired in self-contradictions and absurdities at least as great as those present in the other conception. Where do individual traits and characteristics come from if not from human evolution within the environment of the natural and social world? And where do societies come from if not from the conditioned activities of their individuals? It is hard to see how either view can wholly dispense with the other. The range of indeterminacy between the two views is large, and neither psychological nor historical tests seem to be able to set the limits to the weightings of the two elements in the total social action.

It should be realized that the difference between the two views is not precisely that between an idealist and a materialist conception of the universe. The individualistic view can be materialistic in arguing that human actions are ulti-

When one sort of institution, one sort of character structure, or one value system of the society grows too rapidly, it must provoke restlessness and discontent and eventually a breakdown, or thorough readjustment, within the social whole.

In these terms it is possible to feel that the European economies grew *too* rapidly in the later nineteenth century. The opportunities were too broad, the responses too vigorous. International capitalism threatened to abolish national frontiers, and the large-scale economic organizations of capital and labor, whether at or beyond the point of economic efficiency, formed powerful controlling units threatening society as a whole. The labor movement in Europe must be viewed partly as a cause of, and partly as response to, this development. It was built out of fraternal, political, and economic motivations. European labor did not confront management simply with demands for more wages or even for more worker participation in profits. It invoked an alternative concept of society, a less individualistic one, based on an integration of work with politics, social life, and even religion. Given the rising real wages workers were not particularly oppressed. But they were alienated from the economic system based on private property and the acquisitive instinct – at least so their socialist leaders proclaimed. But pre-1914 socialism failed in two respects. First, it was essentially materialist and scientific, an heir to the Renaissance and not to the Middle Ages. Second, it paid too little attention to social elements within the national society which were marginal to the economic struggle of labor and capital.

These points are just the sort that arouse economists to unreasoning skepticism and other intellectuals to excessive credulity. Schumpeter even after a decade at Harvard retained enough of his sensitivity to German sociology to be aware of their value. In the essay on *Imperialism* (1919) he had identified what he called the "atavism" of precapitalist aristocratic and military classes as the truly motivating force. In *Capitalism, Socialism and Democracy* (1942), he added another group, the intellectuals, to the anticapitalist chorus. But he derived the failure of bourgeois capitalism to command the credence and loyalty of its intellectuals from the peculiar and perverse, essentially critical enterprise of intellectual activity itself. If this had been all there was to the

mately reducible to biochemical processes. Indeed it would seem to lend itself to that notion more easily than the socialist view. The latter, while professing itself to be grounded in "historical materialism," appears to have been imprinted by an Hegelian or a humanistic idealism more resistant to a biological reductionism in that its structures are lodged in history, and in social classes or groups. Surely it has proved itself at least as susceptible to utopian ideals as its individualist counterpart.

matter, liberal capitalism would not have been in very deep trouble. Instead, Europeans, I would suggest, seemed increasingly to need in politics, as they once had needed in religion, an intercessor between the individual and the universal, an object of tangible love on a grand scale, national symbols, a national history, language, and culture. The competitive character of the power struggle among nations reinforced the need for the sense of group security; once a great power was created, it was necessary for other would-be great powers to defend themselves. It was not simply a political necessity, but a psychic hunger that the national idea fulfilled, that gave it the emotional energy which toppled all before it – socialists, capitalists, peasants, Christians alike – into the excitement and disaster of war.

In this pre-1914 state of European culture, those who sought power over society, whether "politicians" or "statesmen," sensed this need: the thirst for security, familiarity, a sense of the normal and, no doubt, also for excitement and glory, which a national ideology could give. So it came about that the nation-state which had been an invention of liberalism, which had furnished the banner under which the bourgeoisie had fought down feudal and monarchical power, remained – despite its democratization – the device by which national capitalist groups could aspire to control a monopoly of violence with an ideology that would legitimize it.

After 1870, each nation developed a standard set of mercantilist policies – tariffs, an empire, social welfare schemes, extension and secularization of public schools, and stronger military forces. Each country which had a linguistic group in Europe had also inherited or developed a similar set of institutions and interests within itself – an aristocracy, an army, churches, industrialists, landowners – great and small engineers, intellectuals, workers, small businessmen. But their very similarities across the nations seemed to increase their sense of both national individuality and group rivalry. The organization of these groups horizontally on a pan European or worldwide basis was impossible. What but national spirit could hold these groups together within their national regions so as to defend them all against those outside? To maintain their mutual security or to implement plans of dominance, these nations maintained a shaky peace by means of a precarious balance of power, by honoring treaties among themselves and with the premodern empires in Austria-Hungary and Russia. One need not suppose that the World War I developed directly or inevitably out of fundamental economic or social causes which no alteration of political arrangements could have avoided. It is necessary simply to posit nations and a fragile political situation of opposing nations – ambitious or fearful – and to allow an accident to do the rest, setting in motion the chain reactions of violence.

Certainly by 1914, capitalist owners and managers were no longer engaged in freeing society from feudal and mercantile restrictions; they had themselves become a vested interest. But there were other groups – peasants, white-collar workers, shopkeepers – with a stake in the system. The right of suffrage had been widened, partly from a competition between the liberal capitalist and the older aristocratic classes for mass support, partly out of the momentum of liberal ideology. People held natural rights to own property, to govern themselves, to pursue happiness. But private property had been strongly lodged in fundamental constitutions, in decisions of courts, and in the ideology taught in schools and churches. Would nonpropertied classes claim and use the ballot to expropriate the property owners? This was the hope of democratic socialism, and this hope took the sting out of revolutionary movements and co-opted labor parties and socialist parties inside the liberal national-state. But what would be the case if such groups did not really form the effective majority in the nation, particularly taking into account their relative poverty and inarticulateness?

The mercantilist policies and the strengthened nationalism of the late nineteenth century derived only partly from capitalists' insecurity about the political bases of private property and profit. They issued from the national-states with enough force and legitimacy to be effective because those states had come to form emotional and cultural units in which large masses of the electorate found comfort and support. The strength of the nationalist impulse, as an answer to all threats, foreign and domestic, arose partly factitiously from fear, desperation, fright of small people and their small groups in a segmented and hostile environment, and partly from true sources in history and common social values.[8]

Prewar Europe had much the same problem of international order that is faced on a world scale by the power blocs today. Peace rested on international alliances, not on any organic international solidarities. The problem of internal order also was no different. Order rested in each country on popular support for the control of the monopoly of violence and education on a scale compatible with modern propaganda and military techniques. So strong a state system is easily corrupted from the ideal of a pluralistic justice, ensuring fundamental rights, to an instrument of oppression either of the "vast masses," as socialists claim,

[8]The nationalist impulse is nowhere so visible as in Africa since 1960 in the states formed from former colonies. Here lines had been drawn, some as old as the various partitioning agreements of the 1880s, with minimal regard for linguistic or cultural unity, and the struggle between national power and tribalism has been bloody and intense. Yet the nations appear to be the winners. Each has a flag, an army, an economic plan and policy, and a currency; most have systems of schools and propaganda. The vested interests in national identity strengthen wherever clan and tribe recede in their social roles.

or of minorities (e.g., the Jews or the rich), or – if the majority have a stake in capitalist property, land, jobs, or status – of the poor. This was the dangerous instrument to which all groups in the societies, all the subsocieties of the national society, laid claim. It commanded allegiance from the memory and a promise of order, internal peace, and the measure of comfort and freedom it gave. When it was threatened by another such state – a foreign power – that allegiance strengthened and hardened into fanatical determination.

V

In 1919 following the victories and defeats of the war, the European system returned to principles of national behavior which produced a continuation to more intense degree of the prewar history. With the withdrawal of both Russia and the United States from participation in Europe, each European nation had little alternative but to behave again as though it were the center of the world. Each followed its own national interest with no sense of responsibility for the future of all. What really is surprising in both Italy and Germany is the ultimate weakness of an international communist movement and its failure to hold up under socialist and liberal nationalist pressures. The weakness of international communism reflects the Stalinist strategy – itself a nationalistic one – to build socialism in Russia while fighting socialist parties in Europe. But even a less myopic policy on the part of the left could hardly have overcome the nationalist impulse. The revulsion in Italy from international socialism was a thoroughly popular movement. In Germany one cannot fail to observe how drawn out, painful, and bitter was the collapse of all the older aristocratic, liberal, and socialist forces. Yet fascist revolution occurred in both countries almost without a shot being fired except for blood shed in internecine struggles among fascist groups themselves.

So why, we may ask, were the 1920s and 1930s not repeated in the 1950s and 1960s after a war, more devastating than the first, had torn Europe apart and totally disrupted her economy? One reason often given is simply that the United States behaved better both in the world of finance and in its international relations. Its aid to Europe was intelligently conceived, as too were the monetary arrangements under the Bretton Woods Agreement. The United States also poured money in underdeveloped countries, thereby developing a market for European as well as American goods. To explain this maturity in U.S. policies, one must enter deeply into the recesses of twentieth-century American society. Within the countries of the European Common Market somewhat similar and compatible programs combining state, capitalist managers, and workers were strengthened. Workers' benefit programs, further extension of social security, and schemes of partial nationalization all had a part in preserving labor peace. European enterprise achieved a certain symbiosis with labor and with the state bureaucracies. But while organizing with American aid and advice, Europeans also organized to a degree as a group against the United States. The presence of the two giants, the United States and the Soviet Union, on either side, looking down into Europe as into a pit, dwarfed internal dissension. Perhaps the presence of Britain, the former "hegemon," standing just outside the Common Market for so long, strengthened internal cohesion.

As in all happy upward movements of this sort, success fed on itself. As war damage was restored, cities rebuilt, suburbs expanded, highways extended, incomes rose, and the internal market expanded. At this point, too, the penetrative power of mid-twentieth-century consumer technology made itself felt. Mass social communication ran like a steamroller over local cultures, ancient or Victorian. The phenomenon was known as "Americanization"; as it infected a whole new postwar generation, the shift in values toward private peace and away from national glory became pronounced.

Is it possible to suppose that one sees today in Europe not so much the end of Renaissance expansion as an adjustment in its aim and dynamic to realities of the whole world? Will this work back on the character structure of new generations as they are born to come to power in European countries to produce the possibility of a European society? Developments since 1975 have not been as encouraging as one hoped in 1950 but they are not completely negative. Americanization had scotched the snake of nationality, not killed it; a European culture and even European defense seem to require a strong national component for emotional support. On the other hand it is apparent that a sense of community within Europe alone is no longer enough. The problem of European peace has been translated to a world scale and with it also the problem of the sound functioning of the European economies.

BIBLIOGRAPHICAL NOTE

It is difficult to document selectively a body of generalizations as miscellaneous and wide-ranging as these. They are based on much secondary material: narrative and institutional histories, biographies, and specialist studies of the sort that have commonly been assigned in college courses in modern European history and politics, including my own in European economic history. Most of my reading has been in English, a little in French, and less in German. Below is a list of a few (mostly recent) books in English on some of the topics treated here, which I have consulted specifically in the preparation of this essay, or am conscious of as having influenced my interpretation of the events. In addition I must acknowledge a debt to a large number of colleagues and friends, at Yale and in the economic history profession at large, who have graciously given their time to reading drafts of this paper and who have endeavored to educate me in aspects of this history, particularly in the history of fascist movements and thought, of international monetary arrangements, and of producer combinations and industrial organization.

Aldcroft, Derek M., *From Versailles to Wall Street, 1919–1929*. Berkeley: University of California Press, 1977.

Alford, B. W. E., *Depression or Recovery? British Economic Growth 1918–1939*. London: Macmillan for the Economic History Society, 1975.

Banks, J. A., *Prosperity and Parenthood: A Study of Family Planning Among the Victorian Middle Classes*. London: Routledge, 1965.

Banks, J. A., *Victorian Values: Secularism and the Size of Families*. London: Routledge, 1981.

Banks, J. A. and Olive Banks, *Feminism and Family Planning in Victorian England*. New York: Schocken, 1972.

Berger, Suzanne (ed.), *Organizing Interests in Western Europe: Pluralism, Corporatism and the Transformation of Politics*. Cambridge: Cambridge University Press, 1981.

Brinton, Crane, *The Anatomy of Revolution*. New York: Knopf and Random House, 1938, 1965.

Brogan, Denis W., *The Development of Modern France, 1870–1939*. Rev. ed., London: H. Hamilton, 1967.

Brunner, Karl, *The Great Depression Revisited*, Boston: M. Nijhoff, 1981.

Cairncross, Alec and Barry Eichengreen, *Sterling in Decline: The Devaluations of 1931, 1949, 1967*. Oxford: Blackwell, 1983.

Chandler, Alfred D., Jr., *Strategy and Structure*. Cambridge: M.I.T., 1962.

Chandler, Alfred D., Jr., *The Visible Hand*. Cambridge: The Belknap Press of Harvard University Press, 1977.

Clark, Martin, *Antonio Gramsci and the Revolution that Failed*. New Haven: Yale University Press, 1975.

Croce, Benedetto, *History of Europe in the Nineteenth Century*. New York: Harcourt, Brace & World, 1933.

Dahrendorf, Ralf, *Society and Democracy in Germany*. New York: Norton, 1967.

Dangerfield, George, *The Strange Death of Liberal England*. London: Paladin, 1935, 1966.

Earle, E. M. (ed.), *Modern France*. Princeton: Princeton University Press, 1951.

Feinstein, Charles H. (ed.), *The Managed Economy: Britain since 1929*. London: Economic History Society, 1983.

Feldman, Gerald O., *Army, Industry and Labor in Germany, 1914–1918*. Princeton: Princeton University Press, 1966.

Feldman, Gerald O., *Iron and Steel in the German Inflation, 1916–1923*. Princeton: Princeton University Press, 1977.

Floud, R. and D. McCloskey, *The Economic History of Britain since 1700*, Vol. 2, *1800 to the 1970s*. Cambridge: Cambridge University Press, 1981.

Graubard, Stephen A., *A New Europe?* Boston: Beacon Press, 1967.

Hamilton, Richard F., *Who Voted for Hitler?* Princeton: Princeton University Press, 1982.

Hannah, Leslie, *The Rise of the Corporate Economy: The British Experience.* Baltimore: Johns Hopkins, 1976.

Hardach, Karl, *The Political Economy of Germany in the Twentieth Century.* Berkeley: University of California Press, 1981.

Heim, Carol E., *Uneven Regional Development in Interwar Britain.* Yale University, Department of Economics, Doctoral Dissertation, May, 1982.

Hinsley, F. H. (ed.), *The New Cambridge Modern History, Vol. XI: Progress and World-wide Problems, 1870–1898.* Cambridge: Cambridge University Press, 1962, Ch. 1–3, 9–11, 14, 22, 24.

Kindleberger, Charles P., *The World in Depression, 1929–1939.* Berkeley: The University of California Press, 1973.

Kohn, Hans (ed.), *German History: Some New German Views.* Boston: Beacon Press, 1952.

Kolakowski, Leszek, *Main Currents of Marxism,* 3 vols. (Eng. tr., P.S. Falla.) Oxford: Oxford University Press, 1978.

Kronman, Anthony T., *Max Weber.* Stanford: Stanford University Press, 1983.

Kuisel, Richard F., *Capitalism and the State in Modern France.* Cambridge: Cambridge University Press, 1981.

Latham, A. J. H., *The Depression and the Developing World, 1914–1939.* London: Crown Helm, 1981.

Latham, A. J. H., *The International Economy and the Undeveloped World, 1865–1914.* London: Crown Helm, 1978.

Lewis, W. Arthur, *Economic Survey, 1919–1939.* London: G. Allen, 1949.

Lewis, W. Arthur, *Growth and Fluctuations, 1870–1913.* London: G. Allen, 1978.

Lichtheim, George, *A Short History of Socialism.* New York: Praeger, 1970.

Lukacs, John, *The Last European War, 1939–1941.* New York: Doubleday, 1976.

McCloskey, Donald N., *Essays on a Mature Economy: Britain after 1880.* Princeton: Princeton University Press, 1971.

Maddison, Angus, *Economic Growth in the West.* New York: Twentieth Century Fund, 1964.

Maier, Charles, *Recasting Bourgeois Europe: Stabilization in France, Germany, and Italy in the Decade after World War I.* Princeton: Princeton University Press, 1975.

Mann, Golo, *The History of Germany Since 1789.* (Eng. tr., Marian Jackson.) New York: Praeger, 1958.

Mayer, Arno J., *Dynamics of Counterrevolution in Europe, 1870–1956: An Analytic Framework.* New York: Harper & Row, 1971.

Mayer, Arno J., *The Persistence of the Old Regime: Europe to the Great War.* New York: Pantheon, 1981.

Mayer, Arno J., *Politics and Diplomacy of Peacemaking: Containment and Counterrevolution at Versailles, 1918–1919.* New York: Knopf, 1967.

Merriman, John M. (ed.), *Consciousness and Class Experience in Nineteenth Century Europe.* New York: Holmes and Meier, 1979.

Milward Alan S., *War, Economy, and Society, 1939–1945.* Berkeley: University of California Press, 1979.

Mowat, C. L. (ed.), *The New Cambridge Modern History, Vol. XII, The Shifting Balance of World Forces, 1898–1945.* Cambridge: Cambridge University Press, 1968, Ch. 1, 3, 4, 8, 13.

Postan, Michael M., *An Economic History of Western Europe, 1945–1964*. London: Methuen, 1967.
Schumpeter, Joseph, *Capitalism, Socialism, and Democracy*. New York: Harper & Row, 1942.
Schumpeter, Joseph, *Imperialism and Social Classes, Two Essays*. New York: Meridian Books, Inc., 1954.
Shonfeld, Andrew, *Modern Capitalism*. Oxford: Oxford University Press, 1965.
Skocpal, Theda, "Bringing the State Back In: A Report on Current Comparative Research on the Relationship between States and Social Structures," in *Items*, vol. 36, no. 112. New York: Social Science Research Council, June 1982.
Svennilson, Ingvar, *Growth and Stagnation in the European Economy*, Geneva: United Nations (ECE), 1954.
Tilly, Charles (ed.), *The Formation of National States in Western Europe*. Princeton: Princeton University Press, 1973.
Tomlinson, Jim, *Problems of British Economic Policy, 1870–1945*. London: Methuen, 1981.

13

A comment on the papers: personal reflections and some diagrams

The two foregoing papers derive, I believe, from a "schema" formulated in my first cycle of research and amplified and adapted for later purposes. It may be useful to the reader of these papers to have a more explicit statement of this schema, with enough autobiography to show how it has formed and developed during my period of research and teaching in economic history.

I

My introduction into the study of economic history – and its introduction into me – came in 1947–1948, as the response, I fancy, of my mind, my training, and my self-perception to the need, after the Army, to find a suitable and useful career. Propelled into the civilian world in 1945, I circled first for two years to spot my prey. Washington, D.C., at that time, as now, was full of other birds similarly circling, looking hawklike for ripe fruit and small rodents. I flew there to a job, first with a U.S. Senator who was sponsoring the civilian control of atomic energy, then in the U.S. State Department, in the Division of Research for Europe, on economic aspects of a German settlement.

In this matter, as in so much else, American policy was schizophrenic. It was torn between the punitive impulse to "pastoralize" Germany and the American impulse to "get things going." The lawyers in the State Department were troubled about the economic consequences of the peace, recalling dimly what Keynes had so brilliantly – though not wholly correctly – said about Versailles. Germany must be denazified and decartellized, and its war potential kept under permanent scrutiny. The latter came to be defined as the coal and steel industries centered in the Ruhr – a curiously clumsy, narrow, and outdated definition of war potential even in 1948, but one that led to the Schuman Plan in 1950 and to the European Economic Community. In this body of concerns, I, a budding young research economist, became immersed. (Two steps up the bureaucratic hierarchy stood, amazingly enough, the loud and not yet world-famous German philosopher Herbert Marcuse.)

It was an exciting life, and almost a happy one. But as Hamlet said, "I could be bounded in a nutshell and could count myself the king of infinite space, were it not that I have bad dreams." I had left behind me in 1941, when I had gone into the Army, the pledge to write a doctoral dissertation at Harvard in economics. It was an unconsummated marriage, and I knew the bad dreams would continue – nightmares of falling, running, being chased – until I returned to settle them. So I was pulled, by the strong force of the superego, in 1948 to get a travel grant, formulate my topic, and go to the land of Marcuse, the land of poets, thinkers, and heavy industrialists, to work for two years in Essen on a dissertation bearing on Germany industry.

Why, I now ask, did I set my topic historically in the developments between 1900 and 1930, and choose to place it formally within the academic discipline of economic history? It was a choice not well understood by my Harvard advisers. Professor Mason thought history was fine since it dealt with industrial organization. Professor Leontief thought history was fine since it could be tackled with an input-output model. Professor Isard (my contemporary, but already beginning his work in location and space economics) assured me that historical study of the influence of energy sources on industrial location would be a valuable contribution. Paul Sweezy, at Harvard on one of his innumerable visiting appointments, thought history was a wonderful field, if you came out – as you inevitably would – with the right conclusions. All through my life I have found that economic history gets initial approval from almost everyone, but the next comment shows the reason: Each person defines it according to his likes. The reaction of the chairman of the Economic Department – Harold Hitchings Burbank – was the most upsetting of all. I came in one day when he was in a good mood to tell him my choice and he said, jovially, "Fine. The field's wide open." Then I came a week later to tell him again (it was always advisable to tell him things at least twice) and he said, gruffly, "It's a dying field." The only thing I knew that was wide open and received the dying was an open grave. But I no longer had a choice; I had already jumped in and was wrestling with the gravediggers.

I hardly knew at the time the reason for the choice, but I think I know now. A boy's moral nature is formed, the Jesuits are alleged to say, before he is twelve, and I would add, the bent of his intellect by the time he is twenty. As a youthful undergraduate I had majored at Harvard in English literature. That meant that I could never see the world quite as an economist. Yet I had invested two years of graduate training – ferocious fifteen-hour days, months on end – in economics. I had done so out of intellectual restlessness and out of conscience. My mind seemed to need the strong structure that economics claimed to impart and which my conscience had wanted to use to help save the world from misery and want. But now – six years and one war later – the structure of economic theory seemed shallow and contrived, even when expressed awesomely in mathematics, in which I had had no advanced training. And saving the world now meant applying my comparative advantage to the problems of the German settlement. My comparative advantage, so far as I could assess it, seemed to lie not in the ability to write quick papers on current events, but in my affinity for serious and weighty historical scholarship. So from some such rag-bag of impulses, fixed costs, and imprecise self-assessment I selected my field and set out on a cycle of research on the coal and steel industries of the Northwestern European regions.

II

It was a complex interregional problem. I pinched off an inchoate chunk of it to form a dissertation, then, storing the problem in my subconscious for several years, returned to find that I had gained a sense of its structure and dimensions. The need really was to gain a judgment on whether the German regions had been more efficient and dynamic as economic structures than the Franco-Belgian ones. This, it should be emphasized, was no mere academic problem at a time when policies were formed to affect whether, and how, the Ruhr or the French industries would be reconstructed. The research problem in making any judgment lay in the great variety of "factors" involved: the geological deposition and chemical composition of the minerals, the accessibility of water transport, the factor cost rates, the tax levels, the location and depth of markets, the laws governing minerals discovery and firm organization, the organization of industrial research, the character of labor supplies, and that great residual catalyst – entrepreneurship.

Table 1, adapted from an appendix in my book (joint with N. J. G. Pounds) *Coal and Steel in Western Europe,* shows how the huge variety of "factors" arranged themselves in my mind. Reconstructing it now from that effort, I can see several elements implicit in the attitudes I held at that time toward the material. Several were, I think, important for this and later work:

(1) The definitions of industries and regions, and the desire to develop a general framework by which the economic records of several such could be seen as a whole and compared

(2) The notion that within such a defined framework individual causal fac-

Table 1. *Evolution of the "great schema": schema for the comparative study of mining and heavy industrial regions*

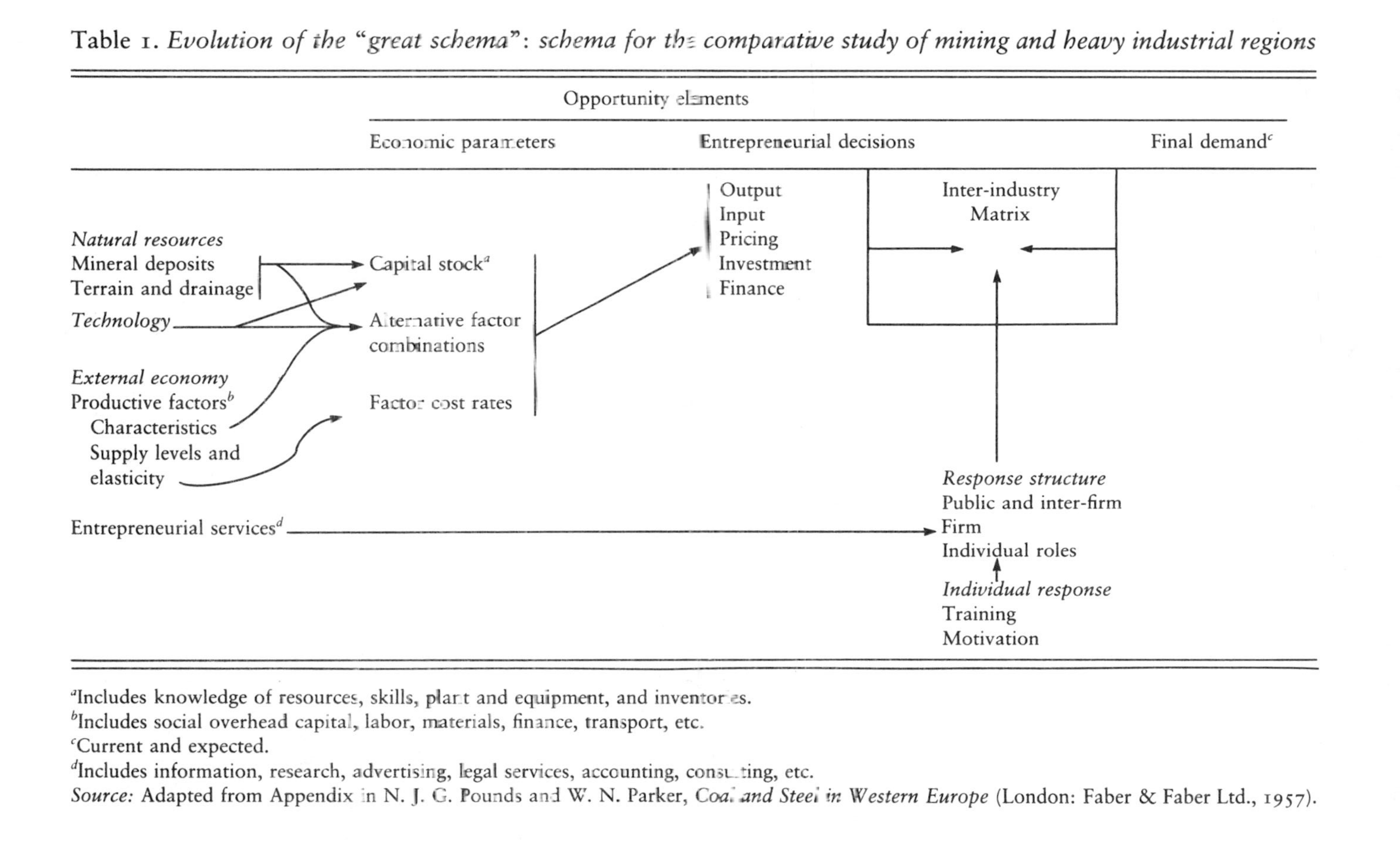

[a]Includes knowledge of resources, skills, plant and equipment, and inventories.
[b]Includes social overhead capital, labor, materials, finance, transport, etc.
[c]Current and expected.
[d]Includes information, research, advertising, legal services, accounting, consulting, etc.
Source: Adapted from Appendix in N. J. G. Pounds and W. N. Parker, *Coal and Steel in Western Europe* (London: Faber & Faber Ltd., 1957).

tors could be studied in isolation and the effects of differences and changes in their quantity or behavior in one regional industry relative to another could be assessed

(3) The separation of "opportunity elements" – given by a growing knowledge of nature or by movements in the economies within which the industries and regions were lodged – from a "response structure," a framework of human organization and motivation

(4) The notion that the records had to be explained in terms of the actions of individuals, working within such structural constraints to opportunities offered by elements exogenous to the regional industries themselves

Looking at such evidence as I could on all these aspects of this problem, I concluded from my structure that several among the items of the opportunity structure moved similarly in all the regions over the period 1870–1914. *Conditions of factor supply* were not very different, not necessarily because labor and capital moved internationally among the regions, but because each national economy was growing vigorously within itself. Labor was a bit cheaper and capital a bit dearer in Germany, but no sharp inelasticities of supply of either labor or capital funds into these regions and industries from the several national economies, no serious bottlenecks of one factor or the other, appeared to arrest expansion. *Technology* moved readily across borders, thanks partly to the professionalism of mining and metallurgical engineers who insisted, despite businessmen's secrecy, in reading papers to one another, publishing new ideas, holding conferences, and making plant visits, after a fashion that would have warmed Thorstein Veblen's heart. The movement of *Demand* was harder to judge, but per capita demand probably grew at about the same rate in all these markets. In finished steel, the German regions had the advantage of faster-growing markets, especially in shipbuilding and construction. Coal and ore moved readily in international trade, impeded only by overland transport costs, which along the Rhine, the Moselle, the Saar, and the Meuse with their related canal systems were not high. This left *natural conditions* as the residual. The Ruhr had much the largest, and cheapest coal reserves of the most varied qualities, and the Ruhr's location was favorable to the use of imported ore and scrap from overseas. An open-hearth steel industry could grow up there much surpassing what the other regions could create. But the French resource discoveries of ore and coal, spurred on by the losses in 1870, were remarkable. A whole new ore field was uncovered in French Lorraine and in the boom around 1900, the Nord and Pas de Calais coalfield, despite its age, yielded large, new, exploitable deposits. Certainly nothing was wrong with the French discovery or investment mechanism in either of these cases. With judgments like these, guided, though not logically demonstrated by my schema, I came to feel I had a grasp on the relative opportunities the industries faced and was in a position to assess the relative effectiveness of the several national economic structures in responding to them.[1]

Ten years passed. I had written the dissertation and done the coal and steel research in Europe. Having returned to teach in the United States, I had specialized in U.S. economic history – a bit out of patriotism but also because, as Willie Sutton said when asked why he robbed banks, "That's where the money was." Money did not mean simply Ford and NSF grants – though they were flowing in abundance, but also the gold of documentary materials, particularly quantitative ones, which lay about in profusion. Why had earlier economic historians never used any modern sampling techniques on the manuscript censuses of agriculture and manufacture? One reason was that as historians trained in those days, they had never heard of sampling techniques. Another was that data couldn't be machine-processed. But it was also true that like the beaver trappers who trapped the California gold streams in the 1830s, the earlier historians – Phillips, Bancroft, and Shannon – weren't looking for gold. Our group of economists felt like 49'ers as looking down we saw beautiful numbers, gleaming at us from every archive. But we were not merely greedy; we were devastatingly ambitious. We wanted to spend our gold on the quest for the Holy Grail of the 1960s – to find the sources of economic growth. My own ambition at the time was to write an economic history of the United States, explaining why, if America wasn't particularly smart, it had gotten so rich.

In the 1960s the academic scene was suddenly swarming with scholars animated by the same *Zeitgeist*. In two conferences of the National Bureau's Conference on Research in Income and Wealth (1957 and 1963) it was possible to organize the disparate work going on in all directions around Kuznets's central questions: How fast had the national product grown? What structural changes had occurred during the growth? What were the underlying historical causes of these economic trends? I brought my best treasure to throw on the fire – the outline from my coal and steel study – a small thing, but (I fancied) mine own. My teaching in both European and American economic history had been organized around its framework, and now I tried to turn it into a scaffold on which the trunk, the branches, and even the leaves of the great tree of growth could – like a piece of stage scenery – be suspended.

[1] My interest was not directly in the opportunities, but in the relative efficiency of the response mechanism – the bureaucracies, cartels, firms, and individual entrepreneurs – in the French and German national economies. This was of interest in the 1950s because of the impression among American students of Europe that the French entrepreneurial structure was old fashioned and decrepit, laced with small firms, and tied up in nets of social relationships among families, among firms, and with the state.

It was necessary in my diagram (see Table 2) to move the mining and transport industries into the interindustry matrix, as part of the mechanism of growth, subject to the price system, leaving the natural facts of geography and physical conditions of resource supply as determinative factors, of whose character, history uncovered the knowledge. Also, factor costs, reducible to labor and interest, became economic variables not given to the economy, but set by markets in which supply of and demand for labor and for capital funds and capital goods met. Behind them, on the supply side, lay the labor force, as derivable from the population, and the capital stock as embodying the technology (also embodied in labor skills), in turn derived, like resource supplies, from the growth of knowledge. This produced the schema shown in Figure 1. For a full model, it would be necessary of course to add a few more pipes and boxes, for the government, export, and financial sectors; to divide the omnibus category "demand" into the Keynesian trinity of consumption, savings, and taxes; and to specify the composition of final demand, as well as, in the financial sector, the demand side of the composition of asset holdings. This was the diagram that my graduate students, groaning as they did so, called the "great schema" when I put it on the board the first day of the class each term. Whatever they thought, I found that its virtue as a teaching device was its open-endedness. It does not, I insisted to them, compel any specific theory of economic growth – unicausal or multicausal. That depends on the weighting of the factors and the number of feedback pipes by which one wishes to interconnect them. It appeared in the 1972 textbook that capped the joint efforts of twelve apostles of the New Economic History, *American Economic Growth: an Economist's History of the United States.*[2]

Now I ask myself, why did it seem necessary at that time to construct so elaborate an edifice, such a plumber's nightmare of boxes and pipes, when I must have known that nearly all of them would remain empty? It is commonly said that the art of theorizing is the art of simplifying. One must pick out a few variables ("key" variables is the cliché) and a few relationships, then construct the model of how they are related systematically to one another. That is the way to success in economics, and we idolize those rare, lean, and efficient spirits who can do just that, and do it with elegance and precision.

But that is not what I want to do at all. Matthew Arnold's ideal for the cultured life was to see life steadily and to see it whole. That was my standard for looking at the economy over time. It is true that, as a gown-clad scholar in a *New Yorker* cartoon complained to a colleague,

[2] L. Davis, R. Easterlin, and W. Parker (eds.), (Harper and Row, New York, 1972).

Table 2. *Evolution of the "great schema": conversion of regional industry schema to the national economy level*

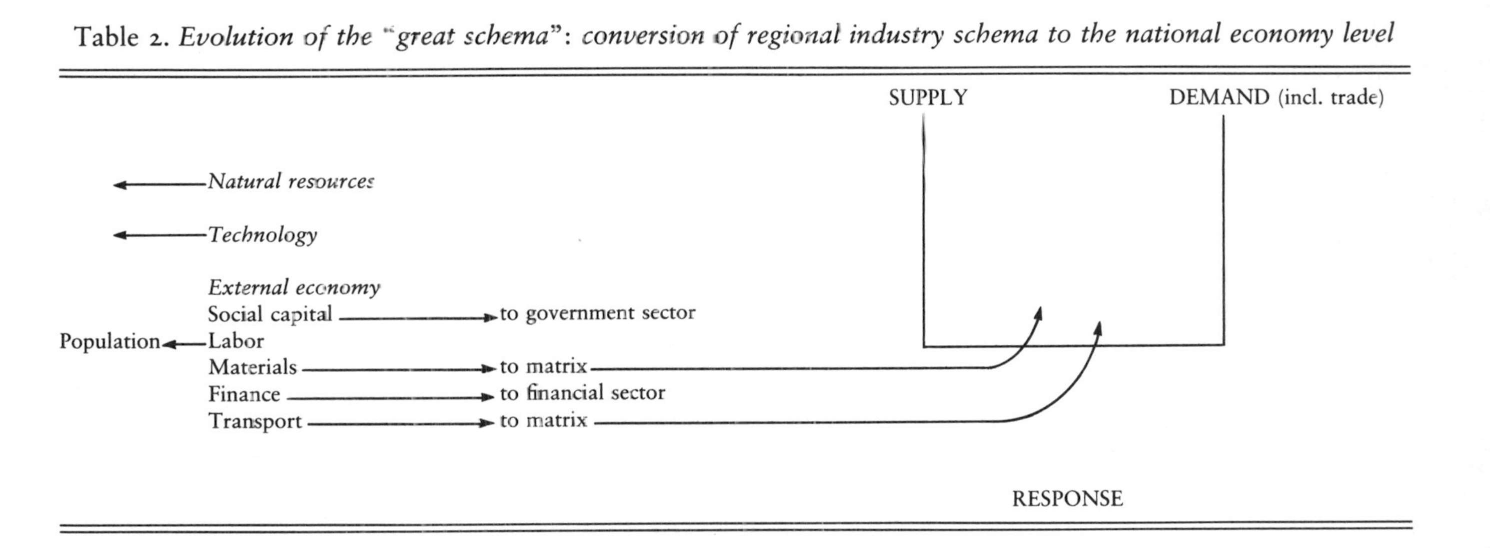

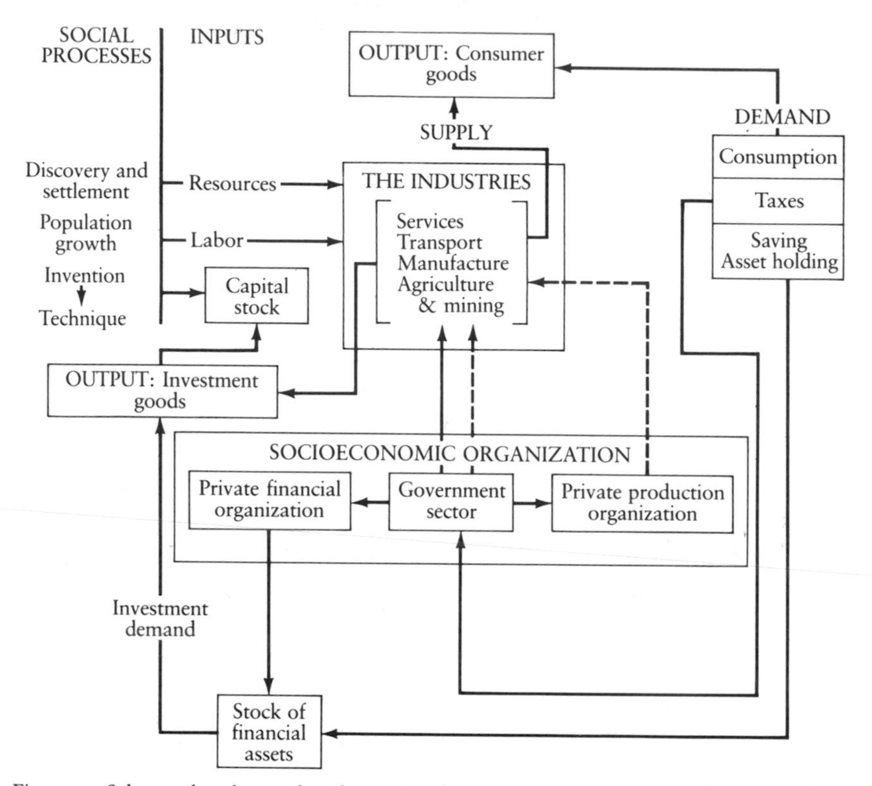

Figure 1. Schema for the study of a national economy. For purposes of simplicity, the foreign sector (exports, imports, and capital flows) is omitted from this figure. (From Davis, Easterlin, and Parker, *American Economic Growth: An Economist's History of the United States,* New York: Harper & Row, 1972, p. 5. By permission.)

"The trouble with a unified theory is that it doesn't explain why the grass is green, why the birds sing or why interest rates are so high." But that is exactly what I wanted a theory to do for the social world. Why this need for completeness, this incapability of working on any one corner of reality without the assurance that that fit into a totality? I know now why, or I think I do. My generation was in a revolt against partial explanations that claimed to be complete, and in revolt at the same time against "mere" literary expositions. We wanted to know the size of the phenomena we were working with, the measure of their dimensions; we thought in our naive empiricism that that information would give some indication of the weight to be given those phenomena in a moving totality. We wanted a picture of the total social reality, a snapshot of all the detail as well as the main features – never mind whether it was in "equilibrium" or not. Then we could turn a time-ordered set of those snapshots into a moving picture – much like the first movies, where the machine flipped through a pile of stills rapidly to create the illusion of motion. *That* is total descriptive history, the dream of Ranke and, in a sense, of Schmoller, if not of Braudel and the current *historiens totalitaires*. Only when that is done – we thought – will we be ready to advance hypotheses, explanations of why the motion is repetitive or stable, speeding up or slowing down, cyclical or revolutionary, showing "long-run growth" or static equilibrium.

A mad dream – but perhaps no madder than the notion that one can say anything useful about social reality with a few equations – the dream of the dynamic growth models developed by theorists at that same time. And of course, like those, it was wedded to a national income approach and the concept of an aggregate production function.

The work produced, I think, valuable pictures but rather banal generalizations. But this is not surprising. It was designed to record history, as by a camera, equipped with both wide-angle and zoom lenses, placed at the point where the economy's final product and set of factor payments issue out from the system. Even on a worldwide comparative basis, the wisdom brought smacked of that of Polonius and produced reactions from graduate students reminiscent of Hamlet's.[3] No, there is no doubt that to explain something, one needs not just a schema, a taxonomy, an infinity of interconnected boxes; one needs some assumptions about behavior and one needs an energizer – or two or three such – working on the system.

III

I come now to the two essays presented here. Each one tackles a very large subject. The first essay tries to explain how it was possible for the European economy to expand in output and productivity more or less continuously – extending ultimately into all its parts between 1500 and 1900. The second asks what went wrong around that date to make the inter-war record appear as a break, or a leveling off of these trends. In both papers, the use of the schema is apparent. In the first one, it is the opportunity side that is emphasized; in the second, it is the social organization of the response.

The argument in the first paper is stated and amplified in the paper's appendix. Given population growth, in the presence of scale economies in industrial and mercantile occupations and not excessively diminishing returns in agriculture, a growth of productivity may occur. And this, in the presence of a growing knowledge of markets, lands, and re-

[3]Polonius: Fare you well, my lord! (Going)
Hamlet: These tedious old fools!

Hamlet, Act II, Scene ii

sources may move an economy from a Malthusian trap into the processes of Smithian productivity growth. That dynamic process having begun, it may then be the case that – in the presence of appropriate attitudes toward science, engineering, and the simple manipulability of the natural world – the density of the nets of trade and communication and the tempo of messages transmitted over them may induce faster, steadier, and better-directed technological change, in a self-supporting and accelerating stream. With this, one is moved out of the Smithian world into the nineteenth century, where the three processes – Malthusian, Smithian, and Schumpeterian – are all at work.

These three processes are in fact the three factors lodged in the supply and demand sides of my "great schema." In the first paper's appendix, I have shown the developments schematically and isolated some of the feedbacks on which its continuous movement depended. At each transition, scale effects are crucial; a large trading world economy derives from a large population and resource base, and that in turn gives both the economic impetus and the dense communications net from which technological change, as a continuous process, can derive. All this, one feels, is a suitable subject for study by an economist seeking to explain history in terms of physical relationships and the drive for profits and accumulation under a capitalist organization.

For the historian the questions do not stop here, and explanations cannot run simply in terms of ill-defined "feedbacks" within an economic model. Demand is not a simple derivate of trading opportunities or production growth, but is composed of many channels each running back to one of the many components of social, cultural, and political life. New generations of a labor force come not out of the economy, but out of familial life. The voyages and discoveries were initiated not largely by merchants but by states and private explorers, from an array of unbusinesslike motives. A society's technology is an artifact not simply of its economy, but of its culture, from which derive also its fine arts and the history of its philosophical and scientific thought. Capitalism itself, defined in my diagrams as the "response mechanism," is a molding of perennial human drives and urges in the complex social and religious environment of sixteenth-century Europe. In the separate histories of all these human activities that lie around the history of the economy, general historians do not endeavor to explain the growth of wealth; insights into that come from their work as a by-product. Other human drives and motives are at the basis of these phenomena, and these act and react according to a different logic from that of the world of business.

In Table 3, I have tried to show some of the processes that surround the economy, in terms of the Parsonian concept of "roles" and in rela-

Table 3. *Relation of social structures and processes to the economy*

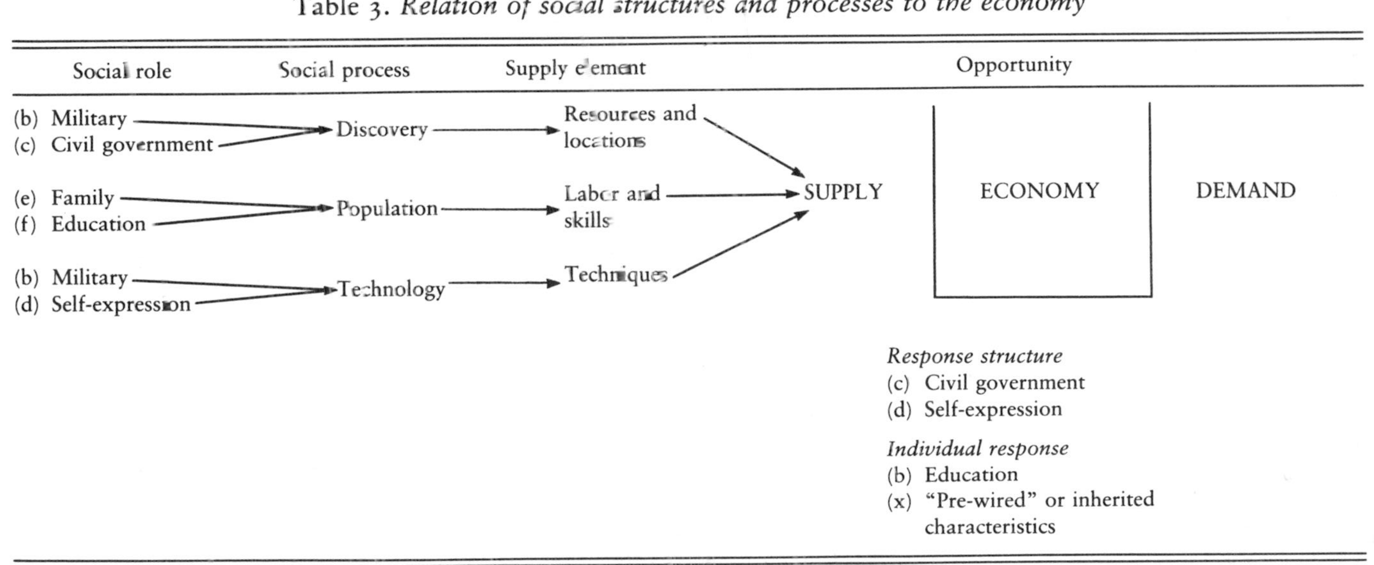

Note: Letters in parentheses indicate role sets shown in Table 4 below.

tion to their function in maintaining social structure. But, as stated previously, the first paper here needs these concepts only for showing the framework of opportunity in which the Western economies could grow. Such a history does not show that Europe had to grow. That depended at every stage on the response structure – on actions of entrepreneurs, governments, explorers, inventors, families, workers to the opportunity, as it filtered down in subdivided fashion into every cottage, field, and workshop, in these economies. But it does show that with a steadily and generally strong response mechanism, called capitalism, the West *could* be led by an encouraging logic immanent in the processes themselves along the historical path we observe.

The second essay, (Chapter 12, on the response), is in a very real sense incomplete. For one thing, it is inartistic. The bare bones of the schema protrude in the formal way it takes up the opportunities, then turns to the response. Furthermore, I was too eager to get to the response. For years I had taught and written about opportunity: resources, trade, population growth, and technology. It was not out of love for those subjects. It was out of that conscience that makes cowards of us all – and perhaps a little out of intellectual insecurity. Those subjects, with their physical and natural components, were real, not psychological; tangible, not spiritual; they did not depend on ideology. People were not free, I felt, except within constraints. One needed to study the most enduring of those constraints – those set by nature, *before* examining the social constraints people had contrived for themselves, or their volatile reactions within them. But my humanistic undergraduate education had never left me. The human being was still to me the measure of all things, and with all my measuring, I still wanted to reach the mysteries of the human heart, the constraints human beings put on themselves in society, and the susceptibilities and drives that caused them to operate within and through those constraints and pushed humanity into altering them, through social erosion or through violent revolution.

So I dismissed the opportunity constraints on economic life since 1920 too lightly. Perhaps I need not have located the entrance of a "Schumpeterian process" as early as the English Industrial Revolution. Science and engineering did begin to enter the economy then. But the science was largely mechanics, and the sponsorship was still compatible with small scale market-oriented firms. Those decades until 1870 I might in the first paper have called proto-Schumpeterian; the large-scale integration of science, engineering, and the economy should be situated in Schumpeter's own century, after 1880. The Schumpeterian dynamic has continued to the twentieth century, while population growth, resource discovery, and trade, though continuing under an international capitalism, have been dominated by it. As engineering has moved beyond the electricity to electronic and atomic engineering and chemistry to biochemistry, with its immense implications for the world's resource and agricultural industries, it is apparent, as the first essay (Chapter 11) concludes, that we are in the hands of the technologists, struggle as we may. Or is it the case that already by 1920 technological change had become so strongly controlled by feedbacks from the economy, both in the demand for inventions and in the supply of funds and risk capital for research and development, as hardly to be an exogenous "opportunity" variable at all? I should have given more and closer attention to this aspect of the contemporary economies before rushing so quickly into suggestions about the response structure and motivations. If indeed technology, for its own good reasons, was experiencing a pause between the two wars, and required the intensity of effort displayed in the Second World War to make the breakthroughs we have seen, then the problems of the interwar period – at least insofar as average growth rates are concerned – are directly explainable here, and no amount of human skill and contrivance could have reduced them. Even so, the path of deceleration surely did not need to be as bumpy as it was. A slowing population growth, vanishing overseas investment opportunities, and an absence of technological breakthroughs did not *need* to produce violent inflations and deflations, prolonged unemployment, and bouts of international economic warfare. Those were human reactions within a social and economic structure to such a structuring of opportunities.

In this paper, too, the problem of modeling the response mechanism, or my inexperience in doing so, shows up. Here one is involved with processes that do not have the wealth of nations but the power, the security, and the cohesion of social groups as their main end. The scale phenomenon, so puzzling in the explanation of the nation-state, is not one of scale of markets or communication among entrepreneurs, but of the scale over which social organizations are deployed, and within which the instruments of the state – laws, educational systems, police, and armies – are utilized. Why did the nation-state grow so strong when international capitalism, technology, and scientific culture extended itself so vigorously around the world? The essay seeks to touch this question, and in touching it readers may feel that they have touched bottom in the ultimate reason for the economic trends since 1870.

Economists move here into very deep water. They must shed the plastic bubbles that have kept them afloat, the inflated wings labeled "economic man" and even "rational behavior." As Shelley wrote, "The massy earth and sphered skies are riven. And I am borne darkly, fearfully afar . . ." into what is for me the black hole of political sociology, ". . . a Serbonian bog" – as Milton says – "where armies whole have sunk." How should I think about what I continue to call the "response mechanism"? Not mechanistically, I suspect, but perhaps electrically, biologically, or chemically. Of one thing I feel a perhaps unwarranted certainty – which may explain, if not excuse, the brashness of my effort in the essay and in Table 4, with its naive references to "drives," reminiscent perhaps of the early Veblen, and to "greed," "love," and other terms an economist shudders to employ. A science of society or of politics can never be stabilized – it seems to me (as it has to many others) – unless like economics it can develop explicitly, firmly, unswervingly some model of the psychological sources of human action, some defined view of human nature. Where are we free, where determined, how does our underlying physiology enter, what can heredity create, how much can social influence do? Given such a view, may one then look at behavior in politics, in society, in cultural life, as well as in economics, as rational individual responses to opportunities? May one sketch out, as in economics, the inner social logic of a process of political or social development as the basis of process-histories following those of the economic historians?[4]

Such an effort begins, no doubt, with the economist's familiar utility maximization, including in the utility function not only profit or wealth, but leisure, self-righteousness, childbearing, creative joy, self-abandonment, or any other of the goals to which we see men and women giving themselves. But the effort must go far beyond such simpleminded rational constructs. For one thing the individual must be seen not as an independent atom with goals and identity firmly fixed, but as a sensitive plant, capable of being swayed and changed in the very direction of his desires, by his activities in the course of obtaining them, and by the content of his satisfactions – seen, that is, as a malleable and social creature. Marxists have been telling us this for years. And an ultimate problem for Marxists and non-Marxists alike (whatever those labels may

[4]It does not become me to prescribe for historians. But may it not be their next task to develop structures of explanation for the history of the activities contained in the other functional "role sets": (b) military, (c) civil government, (d) artistic, intellectual, social, and religious activities, (e) family life, (f) education, comparable to what economic historians have tried to trace for (a) the economy? Some of these histories are much more difficult to visualize since the "product" of the social process in wars and other violence; politics; art, science, and religion; family life including marriage and fertility patterns, and child-raising and socialization is superficially less easily visualized, measured, and specified than is the product of economic life under a price system. Still, we do not consider the measurements of wealth, income, capital, the utility of consumption, and the disutility of labor to be as unambiguous as we once did, and there is no philosophical reason why "process histories" in these other activities should really be more elusive than the meaningful description and analysis of economic behavior.

Table 4. *Psychological drives, social structure, and socio-economic function*

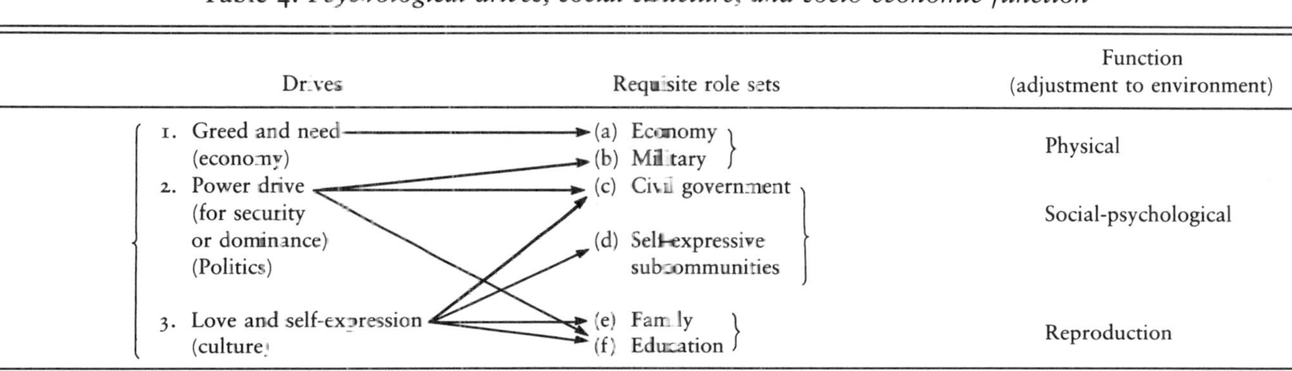

Drives	Requisite role sets	Function (adjustment to environment)
1. Greed and need (economy)	(a) Economy	Physical
	(b) Military	
2. Power drive (for security or dominance) (Politics)	(c) Civil government	Social-psychological
	(d) Self-expressive subcommunities	
3. Love and self-expression (culture)	(e) Family	Reproduction
	(f) Education	

mean) lies still deeper: There must be room in the model of society for irrational or purposeless behavior. Human beings are born into society where roles have been already set. They are poured into them in their youth and compressed within them during adult life. Those structures have been created by people in history and are sustained by the conditioning of people through history. Within them, individuals express values, goals, loyalties, antipathies, turns of mind and of desire. In our conscious lives we pursue these – even perhaps try to maximize on occasion, acting under the magnificent illusion of human freedom. But in the choices we make in creating societies, and in leading lives within them – choices and lives that often strike an outside observer as willful, perverse, self-destructive – is there an ultimate principle, whether rational in a human sense, or otherwise? And if not, how can human reason, which is the social scientist's only instrument, contemplate a "science of society"? What is the ultimate, value-free rationality that a historian or a social scientist brings to his material?

So I am in a sense back to a humanistic beginning. Within this circuit of one scholar's intellectual history, what do these papers, what indeed does the whole cycle of my research, seem to me to say?

For four hundred years following the Renaissance discoveries of new worlds, the European peoples created, within national cultures and societies, economic structures well suited to express and develop unfolding opportunities for the growth of wealth and productivity. After 1920, perhaps beginning even half a century earlier, the opportunities appear – at least from our present vantage point – to have shifted and the structures, particularly the international structures, to have grown transitory, inadequate, and frail. They had new and difficult adjustment problems, but much of the failure surely arose from deeper sources in the layers of civilization below the economy. Profit maximization and wealth creation by the actors in an international capitalism could not be made compatible with either the contesting drives for power and safety of the national states or the simpler needs of twentieth-century men and women for the warmth and security of large, all-embracing societies of subcommunities within the international economy and culture. After 1948, Europe encountered wide opportunities for renewed growth and its structures had altered in many subtle ways to allow their utilization. The twenty-five years after 1948 show a much brighter record than the two decades after 1918. We watch now with bated breath to see how durable and flexible these structures may prove in the situation of altered opportunity developing over the years since 1973. This is, I think, as much as the two essays presented here or indeed the whole body of my thoughts and research on Europe can say.

A comment on the papers

Where will it all end? Writers of discourses such as this lack a sense of completion if they fail to end their books on a note of fashionable pessimism. After all, it is a lazy scholar's "out" to predict an end to history, since then one is under no obligation to go on with the chronicle. But professors who teach students see society in its most hopeful, reproductive phase. It is not uncommon for them, in their heart of hearts, to fantasize a vision of civilizations stretching as far ahead into the future as they have back into the past, and continuing like those past civilizations to reel erratically and convulsively down the corridors of Time. On such a moving panorama of civilizations, they often discern, too, figures of intellectuals, continuing to chase after their societies, a sheaf of rattling papers in hand, as one chases after a busy department chairman, trying to get in a word as he or she rushes off, late for a meeting.

APPENDIX

A. P. Usher: an appreciative essay

The work of the Harvard economic historian, A. P. Usher, will be remembered first of all because it has illuminated limited areas of history. His careful investigation and sound judgment have taught us more about medieval trade and early banking, about mechanical invention, about the influence of resources on industrial location, about the role of public policy in industrialization, about the textiles, the metal trades, the railroads in the Industrial Revolution. In judging Usher's influence on his successors, too, one thinks first of the example set by these separate and substantial contributions to knowledge.[1]

Such concrete achievement points none the less to a consistent attitude toward the scope, the methods, and the meaning of the social sciences. In a review of Nef's *Rise of the British Coal Industry* in 1933, Usher wrote:

> It has long been the conviction of the present writer that this is the way economic history should be written. . . . Whatever may be the merit of the large-scale history of a single period in political or constitutional history, there are grounds for believing that any well rounded achievement of this character is impossible in the field of economic history. A relatively long time period must be treated if the results are to be of real significance, and a larger geographic

Originally published in J. Lambie, ed., *Architects and Craftsmen in History. Festschrift für Abbott Payson Usher*. (Tübingen: J. C. B. Mohr (Paul Siebeck), 1956). Reprinted by permission.

[1]Professor Usher's extensive bibliography breaks down into five major groups of writings: (1) his three major works of research, (2) his two texts, (3) numerous historical articles, (4) review articles and comments on methodology, (5) some semi-popular discussions of problems current at the time. The present discussion draws to some extent on Usher's published comments on methodology (Group 4), but is focussed mainly on the attitudes revealed as shown in his own historical work (Groups 1–3). Perhaps the most fully developed statement of his view of history and history-writing is contained in the revised edition of *A History of Mechanical Inventions* (Cambridge: Harvard, 1954), ch. 1–4.

area must be covered than is adequate for the political or constitutional historian. True, any large work is of value; the real issue is the most effective use of time. Does one contribute as much . . . in the form of a comprehensive period history, as in the form of carefully executed studies of special topics . . . ? Professor Nef's study of the Coal Industry will be accepted as definitive long after Sombart's *Moderner Kapitalismus* has been relegated to the group of books that are significant not for the history of men and events, but only for the history of thought.[2]

Along such lines Usher's own research and teaching have been directed. His three major monographs – on the grain trade in France, on mechanical invention, and on deposit banking – have dealt with single subjects over periods of several centuries. His original treatment of massive but selected and discrete topics in economic experience over rather long periods dominates also his two texts (the *Industrial History of England,* and his substantial contributions to the *Economic History of Europe since 1750*), and a similar attitude toward subject matter is evidenced in the syllabi of his courses at Harvard. Throughout Usher's writing and teaching, the treatment of the material of economic history is topical, being neither exhaustive in the treatment of an age or region, nor connected by any clearly articulated and comprehensive theoretical schema.

In this attitude toward the field, Usher has set himself off sharply both from the narrative-descriptive approach of Clapham and from the "idealistic" approach of the Marxists and of sociologists like Weber.[3] His chief objection to the latter writers has been their lack of interest in empirical description and measurement and their blindness to the complexity of the historical process. To all premature syntheses, Usher has opposed a common-sense, generally slightly amused historical "realism." Of one author's over-simplified description of the Industrial Revolution, Usher commented, "This exhibits all the higher forms of historical inaccuracy."[4]

Usher's criticism of Clapham is the more surprising, considering his

[2]"Two Notable Contributions to Economic History," *Quarterly Journal of Economics,* 48 (Nov., 1933), p. 180. In a review article on Hacker's *Triumph of American Capitalism,* "Institutional Methodology in Economic History," *Journal of Economic History,* 1 : 1 (May, 1941), p. 8 a similar objection to the scale of the work is raised.

[3]References to Marxist and socialist writers, to "ideal-type" sociologists, including Weber, and to "institutionalists," including the "stage" theorists, Schmoller, Bücher, and others are scattered throughout Usher's historical and methodological writings. See, for example, *An Introduction to the Industrial History of England,* (London, 1921), pp. 1–3, 250–251; "The Application of the Quantitative Method to Economic History," *Journal of Political Economy,* 40 : 2 (April, 1932), P. 193.

[4]*An Introduction to the Industrial History of England,* p. 249.

matter-of-fact objections to the Marxists and German "idealists." It is less strong, but is elaborated at considerable length in two review articles. At the basis of it is the feeling that in his own way Clapham too is "unscientific." Not only in an unwillingness to make use of statistics and economic theory, but in an apparent lack of interest even in limited causation, Clapham, for all his realism and learning, resembles a tourist moving through his material.[5] His final judgment is expressed in a 1951 review of *A Concise Economic History of Britain,* along with a full appreciation of Clapham's achievement:

> Statistical analysis of economic and social phenomena carries one rapidly toward substantial analysis of historical process. These developments, however, clearly lay outside the field of Clapham's interests. He was strategically placed to assume leadership in an empirical reaction against the mechanistic and idealistic systems of the Marxians and the ideal-type sociologists, but by temperament and background he became committed at an early date to a limited program, which he carried out with great skill and unusual literary distinction.[6]

As shown in his own research, Usher's attitude then, would seem to exclude an unnecessary interest in the details of social life just as it excludes premature generalization. The complexity of history, he would seem to say, arises not out of its complete formlessness, but out of the hints of limited connections and form which it presents. A method of investigation, therefore, must not aim at describing the whole society or economy and at narrating its movement by artistic selection of events; it must confine itself to a limited activity – banking, invention, and industry – where some causal relations are simple enough to become evident, even though it be acknowledged that such an activity occurs in the complex environment of the whole social process. Understanding of history is always only partial and comes through the understanding of the natures of parts of the social process and their interaction. Unlike the scientist, the historian cannot examine enough evidence with variables strictly enough separated to define comprehensive historical laws. His task rather is to make some sense out of a "particular system of events" – a body of historical data grouped around a common subject – the job of an engineer, faced with the necessity of devising a practical solution to a specific problem, in which, to be sure, relationships of more general validity are evident. Usher's approach to research is the approach of an engineer-inventor to a mechanical-scientific problem.

[5] "The Application of the Quantitative Method," *Journal of Political Economy,* 40 : 2, pp. 186–191.

[6] "Sir John Howard Clapham and the Empirical Reaction in Economic History," *Journal of Economic History,* 11 : 2 (June 1951), p. 153.

"The movement of economic history is due to reactions among three distinct classes of factors: physical resources, the technologies developed for the use of resources and social institutions," Usher writes at the opening of the *Economic History of Europe since 1750*.[7] His own scientific contribution has lain largely in exploring the first two of these classes of factors: the sources and the course of mechanical invention and the fascinating relations between resources and the geographical patterns of economic activity.

Usher's work on the history of inventions[8] is carried out with the sympathy and insight of an engineer to whom not only the mechanical details, but the role of the human mind, is of absorbing interest. For him, invention and technological change is a strain in human evolution, not dependent on the sporadic appearance of heroes, but emerging, like other forms of social life, from the organized and interdependent activities of many men. Within the limits set by the logic of Nature and by work of others, there is room for free human effort, functioning according to a pattern suggested by *Gestalt* psychology. Together this activity, like much other social activity, forms part of a conscious and rational attempt of men to use and adjust to their physical environment.

The adaptability of this concept to other social processes is evident; recently in a general way Usher has permitted himself to extend this important insight to other forms of social change.[9] As an engineer of historical subject matter, he has been drawn toward tangible things – fuel, power, transport routes, climate on the one hand – and statistically measurable magnitudes – population, output, and productivity on the other.[10] Usher's work on resources has helped to show how economic geography sets limits to economic opportunity, limits within which men in society can respond through the development of industrial arts and institutions. The tantalizing insights offered by location theory have particularly intrigued him. Usher, however, has persistently avoided any

[7] *An Economic History of Europe since 1750*, (New York: American Book Company, 1937), p. 1.

[8] *A History of Mechanical Inventions*, (1st ed., New York: McGraw-Hill Book Company, 1929; revised ed., Cambridge: Harvard University Press, 1954). Chapters 1 and 2 of the 1929 edition contain the generalizations on innovation and the process of invention, with which most students are familiar. The 1954 edition expands this material and includes discussion of the emergence of novelty in other sequences of historical events.

[9] See note 8, above.

[10] See, for example, *A Dynamic Analysis of the Location of Economic Activity* (unpublished). "Resource Requirements of an Industrial Economy," *Journal of Economic History* VII S, 1947, Pp. 35–46. "The Steam and Steel Complex and International Relations," *Technology and International Relations* (W. F. Ogburn, ed.), Chicago, 1949, P. 70 ff. *An Economic History of Europe since 1750*, pp. 5, 11–13.

rigid geographical determinism and has remained content to suggest the natural economic bases of patterns of settlement and regional development and the dynamic effects of technological change upon them. Here surely a mind of the cast of Usher's must have been most sorely tempted; in his restraint here, his judgment and balance, his humility as a scholar, and his stature as a social scientist demonstrate themselves most clearly.[11]

If Usher's research is most original in the treatment of technology and resources, his teaching and texts have been most effective through the balance maintained between these and his third factor in economic history: "social institutions." A scholar's influence is most deeply felt through the impress on both his research and teaching of his own system of values; and here Usher's treatment of "social institutions" is most revealing. At the same time, his attitude toward this most human aspect of economic history poses a fundamental dilemma faced by the liberal-minded student of society – economist, historian, or sociologist. This aspect of Usher's thought is, therefore, worthy of closer examination.

"Sophocles in his great chorus described man the inventor and man the high-citied." So writes J. L. Hammond, the English social historian, in a passage quoted by Usher in a review article on Clapham.[12] Historians, according to Hammond, are likewise naturally divided (presumably from birth) according to which of the two human struggles rouses them most: man's "conquest of natural obstacles," or "the attempt to find in one civilization after another the expression of highest desires and character." Usher's comment on this rather banal generalization provides a convenient insight into his own treatment of the social institutions which "man, the high-citied" erects:

> No one would care to deny the importance of the social interests embodied in this concept of "man the high-citied," but it may well be doubted if the history of these interests and problems can be identified with economic history. No more adequate description of the basic problems of economic history can be given than this statement of the interests centering around "man the inventor." The other interests may perhaps be best described as social history. They are obviously related to economic history in many ways, but presentation of economic development from such a point of view can only result in serious distortion of all the values appropriate to the interpretation of the basic phenomena of economic history. The economist is primarily concerned

[11] An excellent example of Usher's interest in scientific work and his restraint in applying it in historical interpretation occurs in an examination of soil exhaustion as an explanation of economic decline. "Soil Fertility, Soil Exhaustion, and their Historical Significance," *Quarterly Journal of Economics*, 37 : 3 (May, 1923): pp. 385–411.

[12] "The Application of the Quantitative Method," *Journal of Political Economy*, 40 : 2, P. 191.

with the study of the struggle for material existence. The use to be made of the individual life in spiritual and general intellectual interests is, after all, a separate subject of investigation.[13]

Now it is never certain that an economist who replies in this vein to the enthusiasms of the sociologist really considers that the "use to be made of the individual life in spiritual and general intellectual interests", is a proper subject of scientific investigation at all. To raise this doubt one need only apply to the ideals of scholarship itself the empirical test to which Usher subjects the ideals of politics and social philosophy. Usher's most recent view with respect to ideals is given in an article in 1949:

> The empiricist is not disposed to challenge the ideals as such; he challenges rather their status as necessary and final ends. Ideals are inevitably a factor in all value systems, but according to the empirical position no particular ideal can be presented as a universal value judgment. . . . The empiricist recognizes the necessity of having ideals, but he also realizes keenly that we must not only have them as concepts, we must learn how to live with them. They are not ends in themselves; they are means to the continuing realization of organic relations between the individual and the various social groups which are the setting for his life.[14]

Not only conscious ideals, but such social processes as invention and statecraft,[15] being in a sense free and purposeful activities, function in furthering the adaption of men in societies to their physical environment, though such processes admittedly have an independent life and logic of their own. Surely the work of the scholar too is in part to help men in society to achieve social control over nature; scientific work, including the writing of history, then may also be a social process similar to invention, with a role of its own in human evolution. But is "the use to be made of the individual life in spiritual and general intellectual interests" itself to be also subjected to conscious social control;

[13] *Ibid.*, P. 191.

[14] "The Significance of Modern Empiricism for History and Economics," *Journal of Economic History,* 9 : 2 (Nov., 1949), P. 155.

[15] The fullest statement of Usher's attitude on social policy is found in his presidential address to the American Economic Association, "A Liberal Theory of Constructive Statecraft," *American Economic Review,* 24 : 1 (March, 1934), Pp. 1–10. This address, like other of Usher's philosophical remarks, shows an historian's desire to synthesize divergent attitudes and strains of thought rather than to follow any to a logical and "unrealisitic" conclusion. It is clearly his purpose here to furnish some satisfactory basis for his faith that the economic historian's work properly conceived can help men adapt their social arrangements to the changing conditions of their environment. His effort to divorce liberalism from a *laissez-faire* concept of state policy is worthy of special attention. See "Laissez-Faire and the Rise of Liberalism," in *Explorations in Economics: Notes and Essays Contributed in Honor of F. W. Taussig,* (New York: McGraw-Hill, 1936), esp. Pp. 408 ff.

if so, how and to what ends are human beings, thus managed, to be adapted? An "empirical" view of the ideals of science would suggest that only if the human personality is to be brought under conscious and purposeful social control are the relations of man to man within "high-citied" walls an appropriate area of study.

To this difficult question the example of Usher's own research career alone furnishes but one rather lmited answer. A general survey of his work suggests the picture of a liberal-minded engineer who neglects, or refuses, to apply his engineering consciously to the manipulation of the thoughts and intimate lives of human beings. Usher's treatment of social institutions in a sense also contributes to this impression. Grain markets, banking, forms of industrial organization, and the state illustrate how social organization helps men in the struggle for material existence.[16] Even monopolies and the state – despite excesses – are viewed as instruments by which men in society consciously gain control, not over one another, but over poverty and famine. The forms within which an economy functions – laws, markets, labor unions, business firms – make up the institutional framework; the ways of behaving that lie at the basis of human response to economic situations within these forms are overlooked. Patterns of consumer demand, time preference, willingness to work, entrepreneurship are left securely outside economic history, relegated to treatments of "man the high-citied" by social historians. If social institutions are simply organizational forms which function to permit achievement of maximum material welfare, no application of psychology – even the introspective insights of the traditional historian – need be made in economic history. Consequently no real insight into the sources of change in institutional forms, much less in modes of behavior, can or need be achieved.

In the treatment of these treacherous aspects of economic history, Usher's vision goes far beyond the example of his own work. Indeed it is possible, when account is taken of his liberal bias, to feel that his neglect of the "human" side of economic history arises, not out of doctrinaire prejudice, but simply out of limitations of time and temperament. His work on invention is the strongest indication of his willingness to go beneath the forms of social institutions to examine individual actions; indeed, it would be difficult to find a better use of

[16]*The History of the Grain Trade in France, 1400–1710*, (Harvard, 1913) demonstrates the "victory of administrative regulation" over natural forces. "The development of social institutions," writes Usher (p. 361), "seems to be the result of conscious individual effort. . . . Progress is not inherent in the environment; it is the result of conscious human effort to deal with concrete problems." This view is found more clearly stated and applied in discussions of tariffs, banking, and social welfare legislation in his two texts.

psychology in the interpretation of a social process in its historical sequence. The reaction between man and nature, the limits set by environment, the role of the individual personality within the evolutionary process – all these are suggested by this work, and their application to the history of innovation in other fields offers an exciting opportunity for research.

A broad view of the scientific treatment of history is implicit also in Usher's criticisms of work on social institutions done by others.[17] His criticisms of the German "stage" theories of Schmoller and Bücher – the sequences of forms which social or economic institutions were said to follow – correspond in a loose way to criticisms that might be leveled against this aspect of his own work. In a number of places, Usher accuses these theorists of an excessive simplicity, an imposed "teleology," and an inability to interpret the change from one stage to another. To their simplicity, approaching that of the "ideal-type" sociologists, Usher would oppose a more accurate measurement of the extent over time and space of each organizational stage in development. This in turn would reveal history not to be a "unilinear" process moving inevitably through a simple sequence of stages to an appointed end. To their "teleology," which at times seemed to identify that end with the "development of the national state and factory system"[18] Usher would oppose his own notion of the function and relativity of all ends and ideals in evolution. The gap between one stage and the next, filled variously by "idealistic", revolutionary, and cataclysmic concepts of the nature of social change, Usher would fill with his own insights into the emergence of novelty in an evolutionary process.[19]

[17]See references cited in Note 3, above; also "The Significance of Modern Empiricism," Pp. 137–140.

[18]*Ibid,* P. 139. Usher's concept of history as a bundle of "systems of events," which he terms "multilinearity" is clearly stated and applied in *A History of Mechanical Inventions,* rev. ed., Ch. 2: "Early concepts of social revolution were expressed as sequences of stages that were presumed to describe the entire social structure. The structures of each particular period were represented as a development out of the totality of the preceding period. The totality of the present was derived from the totality of the past. Many alternative concepts of stages were put forward in the middle and late nineteenth century, but the details are unimportant if the sequences were expressed in this linear framework as a succession of comprehensive social entities. Adequate historical analysis requires concentration of attention on particular sequences of events. . . . We ought not to say that the present is derived from the past and the future from the present. The proposition must be formulated in much more specific terms: every event has *its* past. The principle of historical continuity does not warrant any presumption about the relations among events occurring at the same time. This assumption is very frequently made, but it will be readily seen that it is not warranted." *Ibid.* P. 19.

[19]Ibid., Ch. 4.

Despite such criticisms as these, Usher in a complex way retains respect for the work of Schmoller, Bücher, and Sombart.[20] His sympathy does not rest wholly on his own improved utilization of organizational forms in his treatment of social institutions; it rests also on his appreciation of these German writers' willingness to frame social theory along with their empirical work, and so to point a way betwen the rashness of the Marxists and the timidity of Clapham. To Usher the development of valid social history can be accomplished only by the modern scientist's understanding of the use of theoretical models in relation to empirical work. In a recent and elaborate methodological article,[21] Usher expresses his broad hope for the development of economic and historical work in this direction. In signifying his interest here also in the method and results of Toynbee, he points out signficantly that so purely historical a method as his must be supplemented by the insights into innovation and human behavior furnished by psychology.[22]

It is possible thus to feel that scientifically and intellectually Usher has sensed the direction in which further advance in the social studies may be made. In much the same way that the history of invention is treated by his own work, he had indicated that it may be possible to deal with the history of other human activities through a developed understanding of the psychololological bases of thought, art, and political activity. Is it fair to suggest that, having sensed it, Usher seems to have remained uncertain of the usefulness of such knowledge for human welfare? Is it for some such reason that in his own work, like many an economist, he has shied away from it and remained "primarily concerned with the struggle for material existence?" This attitude, compatible either with a laissez-faire or a socialist concept of the state, has the merit of leaving the spiritual side of life alone, not out of lack of interest in it, nor indeed from the Marxist notion that it is derivative from the material conditions of production, but simply out of a deep regard for its privacy and its freedom.

For the present generation of students, the great advantage of Usher's topical approach to historical material lies in the extremely satisfactory degree of specialization which it permits. It is not necessary, Usher would seem to say, that one master the *minutiae* of all phases of economic life in a particular region or period; nor is it necessary that one

[20] Usher's evaluation of Sombart's work is more complex. See his review article, "The Genesis of Modern Capitalism," *Quarterly Journal of Economics*, 36 : 2, (Feb., 1922) Pp. 525–542.

[21] "The Significance of Modern Empiricism," *Journal of Economic History*, 9 : 2 Pp. 142–144.

[22] *Ibid.*, P. 150.

develop a comprehensive philosophy of history and a complete sociology before interpreting any economic event. It is possible, and much more fruitful to focus on rather large topics in the history of economic life, within the fields of one's own interest, and to look for limited causal relationships within these areas. Specialization, then, is seen to consist not in endless, unplanned fact-finding expeditions into areas with purely arbitrary geographical or chronological boundaries; and generalization does not consist in dreaming dreams and seeing visions of the ultimate vital principles of all human activity. Ultimately, then, a body of knowledge about economic life and its movement can be built up which can be tentatively synthesized, and put to the use of helping free men guide their social activities.

If scientific curiosity continues unbounded, the students of society will be unable to neglect, as the economists of Usher's generation did, the more complex aspects of social psychology. Using the method and attitude of careful scholarship which Usher's own work exemplifies, economists and historians will increasingly be impelled to lay impious hands, not simply on resources, technology, and the forms of "social institutions," but on human beings themselves, their motivations, and their social behavior. Moreover, work in economic theory is focussing increasingly on the long-run movement of the whole economy; the attempt is being made to construct consistent models of economic growth and to connect these at relevant points to other changing social phenomena. Usher has indeed recently stated that: "The time is surely coming when work in theory and history can be drawn much more closely together than at any time in the past." So long as all partial formulations and explanations remain basically unsatisfying to the human mind, these attempts to unify partial studies into comprehensive economic history and to bring the history of economic life into its proper relation with the history of the other forms of human activity will continue. It remains to be seen whether the present generation of social scientists will be disciplined by a concept of the ends of social life as dignified and fruitful as that which has stimulated and regulated the scholarly life of Usher and other historians and economists of the liberal school.

Index